ENCYCLOPEDIA OF THE
BOOK OF MORMON

ENCYCLOPEDIA OF THE BOOK OF MORMON

BY

MARGARET BINGMAN

REORGANIZED CHURCH OF JESUS CHRIST
OF LATTER DAY SAINTS
HERALD PUBLISHING HOUSE, INDEPENDENCE, MO.

Library of Congress Cataloging in Publication Data

Bingman, Margaret.
   Encyclopedia of the Book of Mormon.

   1. Book of Mormon—Dictionaries. I. Title.
BX8627.A1B56   289.3'22'03   78-6591
ISBN 0-8309-0199-X

Printed in the United States of America

INTRODUCTION

Before attempting to use this reference work, readers not familiar with the Book of Mormon should carefully read the following subjects in the book:

Lehites

Lamanites

Nephites

Mulekites

Jaredites

Alma—Church Founder

Nephi—Son of Lehi

Anti-Nephi-Lehies

Zarahemla—City and Land

Cataclysm

Christ in America

The entry on Christ is divided between his Jerusalem appearance as prophesied and his New World appearance as experienced. Both refer to the same Christ.

EXPLANATION OF MARKINGS

Headings

The title of each subject is underlined, followed by a distinguishing characteristic. In parenthesis is the date when that person began his activities in connection with history. All entries labeled "Old Testament" refer to persons whose more complete history is found in the Old Testament. All entries labeled "Ether" refer to persons whose history is in the indefinitely timed history of the Jaredites. Because Lehi prophesied that Christ was to appear 600 years following the exodus of the Lehite family from Jerusalem, a careful record of the time was kept. These dates are easily coordinated with our present dating system, assuming that Christ was born in A.D. 1. The c, before the date of the character indicates that the date may not quite match present dates. It stands for *circa*, meaning "around the time of," translated from the Latin as "about."

References

Using the following reference as a guide, the interpretation given is an example for all references.

References: I Nephi 1:11-12; 3:2; 6:21, 27 (Isaiah 48:14, 20); II Nephi 10:1-54 (Isaiah 13 - 14); 11:17-18, 25; Alma 2:26 - 4:15.

Reference	Indicates
I Nephi 1:11-12	*First Book of Nephi*, chapter 1, verses 11 through 12.
3:2	Same book but chapter 3, verse 2.
6:21, 27	Same book but chapter 6, verses 21 and 27, not including the verses in between.
(Isaiah 13 - 14);	*Isaiah*, chapters 13 through 14.
11:17-18, 25	*Second Book of Nephi*, chapter 11, verses 17 through 18 and 25.
Alma 2:26 - 4:15	*Alma*, chapter 2, verse 26 through chapter 4, verse 15.

A

AARON—Son of Mosiah (c. 120 B.C.)

Aaron and his friends sought to destroy the church headed by his father, King Mosiah. At the time that Alma, one of his friends, was converted, Aaron saw and heard an angel speak. With the help of his brothers, he carried Alma, who had fallen into a trance, to his father. When after much prayer and fasting Alma arose, he told Aaron and his friends what he had experienced during his trance and converted them to the work of the church.

From that time, Aaron and his companions spent all their energy trying to repair the damage they had done to the church. Further, they sought permission of Aaron's father to go to their Lamanite enemies to convert them, also.

When King Mosiah grew old, the Nephites were asked to elect another in his stead. When Aaron was chosen, he refused to be king because of the greater mission he had chosen.

Aaron first went to Jerusalem, of the Lamanites, near the borders of Mormon. After teaching them and receiving no response except jeers, he joined his brother Muloki at Ani-anti. There also their teaching fell on deaf ears, so they proceeded to Middoni. The few converts there fled when Aaron and Muloki were cast into prison. There they remained, without food, water, or clothes, until rescued by their brother Ammon and his friend, King Lamoni the Lamanite.

After his health returned, Aaron and his brothers went to the land of Nephi to the house of the king, father of Lamoni. There Aaron begged to be a servant to the king, but the king insisted that Aaron teach him instead. Through the king's knowledge of the Great Spirit, Aaron was able to convert him so quickly that he fell into a trance of joy.

The queen entered and, thinking that Aaron had slain the king, called her servants to kill Aaron. The servants, knowing what had happened, refused. The queen sent for the people to slay Aaron. Seeing the stubbornness of the queen, Aaron roused the king.

The king explained to the queen what had happened and at the same time declared that Aaron and his brothers should be free to teach among the Lamanites. Because of this preaching thousands were brought into the church and the church was established among the Lamanites. The converted Lamanites were called Anti-Nephi-Lehies.

After much more labor, Aaron returned with Alma to Zarahemla. When Ammon spoke of the joy of the fulfillment of their mission, Aaron cautioned him not to boast. After a good rest, Aaron went with Alma to the Zoramites. Alma ordained Aaron and his fellow workers for this mission. Some of the Zoramites were converted, but only among the poorer class.

References: Mosiah 11:159-181, 203-207; 13:4-5; Alma 12:182; 13:1-22, 31-69, 82; 14:1-12, 17-18, 78, 90; 15:19-20, 28; 16:81-83, 112-119.

AARON—King of Lamanites (c. A.D. 330)

Aaron was king of a warring and ferocious dark-skinned people. He gathered 44,000 of his most bloodthirsty men and led them against Mormon's 42,000 white-skinned Nephites at Joshua, a city near the sea. His troops were soundly defeated there. Later, regrouped and infected by a new spirit of barbaric savagery, Aaron's troops returned to destroy the Nephites to the last man.

References: Mormon 1:31-32; Moroni 9:16.

AARON—Son of Heth (Ether)

Aaron was the grandson of the sixteenth king of the Jaredites. He and his father were kept in captivity all their lives.

References: Ether 1:6; 4:85.

AARON—City

Aaron was located near the lands of Ammonihah and Moroni. Alma, son of Alma, was traveling there when he was told by the Lord to return to Ammonihah to continue to reconvert the Nephite dissenters to righteousness.

References: Alma 6:16-23; 22:15.

ABEL—Son of Adam (Old Testament)

Abel was a shepherd who strove to keep the commandments of God as he understood them. Cain, his older brother, was a farmer who was beguiled by the temptations of Satan, whom he chose to serve. Abel offered a lamb in obedience to God; Cain offered grain because Satan told him to.

Abel's offering was accepted but not Cain's. This made Cain jealous of his brother. Satan told Cain that if he murdered Abel and took his possessions, the act would not be known to the world. The secret combinations that developed from that pact brought about the first murder and brought empires to destruction throughout the ages.

References: Helaman 2:151; Genesis 5:1-26.

ABINADI—Prophet (c. 150 B.C.)

Abinadi was a priest among the Nephites in Lehi-Nephi in the days of King Noah. He preached repentance to his people. When they sought his life, Abinadi disappeared for two years.

He returned in disguise to prophesy again to his people. He told them of their wickedness and their path toward bondage and destruction. The people bound him and took him to be questioned before King Noah.

King Noah had Abinadi cast into prison in an attempt to bring him into submission. When questioned again, Abinadi condemned his judges. When they attempted to slay him, the power of God came upon Abinadi with such strength that his face glowed. He was allowed to continue to speak until all of his message was delivered.

He told the king and his priests of their sins; recounted the commandments; prophesied of Christ, Zion, and the last days, and the ultimate destruction of the Nephites by the Lamanites. Alma, a fellow priest, was converted by his words and tried to plead for the life of Abinadi, but was himself cast out of the land.

Abinadi was again cast into prison and told to deny the words he had spoken against his inquisiters. Refusing repeatedly to do this, Abinadi was bound, scourged, and burned. As he died, he prophesied that King Noah and his fellow conspirators would die in a like manner.

References: Mosiah 7:28 - 9:28, 133, 171-173; 11:50, 51, ↄ4-56, 122; Alma 3:21; 14:68-72; Mormon 1:20.

ABINADOM—Recorder (c. 200 B.C.)

Abinadom, son of Chemish, was one of the keepers of the record of the Nephites. He wrote little and fought much, slaying the hated Lamanites in battle to protect the colony of the Nephites.

References: Omni 1:13-18.

ABISH—Lamanite Woman (c. 90 B.C.)

Abish was a maidservant to the queen of the Lamanites. She was present when Ammon, the Nephite priest, came to the royal court and converted the king, queen, and their servants to the love of God. She alone did not fall to the ground in a trance-like state under the influence of the Spirit. She had been converted long before by her father.

Seeing an opportunity to witness for Christ, Abish ran from house to house declaring the news of the conversions. In joy, she saw the multitude gather. In sorrow, she saw the people misinterpret the sight and accuse Ammon of murder. She took the queen by the hand and raised her from her trance.

When the king was roused by the queen, he called upon the people to listen to Ammon. Slowly, they were at last converted.

References: Alma 12:150-170.

ABRAHAM—Patriarch (Old Testament)

Abraham was called out of Ur of the Chaldees by God to possess the land of Canaan. He was tried often and found to be obedient in all things. He was given a son, Isaac, in his old age, then told to offer his son to God on an altar of sacrifice. He was stopped in the act of compliance and told that this was a similitude of the offering God would make of his Son for the redemption of mankind. He was also promised that through the seed of Isaac all the world would be blessed. The time would come, he was told, that his descendants would be scattered and scourged by the gentiles, but they would be gathered to their inheritance in the latter days.

Abraham came to Melchisedec at Salem and paid him one-tenth of all he possessed in obedience to the law of tithes.

Because of his faith and perfect obedience, Abraham's name was used by the Nephites to define their God. His reward upon his death was a place to sit down in the kingdom of God with garments cleansed, spotless, pure and white, to go out no more.

References: I Nephi 2:4; 4:23-29; 5:132-133, 239-244; 7:19-20; II Nephi 5:71; 11:158; 12:74; Jacob 3:6; Mosiah 5:28-29; 11:26; Alma 3:44; 5:39-42; 10:8; 15:62-65;

14

17:2; Helaman 2:25-26; 3:49-53; III Nephi 2:77; 9:63-65; Mormon 2:49; 4:70; Ether 6:11-12; Genesis 12-25.

ADAM—First Parent (Old Testament)

Adam, with Eve, was the first father. He partook of the fruit of the tree of knowledge even though God forbade him to do so. He thus had the knowledge of all good and all evil. God condemned him to die and cast him out of the Garden of Eden, placing cherubim and a flaming sword on the east to prevent his return.

If he had partaken of the tree of life, he would have frustrated God's plan for the human race; there would have been no opportunity for redemption.

Adam's transgression placed man in a fallen state—that is, separated from the face of God. It also allowed man to have a probationary period of time to repent, learn to do good and reject evil, and to prepare to return to the presence of God.

If Adam had not transgressed, all would have remained in its innocent state, there being no death, good, evil, children, misery, joy, Christ, nor redemption.

References: I Nephi 1:159-163; II Nephi 1:105-106, 111-115; Alma 9:35-53; 12:114; 13:44, 45; 19:82-88; Mormon 4:71; Genesis 2-4.

AGOSH—Plains

Agosh was located near the wilderness of Akish. There Coriantumr, the last Jaredite, killed Lib, the king of those who worked evil by secret oaths. Then

Shiz, brother of Lib, battled Coriantumr in the stead of Lib and drove him and his army from the plain.
Reference: Ether 6:49-51.

AHAH—King of the Jaredites (Ether)

Ahah was the son of Seth. He took over the kingdom from Shiblom, his grandfather, while keeping his father in captivity. He reigned only a few years, using his power to commit sin. These sins are not listed, but great bloodshed resulted from them. He was the father of Ethem who became king after him.
References: Ether 1:6; 4:100-102.

AHAZ—King of Judah (Old Testament)

Ahaz was a stubborn and willful king. He followed the advice of Isaiah, the prophet, by refusing to join the alliance with Pekah and Rezin against Assyria. He, instead, robbed the temple of Solomon and his own treasury to pay Tiglath-pileser III, king of Assyria, to send his army against the allied enemies.

When Ahaz was told to ask for a sign of the Lord, he refused and was rebuffed by Isaiah. He was told of the birth of Christ; death of his enemies, Pekah and Rezin; destruction of Jerusalem; return of the Jews to Jerusalem; and Roman dominance at the time of the birth of Christ.
References: II Nephi 9:23-38; Isaiah 7:10-25; II Kings 16.

AIATH—Old World City

Aiath, also written Ai, Aija, or Hai, was a city of the Canaanites near Jerusalem. When Joshua led the Israelites to possess the land, it was taken for Benjamin's lot.

Isaiah prophesied that the king of Assyria would come to Aiath to destroy it on a march to Jerusalem. Tiglath-pileser III was the king.

References: II Nephi 9:109-110; Isaiah 10:28-29; Joshua 8.

AKISH—Jaredite King (Ether)

Akish was the ambitious son of Kimnor and friend of King Omer. Jared, who became king by flattering away half of his father's kingdom, was overthrown by his brothers and Omer was restored to his throne. The daughter of Jared decided to use the ambitious Akish to regain the kingdom for her evil father. To gain the hand of Jared's daughter, Akish agreed to kill Omer by secret combinations among his kinsfolk. Omer, being warned by God, fled, abandoning the kingdom to Jared.

When Akish took Jared's daughter for a wife, he decided to take the kingdom as well. He used the same secret combinations that drove away Omer to rid himself of Jared.

As Akish reigned, he became jealous of his own son and had him imprisoned and starved to death. He continued his evil reign using secret oaths to keep order until his sons drew away a portion of the people by bribery and began a war with Akish.

After many years of war and destruction, only thirty souls of the kingdom of Akish remained;

Akish himself had been slain. Omer was restored to his throne and inheritance.
References: Ether 3:82-91; 4:2-14.

AKISH—Wilderness

Gilead, brother of Shared, in an attempt to overthrow King Coriantumr, pursued Coriantumr to the Jaredite wilderness of Akish. After a vicious battle, Gilead slew enough of Coriantumr's army to place himself on the throne.

Coriantumr continued to live in the wilderness two years until his army became sufficiently strong to pursue the battle once more. By this time, Gilead had been secretly slain by Lib, his high priest. Coriantumr fought Lib on the plain of Moron, but was beaten back. He retreated into the wilderness of Akish, taking with him all the people that he could gather. These battles occurred near the end of the existence of the Jaredites.

The wilderness of Akish was named after King Akish, son of Kimner. This area probably lay near the valley of Gilgal, the plains of Heshlon and Agosh, and the land of Moron, because the armies moved back and forth within these areas as they struggled.
References: Ether 6:37-51.

ALMA—Church Founder (c. 148 B.C.)

Alma submitted to the rule of Noah, living off the taxes extracted from the people of the city of Nephi and preaching the soothing words King Noah wanted to hear. When Abinadi, the prophet, came among the people to declare the truth and warn the people of their judgment, Alma was converted. When Abinadi was brought to trial and condemned, Alma pled for the life of Abinadi and because of this was cast out of the city of Nephi.

While Alma hid from the searching army of King Noah, he wrote the words of Abinadi. Quietly, he returned to the people of Nephi to preach the words of Abinadi. The people who were converted met often at the waters of Mormon, near this city, to learn the words of Abinadi concerning Christ. When they desired baptism, Alma first baptized Helam and was baptized at the same time. Then, with the help of Helam, the rest of the converts were immersed. Under his authority as priest, Alma ordained other priests and established the church of Christ among them.

Upset by what was going on, King Noah sent spies, then an army, against Alma and his people. Apprised of this, Alma took his 450 converts and departed into the wilderness. They built the city of Helam near a beautiful stream along the way. The people asked Alma to be their king, but he refused, warning the people of the evils brought on by kings.

A party of Lamanites, seeking the evil priests of Noah who had escaped from Nephi during an invasion, became lost and wandered into Helam. Alma promised to show them the way back to Nephi upon a promise that his people could retain their freedom. No sooner had Alma showed them the way than the Lamanites set Amulon, a deceitful priest of Noah, over them to rule the city. Amulon recognized Alma as a former priest and enemy of King Noah and decided to enslave the people of Helam in revenge.

The people lived under severe bondage for a time. They were released only by the power of God when he set a deep sleep over their Lamanite guards. The people of Alma fled toward Zarahemla, stopping again in a valley they named Alma. God prodded them on to complete their journey to Zarahemla. They joined the Nephites there, giving the records of Alma to Mosiah, the king.

Alma remained in Zarahemla, establishing the church among the Nephites. His own son, Alma, worked against him, but was stopped by the prayers of the faithful. The sons of Mosiah brought the prostrate form of his son to Alma to be healed. The conversion of his son was so complete that Alma appointed him high priest. Alma died at the good age of 82.

References: Mosiah 9:2-7, 28-74, 171-173, 178; 11:1-43, 54-158, 167-169, 179-186; 13:63-68; III Nephi 2:96.

ALMA—Son of Alma (c. 120 B.C.)

Alma, disbelieving what his father taught concerning the church, sought to destroy it. The people of the church prayed for his welfare until God sent an angel to stop him. The experience was so overwhelming that Alma was left in a trance-like condition. The sons of Mosiah who were with him took his body to his father. Further prayer on his behalf broke the spell. He stood to testify of the many wonderful things that had been revealed to him and to confess his sins. From that time his leadership abilities were spent converting the people he had before led astray.

Alma's conversion was so complete that his father gave him the high priesthood over the church and King Mosiah gave him charge of the plates of brass and the plates of Nephi. He was elected the first judge of the Nephites.

As judge, the case of Nehor, the murderer and teacher of priestcraft, was brought to Alma. Alma condemned Nehor to die. As leader of the Nephites, he headed an army against the Amlicites, followers of Nehor, and slew Amlicki with a sword. He led another army against the invading Lamanites and fought their king face-to-face.

When peace was won, Alma established the church more fully in Zarahemla, baptizing many and consecrating priests to serve them. He gave up the judgment seat to go into the mission field. His travels led him into Gideon, Melek, Ammonihah, land of Zoramites, and Jershon. With the help of the sons of Mosiah, many were converted.

Korihor, who preached against Christ, was brought to Alma after Alma's return to Zarahemla as head of the church. After a long debate with Alma, the unrepentant Korihor was struck dumb as a sign to him that Christ lived and would come to the world.

Tired and worn, Alma blessed each of his sons and assigned the keeping of the records of Nephi and other relics to his son, Helaman. Alma was last seen traveling between Zarahemla and Melek before he disappeared.

References: Mosiah 11:159-202; 13:1-2, 63-65; Alma 1:3, 14-23, 71, 76, 77, 87-92, 123-125; 2:4-5, 11-12, 22-28; 3:1-7:51; 8:46, 64-66; 9:1-10:111; 11:4-14, 22-33; 12:1-4; 16:36-71, 78-84, 95, 100-246, 256-257; 17:1-20:1, 27; 21:1-22; 30:1-2, 16, 21; Helaman 2:54-57, 107, 149; Ether 5:14.

ALMA—Valley

When Alma retreated with his people from Helam, which had been captured by the Lamanites, they traveled in the wilderness toward Zarahemla. Satisfied that they were out of reach of the pursuing Lamanites, they stopped in the valley to praise God for their deliverance. Alma was told to take his people and hasten on to Zarahemla. God promised that he would stop the pursuit of the Lamanites in this valley.

The valley of Alma was located nine days' travel from the land of Nephi and twelve days' travel from the city of Zarahemla.

References: Mosiah 11:69-76.

ALTAR

At first, altars were mounds of unhewn stone prepared by a high priest or patriarch for worship. The first mentioned is that altar built by Noah when he left the ark, but Abel probably built one when he made his sacrifice of meat to God.

Abraham built several altars as memorials of some event as well as places for worship or sacrifice. He built one on which he prepared to offer Isaac before he was stopped and given a ram instead.

In a vision, Isaiah saw an altar served by seraphims. Coals from this altar were used to purify Isaiah and prepare him as a prophet.

When Lehi and his family were sent away from Jerusalem before its overthrow, he went three days' journey into the wilderness, pitched his tents, and built an altar of stones similar to the altars of Abraham to praise the Lord for his goodness.

When Moses was commanded to build the tabernacle, he was instructed to prepare an altar for it. It was to be five cubits square (2.25 meters) on top and three cubits high (1.35 meters) with horns at each corner and overlaid with brass.

Altars of this type were built in temples by the Lehites. It was to these altars the people were called to publicly repent.

References: I Nephi 1:34; II Nephi 9:1-8 (Isaiah 6:1-8); Alma 10:107-110; 12:6-7; Genesis 9:4; 2:6, 7; 13:15; Exodus 27:1-8.

AMALEKI—Recorder (c. 180 B.C.)

Amaleki, the son of Abinadom, a writer before him, was born in the days of the first King Mosiah and lived to see the death of the king and the beginning of the reign of King Benjamin. Having no children, Amaleki gave the keeping of the records to King Benjamin.

He wrote of the days of King Mosiah and the finding of the records of the Jaredites.

References: Omni 1:18-54.

AMALEKI—*Brother of Ammon (c. 121 B.C.)*

A group of Nephites had gone from Zarahemla to Lehi-Nephi to reinhabit the land. Nothing had been heard from them for many years. Amaleki was among the sixteen men chosen by King Mosiah to find out what had become of them. Amaleki's brother, Ammon, was selected by Mosiah to be the leader of the expedition.

They traveled in the wilderness for forty days, suffering hunger and fatigue, until they came to a hill north of Shilom where they pitched their tents. Amaleki went with Ammon to the land of Nephi to see if their brothers were still alive.

Suddenly they were surrounded by guards of the king of Lehi-Nephi, bound, and taken to prison where they were kept for two days. They were brought out to be questioned by King Limhi, a Nephite, who wanted to know who they were before they were executed.

Ammon spoke for the group. Limhi was so delighted to hear they were his brothers that he loosed them and told them to get the others and bring them into the city for a feast, to be prepared in their absence, in celebration.

References: Mosiah 5:1-24.

AMALEKITES—*Dissenters (c. 90 B.C.)*

The Amalekites were Nephites who preferred the ways of the order of Nehors, who believed there would be no Christ and that all men would be saved no matter what they did during their lives. They built Jerusalem in which sanctuaries were constructed to be used for the worship of God. When the sons of Mosiah came to them and preached the truth, only one Amalekite was converted.

When the Anti-Nephi-Lehies, a group of Lamanites led by Ammon, were converted, the Amalekites moved the uncivilized Lamanites to come against them in battle. Many of the Lamanites were converted on the battlefield because of the nonresistance of the Anti-Nephi-Lehies, but not the Amalekites who led them. The Amalekites continued their wanton destruction of their brothers until the Anti-Nephi-Lehies were removed from the Lamanite territory and taken in by the Nephites.

Biding their time and becoming more wicked and murderous, the Amalekites spurred the Lamanites to battle the Nephites. The Amalekites were appointed captains over the Lamanites in battle at Jershon, a land given to the Anti-Nephi-Lehies near Zarahemla. Seeing that the Nephites were prepared and well armed for their defense, they left without battle. Planning for a sneak attack, the Amalekites led the Lamanites through the wilderness to Manti.

Moroni, being warned by God through Alma, son of Alma, made ready for them. When the Amalekites entered the arena, they were surrounded by Lehi's divisions of Nephites on the east and Moroni's divisions on the west. After a period of intense battle, the Nephites pulled back and offered peace to the Lamanites if they promised never to come to battle against the Nephites again.

Many of the Lamanites laid down their weapons and retreated. Their leader, Zerahemnah, declared that the arms of the Nephites, not the power of God, had preserved them. At this, Moroni returned their weapons to the Lamanites and the Amalekites and they fought on. The Nephites descended upon the remaining warriors with fury. Just before the Lamanites were completely destroyed, the covenant to war no more was made with the small remnant of Lamanites and Amalekites.

The battle over, the warriors from both sides returned home. The bodies of the many dead were cast into the Sidon River and carried out to sea. The living Amalekites diffused among the Lamanites.

References: Alma 13:2-15, 21, 39; 14:15-16, 56-58; 15:1-3, 12; 20:6, 14-15, 25, 37-97.

AMALICKIAH—Nephite King (c. 73 B.C.)

Amalickiah refused to listen to Helaman and his brothers concerning the establishment of the church. He was a cunning man, full of pride because of his great riches. He wanted to be king of the Nephites.

Using flattery, Amalickiah convinced the other noble rich to join him in his attempt to take over the leadership of the Nephites. He promised the lesser judges that he would give them more power.

When Moroni heard of this, he gathered the Nephites who wanted to maintain their liberty to go against Amalickiah and his army. When Amalickiah saw that the liberty seekers were more numerous than the kingmen and that some of his own people began to doubt that he was right, he feared for his life. Amalickiah departed with what followers he could muster to the land of Nephi.

Moroni gathered his people and chased Amalickiah and his followers to capture them rather than have them stir the Lamanites to further war. Most of Amalickiah's followers were captured and returned to Zarahemla, but Amalickiah and his closest companions escaped.

As expected, once in Nephi, Amalickiah began to stir the Lamanites to battle against the Nephites. The Lamanites, fearing the Nephites and knowing of their strong defenses, refused to go. Amalickiah was given command of the obedient portion of the Lamanite army by the king of the Lamanites. He was commanded to compel the dissenters to join in the war.

By subterfuge, Amalickiah had the Lamanite army chief killed by poisoning his food, the king of the Lamanites murdered by stabbing, and the queen taken for his wife by deceit. With the kingdom in his hands, Amalickiah slandered the Nephites to inspire the Lamanites to gather to battle against them.

Amalickiah sent an army to Ammonihah to destroy it. When the Lamanites found the city fortified, they retreated and refused to return to the proposed battle scene. Because of this, Amalickiah swore in wrath to drink Moroni's blood.

AMALICKIAH

Amalickiah gathered the Lamanite army again, but this time he headed the troops himself. He went to the land of the Nephites and, by attacking their weakest point, he captured city after city until he came to the borders of Bountiful. Teancum, a Nephite captain, gathered his forces and went after Amalickiah and drew him out to battle. The brave Teancum and his army repulsed the Lamanites by strength alone. As the two armies rested by the sea Teancum and his servant stole into Amalickiah's tent and slew him.

References: Alma 21:27-39, 61-68, 78-130, 160, 161, 181-183; 23:10-14, 28-44.

AMALICKIAHITES—Dissenters (c. 73 B.C.)

When Amalickiah made his bid to be king of the Nephites, the minor judges and some other rich folk joined him because they felt he could add to their power and prestige. When Amalickiah attempted to escape to Nephi, they went along, but were captured by Moroni along the way and returned to Zarahemla. They were commanded either to covenant to maintain the freedom of the Nephites or to give up their lives. Many died because of their stubbornness.

References: Alma 21:27-72.

AMARON—Recorder (c. 318 B.C.)

Amaron received the keeping of the record of the Nephites from his father, Omni. During his period he wrote only that the more wicked part of the Ne-

phites were destroyed. He delivered the plates to his brother, Chemish, for keeping.
References: Omni 1:5-10.

AMGID—King (Ether)

King Amgid held the sons of the ancient line of the Jaredite kings in captivity for many years. Com, one of these sons, gained half the kingdom from him. When Amgid lost the kingdom, he faded from popularity into oblivion.
References: Ether 4:87.

AMINADAB—Dissenter (c. 30 B.C.)

Aminadab had been a member of the church of God, but had been led away to dissent. He was in Nephi among the Lamanites when Nephi and Lehi, the Nephite evangelists, were imprisoned. He alone could see Nephi and Lehi through the cloud of darkness that surrounded those Lamanites who had come to slay them in prison. He called to the crowd in the prison to turn and look at Nephi and Lehi, who were conversing with angels. He explained to the Lamanites what they saw and convinced them that they should repent and listen to the evangelists.
References: Helaman 2:99-107.

AMINADI—Descendant of Nephi (Unknown)

Aminadi interpreted the writing on the wall of the temple written by the finger of God. He lived before Ishmael and after the first Nephi, and was a progenitor of Amulek, the preacher.
References: Alma 8:1-3.

AMLICI—Dissenter (c. 87 B.C.)

Amlici used his cunning to draw away people from the church of God, aspiring to become a king. When many Nephites succumbed to his flattery, the leaders in the government became alarmed and an election was called. The people voted against Amlici and refused to make him king. The followers of Amlici made him king nevertheless and drew up an army to destroy the Nephites who refused to recognize him.

Alma, leader of the Nephites, gathered an army of the loyal citizens to defend themselves against Amlici's forces. A battle ensued in which many from both sides were slain. The remainder of the Amlicite followers joined the Lamanites for another encounter with Alma and his army. This time Alma slew Amlici in hand-to-hand combat.

References: Alma 1:53-89.

AMLICITES—Dissenters (c. 87 B.C.)

The Amlicites were the followers of Amlici, who made him their king. They fought the Nephites, losing many men; joined the Lamanites; fought the Nephites again, losing their leader; and finally were driven out of the land of the Nephites with the Lamanites in a decisive battle.

After joining the Lamanites, they unknowingly took the curse of God upon themselves by painting their foreheads red like those of the Lamanites, but did not shave their heads. They mingled with the Lamanites and lost their identity.

References: Alma 1:64-102, 111, 117-125.

AMMAH—*Preacher* (c. 90 B.C.)

While Ammah, a Nephite, was in Ani-anti peaching among the Lamanites, he met Aaron, his old friend. He hoped to convert the Lamanites to righteousness, but all his efforts were in vain. He went with Aaron to Middoni to preach.

In Middoni the two evangelists met with even more opposition. The aroused citizens bound them and cast them into prison to starve to death. Before the men succumbed to this maltreatment, Ammon, brother of Aaron, and King Lamoni, converted king of the Lamanites in Ishmael, arrived to obtain their release from the king of Middoni, friend of King Lamoni.

After their deliverance, Ammah and Aaron went to the Amalekites. This time they were blessed with more success.

References: Alma 12:182; 13:14-22.

AMMON—*Children* (Old Testament)

Ammon was the son of Ben-ammi, son of Lot who came out of Ur with Abraham. God gave Lot a land of promise next to the land of promise given to Abraham.

Moses was commanded to leave the Ammonites, descendants of Ammon, alone when he took the children of Israel out of Egypt toward their inheritance. When Moses came to the land of Moab, brothers of the Ammonites, the Israelites were refused the water and safe passage they needed. Instead, they sent Balaam, the prophet, to curse them, in collusion with the Ammonites. As a

31

result of this, the Lord refused to allow the Ammonites or the Moabites to worship with the Israelites in their tabernacle to the tenth generation.

Over the years that followed the establishment of Israel in the promised land, the Ammonites battled and were subdued by the Israelites many times. The prophets cursed the children of Ammon because of their idolatry and continued wickedness.

Isaiah says that Ephraim and Judah are to join in battle against Israel's enemies. The children of Ammon will be subdued and obey them in the latter days.

References: II Nephi 9:128-129; Isaiah 11:14; Genesis 19:44; Deuteronomy 2:19-20; 23:3; Judges 11; I Samuel 11:11; II Samuel 10; 12:26; Jeremiah 25:21; 49:1; Ezekiel 21; 28:25; Amos 1:13; Zephaniah 2:8.

AMMON—Son of Mosiah (c. 120 B.C.)

Ammon and his friends sought to destroy the church headed by Alma. To stop their wanton desecration, the members of the church appealed to God for help. God chose to send an angel to stop them. Alma, son of Alma, leader of the gang, fell to the ground as if dead. Ammon, with the help of his friends, took Alma to his father. After prayers on his behalf, Alma arose and told his friends what had happened to him while he was unconscious. Ammon was converted by his testimony. He could no longer bear that anyone be without the knowledge of the gospel. Ammon and his friends spent their remaining years trying to repair the damage they had done to the church and to bring back those they had led away to paths of evil.

When the church was set in order in Zarahemla, Ammon and his companions asked King Mosiah's permission to go to the Lamanites to convert them to the church. After inquiring of God and receiving assurance that the companions would return safely, King Mosiah granted the request.

As King Mosiah became old, he asked the people who they would have as their next ruler. When the vote of the Nephites called Ammon, he refused because of his mission to the Lamanites.

Ammon took his mission work to Ishmael. When the Lamanites saw him, they bound and carried him to King Lamoni. When, after questioning, Ammon agreed to live among the Lamanites, he was loosed. Though the daughter of the king and a place in the king's house were offered, Ammon refused, to take a job as a shepherd servant to the king.

The Lamanites gathered to torment the shepherds of the king as Ammon and his fellow servants took the sheep to water. Ammon defended the sheep and the servants by killing the enemies of the king and cutting off the arms of those who dared to raise them against him.

When they returned, the servants carried the arms to the king and told him of Ammon's valor, while Ammon went on to care for the horses as he had previously been commanded. Because of the obedience of Ammon to every command of the king, he got King Lamoni's full attention and was able to teach him the gospel and convert him to righteousness. At his conversion, the king fell in ecstasy.

Thinking the king dead, the servants tried to bury him. The queen asked Ammon what to do. Ammon told her to wait; the king would revive.

When the king arose, he told the queen of his experiences. Both the king and queen fell into a trance. Seeing this, Ammon and the servants fell too. Akish, the maidservant of the queen, alone was not overcome. She sent for the citizens, who gathered around the scene and blamed Ammon for mass murder. When they were about to slay Ammon, Akish broke the spell, raising the queen and the king to their feet.

The king and Ammon explained to the gathering the wonderful things they had witnessed and converted many. Ammon ministered to them and baptized the converted.

Lamoni wanted Ammon to go to his father at Nephi for a feast, but the Lord told Ammon to go to Middoni to rescue his brothers from prison. Lamoni decided to go with Ammon because the king of Middoni was a friend of his. On the way, they met and argued with the father of Lamoni, king of all Lamanites.

Lamoni's father saw only that Ammon was a Nephite, so he told his son to slay Ammon. When his son refused, Lamoni's father decided to kill Lamoni for his disobedience. Ammon stepped in and fought Lamoni's father, injuring him so that he could no longer fight. The father of Lamoni begged for mercy, which Ammon granted on condition that he release Ammon's brothers from prison and spare Lamoni. The father of Lamoni acquiesced, then went on to free Lamoni from his rule.

Ammon and Lamoni continued to Middoni, where his brothers were released from prison and cared for until they returned to health. Lamoni and Ammon returned to Ishmael where Ammon preached to the Lamanites in synagogues built for that purpose. Under the protection of the father of Lamoni, Ammon and his brothers preached with such power that those Lamanites converted to righteousness never did fall away to sinning again.

When the uncivilized Lamanites outside the realm of the father of Lamoni heard of the conversion of their civilized brothers, they gathered and descended upon the believers to destroy them. The converted Lamanites laid down their weapons and refused to defend themselves. Many were slain. As a result, Ammon called upon the Lord for advice. He gathered the survivors and took them and their possessions to the city of Zarahemla.

The Nephites in Zarahemla voted to give Jershon, an adjoining land, to the followers of Ammon and to defend them against the Lamanites if the Ammonites agreed to pay tribute to defray the expenses of the Nephite guard.

Ammon was called to be high priest over the Ammonites. During his rule, Korihor, the antichrist, was brought before him. Ammon cast Korihor out of Jershon.

Later Ammon was called by Alma, his old companion, to preach among the Zoramites. There he was able to provide a great ministry, but only among the poor class because only they would listen.

References: Mosiah 11:203; Alma 12:26-221; 13:23-31; 14:1-15:43; 16:1-5; 17:38-39; 21:141, 185-186; 24:63-66; 26:3; Helaman 2:83; Ether 5:16.

AMMON—Descendant of Zarahemla (c. 121 B.C.)

Ammon, at King Mosiah's bidding, led a party of sixteen strong men to the land and city of Lehi-Nephi. A group of Nephites had returned to that land to reinhabit it, but had not been heard from for many years.

Ammon's party wandered in the wilderness forty days. When they came to a hill north of Shilom, most of the party remained there while Ammon and three men entered the land of Nephi. They came upon King Limhi, who was enjoying an outing. The king ordered his guards to capture and imprison Ammon and his companions because he thought they might be Lamanite spies.

After two days, Ammon and his friends were released and brought before the king to answer questions. Ammon humbly answered for his party, telling King Limhi that they were the king's brothers. He informed King Limhi of their mission from King Mosiah and of their joy in finding them safe.

King Limhi rejoiced at this news and poured out his troubles to Ammon concerning their bondage to the Lamanites. He then sent Ammon to fetch the rest of the party from their hill camp.

The following day an announcement was made by King Limhi that Ammon had come to Nephi from their fatherland. Ammon related to the citizens at Nephi, who had gathered at the temple for that purpose, news from Zarahemla.

After the celebration, King Limhi gave Ammon the record of Zeniff, concerning the history of the people at Nephi, and asked if he could interpret languages. Without giving Ammon time to reply, Limhi explained that a strange record had been unearthed by some of his people who had been sent in search of Zarahemla which related the history of a lost and destroyed nation. Ammon told Limhi of Mosiah's gift of interpretation of tongues. Limhi rejoiced again to know that this gift had been given by God.

Ammon encouraged the Nephites to deliver themselves from the Lamanites and return to Zarahemla. Gideon, a servant, quickly offered to guide Limhi's people out of the city through the city's back wall by night. The Lamanites, paid their tribute in wine, drank and fell into a deep sleep. Then Gideon led the people out of the city as he had promised and Ammon led the way back to Zarahemla.

King Mosiah gladly received both the citizens of Nephi and their records. He translated the record of the lost people and found it to be the Jaredite record written by Ether.

References: Mosiah 5:1-24, 53-86; 9:163-181; 10:1-2, 14-19.

AMMONIHAH—Dissenter (Before 82 B.C.)

Ammonihah was a Nephite dissenter after the manner of Nehor, who believed that all men would be saved no matter what they did in life. He first possessed a land and city called Ammonihah in his honor.

References: Alma 6:8.

AMMONIHAH—City

Ammonihah was located three days' journey north of Mulek and near Zarahemla. It was one day's journey from Aaron. Ammonihah was destroyed by the Lamanites in about 81 B.C.

Later it was rebuilt and fortified by Moroni, the war chief of the Nephites. The Lamanites were turned back in their invasion attempt, because of the strength of the fort built there, during the reign of Amalickiah in about 72 B.C.

References: Alma 6:7-10, 16, 20, 24; 11:1-3, 14-15; 21:149-167; Helaman 2:72.

AMMONIHAH—Land

Ammonihah surrounded and included the Nephite city of Ammonihah. It was named for the follower of Nehor who first possessed it. The Lamanites destroyed the land and slew all of its inhabitants in about 81 B.C., burying the dead in a heap in a shallow grave. The stink caused by the decaying bodies made the land uninhabitable for many years. Because of this it was called the desolation of the Nehors. The Nephites repossessed it about eight years after the destruction.

References: Alma 6:7-10; 8:1-2; 11:18-19; 14:59-60; 21:149.

AMMONIHAHITES—Dissenters

Alma, in his missionary efforts among the Nephites, preached among the Ammonihahites. Satan had great hold on them; they did not believe in the traditions of the Nephites but held to the belief of the Nehors that all would be saved no matter what was done during a lifetime. The Ammonihahites cast Alma out because they did not recognize his authority as high priest.

In dejection, Alma left the city, traveling toward Aaron. He was stopped by the Lord and sent back to warn the Ammonihahites that if they refused to repent they would be destroyed. Upon his reentry into the city, Alma was met by Amulek who took him into his home and cared for him.

Alma began to preach again and was again rejected. Amulek, a converted Ammonihahite, preached to them also. He too was attacked by the lawyers including Zeezrom, chief among them. Zeezrom was converted, but Antionah, the chief ruler who questioned Alma and Amulek, was not.

The citizens took Alma and Amulek to the chief judge along with the few Ammonihahite converts. All the believers were cast out of the city to be stoned, but escaped to Sidom. The families of the converts were gathered and burned and Alma and Amulek were forced to witness the conflagration. The Lord did not prevent the burning of the converts but took them to himself to spare them further humiliation, lest they revert back to their old ways of sinning.

Alma and Amulek were beaten and cast into

prison. After three days, the Ammonihahites came daily to the prison to continue badgering their prisoners. They took away their food, water, and clothes in order to increase their humiliation.

After many days of this treatment, Alma stood before his tormentors and cried to the Lord for deliverance. The Ammonihahites tried to escape, but were paralyzed with fear. The prison collapsed on their persecuters; Alma and Amulek walked out to return to the city. The remaining Ammonihahites commanded them to depart their city and never return. Together, Alma and Amulek headed to Sidom to meet the converted Ammonihahites who had found refuge there. Zeezrom called for them to come to him and Alma healed and converted him there.

The remainder of the Ammonihahites never repented but were slain by the Lamanites in about 82 B.C. Their bodies were heaped up and buried in a common grave. The stench from their rotting bodies made the land uninhabitable for eight years.
References: Alma 6:9-10; 8 - 9:87, 105-107; 11:1-3, 14-17; 14:59-60.

AMMONITES—See Anti-Nephi-Lehies

AMMORON—King of the Lamanites (c. 66 B.C.)

When King Amalickiah was slain by Teancum, Ammoron, his brother, was made king in his stead. The Lamanites were in the midst of a battle against the Nephites. They had captured many of Moroni's fortified cities.

Ammoron left to tell the queen what had become of her husband. He gathered more Lamanite warriors and returned to battle with the Nephites on the borders by the west sea.

After a long and fruitful battle, Ammoron sent a letter to Moroni to ask for an exchange of prisoners. Moroni consented on condition that a Nephite family be exchanged for each Lamanite prisoner released by the Nephites. Ammoron consented to the exchange on condition that the Nephites surrender and make him governor over all the Nephites. Instead of sending another letter, Moroni sent a Lamanite soldier, who had deserted to the Nephites, with a gift of drugged wine to the Lamanite troops to gain access to one of the forts held by the enemy. While the Lamanite guard slept, the Nephites under Moroni surrounded their camp, gained their surrender and freed the prisoners. This was the turning point in that long and terrible war.

The Lamanites were slowly driven from the land to Moroni where, in a last great struggle, Teancum slew Ammoron with a javelin and was himself slain by the servants of the king.

Ammoron's son Tubaloth reigned in his stead.
References: Alma 24:3, 4, 14-15; 25:1-63; 26:19-21, 72-93; 27:5-7; 29:38-44; Helaman 1:16-18.

AMMORON—Recorder (c. A.D. 305)
Ammoron was given the plates of Nephi by his brother, Amos. Because of the wickedness of the people, Ammoron was told by the Holy Ghost to hide the records of the Nephites. He did as he was instructed, then went to Mormon, a faithful ten-

year-old, and told him where the records were and to dig them up in fourteen years. In the meanwhile, Mormon was to observe the works of the people and remember to record them after he had received the plates.

References: IV Nephi 1:56-59; Mormon 1:2-6, 43, 44; 2:25.

AMNIGADDAH—Line of the Jaredite Kings (Ether)

Amnigaddah was of the lineage of the kings of the Jaredites, though he lived in captivity all his life. His great-grandfather, Hearthom, had been king but had been overthrown. His grandson, Com, regained the kingdom much later. Amnigaddah's father was Aaron, and his son was Coriantor.

References: Ether 1:6; 4:85.

AMNIHU—Hill

Amnihu was east of the river Sidon. The Amlicites came there to fight the Nephites in about 87 B.C.

References: Alma 1:70, 71.

AMNOR—Spy (c. 87 B.C.)

Alma sent Amnor and others to watch the Amlicites at rest after a long and strenuous battle. They returned to report that the Lamanites were coming to join the Amlicite dissenters to destroy the Nephites. Alma gathered the Nephites and, calling upon the Lord for strength, pursued the battle until the leader of the Amlicites was slain and the Lamanites were driven back.

References: Alma 1:77-86.

AMORON—Reporter (c. A.D. 400)

Amoron wrote a letter to Moroni to report the horrible conditions under which the Nephite captives were held by the Lamanites in the last long war of the Nephites. The Nephites were forced into cannibalism through thirst and starvation.
References: Moroni 9:8, 9.

AMOS—Recorder (c. A.D. 110)

Amos, son of Nephi, kept the record of the Nephites during the years of peace following the coming of Christ, before the last apostasy.
References: IV Nephi 1:22-24.

AMOZ—Father (Old Testament)

Amoz was the father of Isaiah, the great prophet of Judah. He is not to be confused with Amos, the prophet.
References: II Nephi 8:17; 10:1; Isaiah 2:1; 13:1.

AMULEK—Preacher (c. 82 B.C.)

When Alma, son of Alma, was sent by the Lord back to Ammonihah, he was met by Amulek, a rich citizen of the city who took Alma home to live with him. He went with Alma to preach among his fellow citizens to act as a second witness of the gospel for Alma. They were accosted by lawyers because they spoke the unbearable truth against the Ammonihahites. Zeezrom, the chief among the lawyers, challenged Amulek and was so confounded by the answers that he was eventually converted. Nevertheless, few other Ammonihahites joined the ranks of the believers.

Instead, Alma and Amulek were taken to the chief judge in the city. When Zeezrom began to defend them, he, along with the few other converts, was cast out of the city of Ammonihah to be stoned. The families of the believers were gathered and burned before the eyes of Alma and Amulek. Amulek begged Alma to stop the carnage, but Alma refused, telling Amulek that the Lord was prepared to receive these people in glory, to act as witnesses against the citizens of Ammonihah, and to prevent them from being coerced into sin again.

When the rage of the pyre burned down, Amulek and Alma were cast into prison with insults and injury. After three days, the chief leaders of the Ammonihahites came to taunt them. The Ammonihahites returned daily to scoff and demonstrate their satanic subjection by gnashing their teeth, spitting, and mocking. After many days of continuous mistreatment, Alma and Amulek stood and called upon the Lord for help. They were loosed by the power of God from their bonds and from prison. Their tormentors were stoned by the rubble from the disintegrating prison, but Alma and Amulek walked forth unharmed. In terror, the citizens of Ammonihah thrust them out of the city.

Together, Alma and Amulek went to Sidom to visit among the converts who fled from Ammonihah. Among them was Zeezrom, suffering from remorse and guilt. Alma and Amulek came to Zeezrom and prayed for him. Zeezrom was immediately healed.

With the help of Amulek, Alma converted many

and established the church in Sidom. When the church was thriving, Alma took Amulek to his home in Zarahemla to continue to strengthen Amulek in his faith.

As the years went by Alma took Amulek often with him to serve as a second witness of the gospel. They, with other church leaders, took a special envoy to the Zoramites who worshiped upon their Rameumpton only once a week. Seeing the pride of these people, Alma ordained Amulek and a few other chosen leaders of the church with a special endowment to preach without harm but with great power. Nevertheless, they were able to reach only the poorer people to convert them. Amulek preached on the hill Onidah to a multitude of the poor but humble people, offering his second witness to the gospel alongside Alma's first witness.

Following this, Alma and Amulek went to Jershon to the faithful Ammonites. After visiting among the Ammonites, they returned to Zarahemla to rest.

References: Alma 6:25 - 10:111; 11:21-24; 16:83, 100-123, 201-241; Helaman 2:72, 107; Ether 5:14.

AMULON—Priest of Noah (c. 125 B.C.)

Amulon was the leader of a group of wicked priests who had escaped the first destruction of his fellows. He led his followers to a place in the wilderness and began to till the ground.

When the Lamanites, lost on their way to Nephi, stumbled upon the city of the priests, Amulon sent forth their Lamanite wives they had kidnapped, after abandoning their Nephite wives and children in an earlier invasion, to plead for them. The Lamanites spared them for their wives' sake and allowed Amulon and the priests to join them.

In their continued search for the city of Nephi, the band of Lamanites came to Helam, the city of the followers of Alma. Alma promised to show the Lamanites the way to Nephi on a promise that they would leave the city undisturbed. The promise was made, but broken as soon as the Lamanites were given their directions. Amulon was left to be a king over Helam but under the supervision of the king of the Lamanites.

Amulon and his fellow priests gained favor with the king of the Lamanites. They became teachers among the Lamanites, instructing them in the language of the Nephites, to read, to write, and to keep a history of their people. However, the Law of Moses, the words of Abinadi, and service to God were not taught.

Amulon, as king, began to persecute Alma and his people because he remembered Alma as the enemy of King Noah. He tried to stop the citizens of Helam from praying. The people simply changed from vocal prayers in their synagogues to silent prayers at home.

Because of their faithfulness, the people of Helam were released from their bondage to Amulon when the Lord caused a deep sleep to come upon the guards of the city. Alma and his followers gathered all they possessed and walked past their sleeping guards out of their reach. The original families of Amulek and the priests of Noah were with Alma

when they arrived safely at Zarahemla.
References: Mosiah 11:36-68, 88-89.

AMULON—Land

Amulon was located in the wilderness, probably between Nephi and Helam. It was established by Amulon and the priests of Noah in their attempt to hide themselves from the wrath of the Lamanites and the Nephites.

When Amulon and his fellow priests joined the Lamanites, using the skirts of their stolen Lamanite wives to protect themselves, the land of Amulon fell into the possession of the king of the Lamanites.

Much later Aaron came to the city of Jerusalem in the land of Amulon to preach. In it were many synagogues built by the Nehors who had moved into the land.
References: Mosiah 11:35, 44-47.

AMULONITES—Dissenters

The Amulonites were the descendants of the priests of Noah by their Lamanite wives who came out of Nephi to live in Amulon. They built a city called Jerusalem, filled with synagogues in which they taught their religion. They believed that all men would be saved from eternal punishment for their crimes and there would be no Christ to come to redeem them from hell. They were even more hardened in their hatred for the Nephites than the Lamanites.

Though Aaron and Ammon went from the Nephites to preach among them, none were converted. Instead they gathered the uncivilized Lamanites to war against the converts, the Anti-Nephi-Lehies. When the battle was full upon them, the Anti-Nephi-Lehies refused to lift their weapons in their own defense. The Lamanites, ashamed of hacking away at their defenseless brothers, laid down their weapons and were converted. The Amulonites, however, gave up the battle only because there was no challenge and went in anger to exterminate the citizens of Ammonihah, who at least would stand up and resist.

After that, they were driven back by the Nephites and most of the Amulonites were slain. When some of the Lamanites had time to consider what they had done and began to remember the words of Aaron and repent, the Amulonites condemned them to death.

Those acts of infamy stirred the Lamanites to realization of the pure evil of the Amulonites. The Lamanites from that day burned any of the Amulonites they could find, thus fulfilling the prophecy of Abinadi concerning their fate. The Amulonites could no longer find safety anywhere. References: Alma 13:2-5; 14:15-16, 21-22, 56-72.

ANATHOTH—Old World City

Anathoth was a city of Benjamin's lot in the promised land of Israel given to the children of Aaron for a city of refuge. Jeremiah, the prophet, was born there, yet the men of Anathoth conspired to kill him. For this idolatry, Anathoth was destroyed. The men were to die by the sword and the women by starvation.

Anathoth was located on the road to Jerusalem from Damascus, about three miles north of Jerusalem.

References: II Nephi 9:111; Isaiah 10:30; Joshua 21:13, 18; Jeremiah 1:1-2; 11:21-23.

ANGELS

Angels are messengers of God who are sent to men. They are slightly higher in order than men, having free agency and therefore subject to temptation and sin. They have a language pure and plain that, when men are prepared, may be spoken by men in praise to God. Their robes are white or colored depending on the kind of message they bring. Their faces glow with an exceeding whiteness and they are free to go and come as required.

Angels in Lehi's vision surrounded the throne of God and sang praises to him continually.

When Laman and Lemuel became so angry with their brothers, Nephi and Sam, because of the loss of their treasures to Laban in an attempt to purchase the plates of brass that they began to flog them, an angel stopped them. Laman and Lemuel were reprimanded and told to try once more to obtain the records. They were promised success; then the angel departed.

When Nephi prayed for understanding concerning his father Lehi's vision, an angel was sent to teach him. When Nephi tried to explain what he had been taught to his brothers, Laman and Lemuel became jealous and tried to kill him. Nevertheless, Nephi was preserved from their hatred and received further angelic ministry as needed.

Others taught by angels included Jacob, the younger brother of Nephi; King Benjamin; Helaman, son of Alma; Samuel, the Lamanite prophet; Nephi, son of Helaman; Nephi, son of Nephi; and Moroni, who later was promoted to be an angel.

Satan was an angel in heaven who rebelled against God and tried to conquer the throne for himself. He and his angels were cast down to dwell with men although Satan retained his immortality. Angels of the devil, or Satan, delivered his messages to men. For these angels, God has prepared everlasting fire. In the form of an angel of God, an angel of Satan deceived Korihor and cost him his life.

Alma, son of Alma, and his companions, the sons of Mosiah, who tried to destroy the church established by Alma's father, were stopped by an angel. Memory of this event went into much of the witnessing of Alma to those to whom he preached and to his sons. Later, as Alma was traveling among the dissenters trying to call them to repentance, an angel came to him to lift his spirits and to send him back to Ammonihah to find Amulek, who became his lifelong companion. Amulek had been told by the same angel to receive Alma.

When Ammon, son of Mosiah, went to the Lamanites, he taught King Lamoni and his servants the gospel of Christ. As a result the servants of King Lamoni were prepared to be taught by angels to repent.

Those of the multitude that gathered to hear Christ after being prepared by gospel teaching were ministered to by angels. The twelve disciples chosen by Christ as special witnesses received added angelic ministry. Three of the twelve asked to remain on earth until the second coming of Christ. They were granted their request and later became as angels, able to move about unimpeded and to appear to those who need them.

We have been given a promise that if men are prepared through prayer and study, and if they need the ministry of angels, they too can receive it.

References: I Nephi 1:7, 91-97, 101; 2:16; 3:54-256; 4:47; 5:48-49, 145-147, 233-256, 240; II Nephi 3:39; 5:24-29; 6:20-40; 7:5-7; 11:35-36; 13:16-18; 14:2, 3; Jacob 1:64-65; 5:7, 30; Omni 1:43-45; Mosiah 1:92-130; 2:1-2, 18-23; 3:5-6; 11:135-178, 200-202; Alma 6:17-23, 26-27; 7:30, 39-45; 8:10-17, 29, 30, 83, 84; 9:47-48; 10:18-26; 12:2-4, 107-110, 175-177; 13:6-7; 14:37-38 15:5-6, 52-58; 16:67, 145, 146; 17:5-12; 18:7-8; 19:27, 43; Helaman 2:73, 100, 113; 3:119; 5:8, 49, 63, 81-84, 125-126; III Nephi 3:56-61; 4:26-27; 8:25-27; 9:13-16; 13:7, 42-44; Moroni 7:14-16, 21, 24, 30, 38, 41-43; 10:11.

ANGOLA—City

In the last wars between the Lamanites and the Nephites, Mormon led the Nephites in battle. At one point in the war in A.D. 327, the Nephites fled northward from the Lamanites. They came upon the city of Angola and took possession of it for a fort. Nevertheless, the Lamanites came upon them and drove them out of the city and the land of

David in which it was located.
References: Mormon 1:24-27.

ANI-ANTI—City

Ani-anti was a small village of Amulonites and
Amalekites near the city of Jerusalem. In disgust,
Aaron left the unrepentant in Jerusalem and came
to Ani-anti where he joined Muloki. Together they
could not convince the citizens of that village to
repent, so Aaron and Muloki left to go on to
Middoni.
References: Alma 13:14-16.

ANIMALS

The Jaredites came out from the tower of Babel
to the new world. They brought with them flocks of
every kind, including birds, fresh water fish, and
bees. After they were here for four generations,
they listed their domestic animals as cattle, oxen,
cows, sheep, swine, goats, horses, asses, elephants,
cureloms, and cumoms. Whether they brought all
of these with them is not certain, but the skeletal
remains of many of these animals are still found in
archaeological digs and fossil pits.

In the ninth generation, the days of Heth, a
drought killed off many of the species. Serpents
who ordinarily kept themselves hidden in the rocks
showed themselves to the people in their search for
food. They added to the destruction of both men
and beasts. By the seventeenth generation, the days
of Lib, the serpents were seen no more, as the
drought abated and the serpents returned to hiding.

The Jaredites moved southward to hunt for animals in the forest and stayed there.

When the Jaredites fought a civil war that caused them to become extinct, their animals roamed free and became wild. When the Lehites arrived in about 588 B.C., they found the animals in the forest and redomesticated them. They listed the cow, ox, ass, horse, goat, and wild goat among the beasts they captured. Though swine were probably still there, the Lehites, being Jews did not domesticate them.

Later the Lehites divided into the Lamanites and the Nephites. The Lamanites were distinguished from Nephites by their habit of eating beasts of prey and raw flesh which was against the Jewish tradition taught them by their father, Lehi. The more civilized Lamanites kept sheep and horses.

The Nephites continued to keep domestic animals such as cattle, goats, wild goats, and horses. In times of great war, the Nephites gathered their animals and kept them with them to provide necessary food and prevent their enemies from taking them for provisions.

For more information, see the articles on asp, ass, bat, bear, bee, bittern, bull, cattle, chicken, cockatrice, cow, cumom, curelom, dog, dove, elephant, fish, fly, fowl, goat, horse, insect, leopard, lion, mole, moth, owl, oxen, roe, serpent, sheep, swine, whale, wolf, and worm.

References: I Nephi 5:216; II Nephi 4:16; 9:121-123; Enos 1:31-34; III Nephi 2:29-31, 42-45; 3:1-3; Ether 1:21-24; 4:18-21, 35-40, 66.

ANTI-NEPHI-LEHI—*Lamanite King (c. 90 B.C.)*

The father of Lamoni, king of all the civilized Lamanites, conferred his kingdom upon his son, Anti-Nephi-Lehi, shortly before his death. When Ammon called a council with Anti-Nephi-Lehi and Lamoni, his brother, to plan a defense for the people against the uncivilized Lamanites, Anti-Nephi-Lehi refused to consider any kind of defense. He commanded his people to remember their oath to war no more and bade them bury their weapons as a testimony of their covenant.
References: Alma 14:23-47.

ANTI-NEPHI-LEHIES—*Converts*

Ammon, son of Mosiah, went up to the land of Ishmael among the Lamanites to convert them. He became a friend of their king, Lamoni, and later a friend of his father also. Both Lamoni and his father were so converted that a decree was sent out that Ammon and his brothers were to be allowed to preach freely the word of God to the Lamanites of the land.

The resulting conversion was so great that these people never did fall away, for they became a righteous people. They laid down all their weapons and buried them so that they might not take them up again in anger against their brothers even in self-defense. The name Anti-Nephi-Lehies was given to distinguish the converts from the rest of the Lamanites.

King Lamoni's father died and his son, Anti-Nephi-Lehi, ruled the land in his stead. When the

Lamanites did come upon them, they refused to defend themselves. They prostrated themselves upon the ground before their enemies, begging mercy, not from their destroyers but from God in behalf of those who were slaying them. Seeing this, many of the Lamanites were converted and joined the Anti-Nephi-Lehies in greater number than those who had been slain.

The armies of the Lamanites turned away from battle with the submissive Anti-Nephi-Lehies and turned in full vengeance upon the Ammonihahites. Even after this carnage, many Lamanites turned back and, seeing the peace of the Anti-Nephi-Lehies, came to dwell in Ishmael to bury their weapons and repent.

The Amalekites, Nephite dissenters, because of their inability to destroy the Nephites, stirred up the Lamanites who were yet unrepentant to destroy the Anti-Nephi-Lehies. Again the Anti-Nephi-Lehies refused to resist. In order to preserve them, Ammon gathered those who remained alive and took them to Zarahemla.

The Nephites in Zarahemla gave them the land of Jershon and a protecting army on condition that they pay tribute to support their defense. The conditions were accepted and the Anti-Nephi-Lehies moved in. They were renamed the people of Ammon, or Ammonites.

The Ammonites were unique in their zeal to obey God and their demonstration of love for their fellowmen. They were perfectly honest and upright and firm in their faith. Nothing could make that generation take up arms against their brethren, even in self-defense. They did not fear death, but looked forward to it as a victory. The Nephites grew to love the Ammonites and to keep them in high favor. They became exceedingly prosperous and generous.

When Korihor, the antichrist, came among them to preach against the coming of Christ, he was taken to Ammon, who had him cast out of the land. The Ammonites refused to tolerate any who taught unrighteousness.

When the Lamanites, led by King Ammoron, a Nephite dissenter, came into the land and a great destruction of the Nephites began, the Ammonites moved out of Jershon. Late in the war, Helaman came to the Ammonites for help. Rather than let those who had covenanted to keep peace take up arms and break their oath, Helaman chose two thousand young men from among them who had not taken that oath. These two thousand men served valiantly; though wounded, not one was slain in combat. They returned to Jershon with their people at the end of the war with more than four thousand defeated Lamanite warriors who entered the covenant of peace.

Some of these people later migrated to the land northward.

References: Alma 14:7-60, 73-74; 15:3-44; 16:20-22; 20:9-15; 21:111-112; 24:63-78; 26:3-21, 68-69, 75-76, 165-167; 29:19, 31-33; Helaman 2:11; 5:91-104; III Nephi 1:52-53; 5:1-8.

ANTIOMNO—*Lamanite King (c. 90 B.C.)*

Antiomno was the king of Middoni. He had put Aaron and his brothers into prison for preaching against the local beliefs. King Lamoni, his Lamanite friend, and Ammon, brother of Aaron, came to Antiomno and convinced him that he should release Aaron and his brothers. Aaron and his brothers were released from prison, clothed, fed, and strengthened before they were sent on their way.

References: Alma 12:182-185.

ANTIONAH—*Apostate (c. 82 B.C.)*

Antionah was the chief ruler among the Ammonihahites, dissenters from the Nephites who believed that all would be saved in heaven no matter what they had done during their lifetime. Alma and Amulek came to Ammonihah to preach to them in hopes of their repentance. Antionah questioned Alma concerning eternal life, trying to trap him in a controversy. When he could not accomplish his desire, he saw to it that Alma and Amulek were imprisoned anyway.

References: Alma 9:33-37; 10:32-39.

ANTIONUM—*Captain (c. A.D. 385)*

The ten thousand men led by Antionum, a Nephite captain, against the Lamanites in the last war of the Nephites were annihilated in a single battle near the hill Cumorah where the plates of

Nephi and the relics of the Nephites were later buried by Mormon.

References: Mormon 3:15.

ANTIONUM—Land

Zoram gathered believers in idols and moved with them to Antionum, a land east of Zarahemla, south of Jershon, and bordering along the seashore. Rameumptons in synagogues dotted the land for worship centers. Later the Lamanites gathered in Antionum to prepare for war against the peace-loving Anti-Nephi-Lehies in Jershon. The Lamanites were frightened away from battle by the great defense and stronger arms of the Nephites. They slunk back into the wilderness without fighting and left Antionum, to try again to charge the Nephites at Manti in a surprise attack on their enemies.

References: Alma 16:80; 20:5, 17, 25.

ANTIPARAH—Nephite City

In the Lamanite wars from 66 to 64 B.C., the city of Antiparah was captured. The turning point of this Lamanite war occurred at Antiparah when Antipus, captain of the Nephite forces, and Helaman with his two thousand Ammonite youths recaptured Antiparah and began to break the defenses of the Lamanites.

References: Alma 26:15, 36-73.

ANTIPAS—Mountain

Antipas was located near the hill Onidah, near Antionum of the Zoramites. The Lamanite armies of Lehonti, military chief, gathered there in retreat from an unsuccessful battle with the Nephites in disobedience to their king. The king sent Amalickiah's troops to force the Lamanite army to return to war with the Nephites.

Instead Amalickiah, a Nephite dissenter, surrounded the troops on Antipas and drew Lehonti down from the mountain with a promise of a treaty. Amalickiah promised Lehonti safety in return for an appointment as the second in command of the whole Lamanite army. As soon as Lehonti agreed to these terms, Amalickiah began having him poisoned until he died. Thus, Amalickiah gained control of the whole Lamanite army at Antipas.

References: Alma 21:80-100.

ANTIPUS—War Chief (c. 66 B.C.)

In the midst of a great war with the hated Lamanites, Antipus was appointed leader of the Nephite forces at Judea. Helaman joined his two thousand Anti-Nephi-Lehies to the troops at Judea where Antipus was fortifying the city. This preparation frightened the Lamanites and kept them back from taking the city.

To break into the defenses of the Lamanites, Antipus sent Helaman and his warriors to pretend to be carrying provisions to a neighboring city. When Helaman passed by Antiparah, the Lamanites sent their strongest warriors against his inexperienced youth. Antipus brought his men up on the rear of the Lamanites and thus closed off their retreat. The army of Helaman fled before the

Lamanites until they were a great distance from the city. Then, gaining courage, Helaman's army turned upon the Lamanites. Antipus, coming up from behind, completed the circle. The Lamanites were captured, but not without first having slain Antipus.

References: Alma 26:10-64.

ANTUM—Nephite Land

In the land of Antum, near Jashon, upon the hill Shim, Ammoron, the recorder, in A.D. 320, hid the record of the Nephites and their religious relics to prevent their falling into unrighteous hands and being lost. Many of the plates were of fine gold and could have been melted to make useless ornaments.

Ammoron told Mormon, a child of ten, where the records were buried and that he should, when he was twenty-four, dig them up and continue the record.

Mormon did as Ammoron commanded, then was later forced to bury the records himself, at hill Cumorah, for the same reason.

References: Mormon 1:2-4, 43, 44.

APOSTLES—Old World Witnesses

Twelve men were chosen by Christ in Jerusalem of Judea to act as special witnesses to the world of Christ. These men, known as the Apostles of the Lamb to Nephi, son of Lehi, were to write the record of Christ and his church in the Old World, to administer to believers for receiving of the Holy Ghost, and to act as judges of the twelve tribes of

Israel in the resurrection and the twelve disciples of the New World. These men were also made known to Mormon and Moroni.

References: I Nephi 1:9; 3:88-95, 115, 165-167, 190-200, 238-239, 246-251; Mormon 1:84; 4:80; Ether 5:41; Moroni 2:2.

ARCHEANTUS—Choice Warrior (c. A.D. 400)

Archeantus was a great warrior in Moroni's Nephite army in the last war of the Nephites as they were being exterminated by the Lamanites. Though he fought valiantly, he was slain.

References: Moroni 9:2.

ARMS—See Weapons

ARPAD—Old World City

Arpad or Arphad was a northern Syrian city east of Antioch and north of Mamath. In 723 B.C., it was destroyed by the Assyrian King Tiglath-pileser III, father of Sennacherib. Evidence of its destruction was used by Sennacherib to threaten Hezekiah, king of Judah. Isaiah told Hezekiah not to worry. God would take care of Assyria for him.

Assyria was overthrown by the Medes in 609 B.C.

References: II Nephi 9:86-95; II Kings 18:9-37; 19:1-13; Isaiah 10:5-14.

ARROW—Weapon

The arrow was a straight wooden shaft tipped at one end with a sharpened metal or stone head and at the other end with feathers. The feathers were split and tied with thin strips of tendon along the end of the shaft in parallel lines in order to make the arrow fly straight toward its target. Markings on the arrow identified the owner.

Arrowheads were shaped by slamming a heavy hard stone point against a small piece of flint or steel. Indians later lost their ability to work steel. The shape of the arrowhead indicated its purpose. Barbed heads were used in war to make their removal more difficult. Smooth edged arrows were used when the hunter wanted to recover his arrow quickly for reuse in hunting small animal targets. Arrowhead shapes varied from family to family.

Arrows were used by the Lehites to hunt for food as they traveled in the wilderness along the Red Sea on their way out of Jerusalem. When Nephi ran out of arrows along the way, he fashioned new ones. His wood bow, made after the steel one broke, was too light for the steel arrows he had used before.

Arrows were also used in battle by both the Nephites and the Lamanites. There is no mention of arrows among the Jaredites.

References: I Nephi 5:17-41; II Nephi 8:96-98 (Isaiah 5:26-28); 9:37 (Isaiah 7:24); Jarom 1:19-21; Mosiah 6:19-21, Mosiah 6:37-38; Alma 1:63-76, 103; 12:10-13; 20:23; 21:150-179; 22:4; Helaman 1:15; 5:111-119; Mormon 3:11.

ASP—Animal

An asp is a poisonous snake, revered by the Egyptians, whose venom kills instantly after striking its victim. It was mentioned by Isaiah to represent the extent to which safety from the deadly will be accorded man during the period after judgment and during the reign of Christ.

References: II Nephi 9:120-124; 12:91-95; Isaiah 11:5-9.

ASS—Animal

The ass or donkey is a horse-like creature. It is smaller and has unusually long ears. Its mane or neck hair is short and stands straight up, while the mane of the horse is long and flowing. Asses are domesticated for use as beasts of burden, carrying bundles or men. The ass is much more intelligent than the horse and is easily trained; however it becomes obstinate when overloaded or mistreated.

Brought by the Jaredites to the New World, the asses were domesticated and flourished. When the Jaredites destroyed themselves in a long civil war, the asses continued to thrive in the wilds.

The Nephites found the asses in the wilderness when they arrived and domesticated some for beasts of burden. Both wild asses and tame asses are still found today in use, particularly in South and Central America.

References: Ether 4:21; I Nephi 5:216; Mosiah 3:18; 7:124; 9:142.

ASSYRIA—Old World Land

Assyria was an ancient land on the east of the middle Tigris between 35° and 37° north latitude. Assur was its capital and the only town of any consequence.

Despite its short existence, the Assyrian empire has had a great influence on Israelite history. Assyria became an empire under Tiglath-pileser III, also known as Pul, during his reign from

744-727 B.C. The empire was as swiftly lost under Ashurbanipal by 639 B.C. By 609 B.C., the last remnant of their mighty army was scattered, to recover no more. Assyria was effectively swallowed by Babylonia and later Persia.

In a quotation from Isaiah, Nephi told his brothers of the use of the prideful Assyrian to overthrow and scatter the Israelites and to punish them until their hearts returned to sound belief in God. Later God was to overthrow the Assyrian and return the Jews to their inheritance.

This Assyrian was Shalmaneser, who in 722 B.C., conquered Israel and scattered the ten northern tribes. Judea was conquered by Nebuchadnezzar, the Babylonian king, about 587 B.C.

Both Babylonia and Assyria were conquered by the Persians under Cyaxares. Later Cyrus and Darius were responsible for the return of the Jews to Jerusalem. The ten northern tribes were scattered but are to be gathered again in the last days.
References: II Nephi 9:30-131; 10:46-47; Isaiah 7:17 - 11:16; 14:24-25.

AX—Weapon

An ax, or axe, consists of a strong thick shaft of wood headed with a large flat sharpened stone or metal plate. In former times it was used either for hacking or throwing at an enemy. In peaceful times it was used for chopping wood or butchering meat. Axes were also called hatchets by the Indians who used them. Axes are now distinguished from hatchets by their longer handles and heavier heads.

Axes were mentioned as weapons among the Nephites and the Lamanites in their wars. Jaredites did not mention them in their list of weapons.

References: II Nephi 9:96 (Isaiah 10:15); Enos 1:31-32; Alma 3:90; Mormon 3:11.

B

BABEL—*Old World Tower*

When the family of Noah left the ark, they moved down the mountain toward the sea. When they reached the plains they stopped. There Satan plotted with the people to build a great tower so that they might get to heaven by their own strength. The Lord put a stop to this useless endeavor by causing the people to be divided by language and scattered over the earth. The structure itself was destroyed. There is no sure evidence to locate it exactly, but it is thought to be near Babylon.

Among the people at the tower was the family of Jared. Jared had his brother pray to the Lord that their language not be confounded, but that they, their families, and their friends maintain their langauge and be sent away together. The Lord heard the brother of Jared and had him gather the people to go to the New World to live, as long as they were righteous.

They brought with them many seeds and animals from the Old World to populate the New World.

References: Helaman 2:153-155; Ether 1:5, 7-24; Genesis 11.

BABYLON—*Old World Land*

Babylon was an ancient city located on the western bank of the Euphrates river, south of Bagdad.

Lehi told his children that Jerusalem would be destroyed and the people carried captive into Babylon. They were to return to Jerusalem in God's own due time. Lehi and his family were sent away to the New World prior to the invasion of the Babylonians.

A few years later a small group of people joined Mulek to go to the New World, and to escape Babylonian captivity. This group was eventually discovered by the Lehites.

After seventy years of captivity, the Jews were allowed to return to Jerusalem by the Persian rulers who had defeated the Babylonians. In accordance with prophecy, the temple fittings were returned to Jerusalem and Babylon was finally destroyed by Xerxes in about 478 B.C. Though a few attempts at restoration were made, none were successful. The city lies in ruin. No animals except the doleful owls and bats remain there to rest. Man comes and goes in search of artifacts but does not stay.

References: I Nephi 1:11-12; 3:2-3; 6:21, 27 (Isaiah 48:14, 20); II Nephi 10:1-54 (Isaiah 13-14); 11:17-18, 25; Omni 1:26-31.

BARGES—Boats

Barges were built by direction of the Lord to carry the Jaredites and their possessions across the lakes and seas in their journey toward the promised land in the New World. Eight special barges were prepared for the ocean voyage. They were described as small, buoyant, and watertight on all sides including the bottom and top. The ends were peaked. The length was given as the length of a tree. The door, when shut, sealed the vessel. Holes cut in the top and bottom to admit air could be closed to allow the vessel to sink into the depths of stormy seas. Light was provided by phosphorescent balls energized by power from the finger of God, since no fire could be used.

The Jaredites rode the churning ocean in the barges for 344 days before they arrived at the new continent.

References: Ether 1:28, 43-58; 3:2-14.

BARLEY—Plant

Barley is a grain crop from which bread was made for the Nephites. Barley was the basis for their money system and a symbol of the wealth of the land. When they were in subjection to the Lamanites, the Nephites paid a tribute of their crop. The seeds were probably brought over from Jerusalem with Lehi when they escaped the wrath of the Babylonians.

Though barley is only one-half as nutritional as wheat, it ripens first. When the wheat ripens and is ready for use it replaces barley in the making of bread. The remaining barley is kept for seed or given to stock.

References: Mosiah 5:35-36; 6:12; Alma 8:58, 61.

BASHAN—Old World Land

As Moses led the Israelites the second time toward the promised land, the king of Bashan came out to war with them. Israel defeated the king's armies slaying them all, and possessed their land.

The land of Bashan lies east of the Jordan near the sea of Galilee. This large and fertile area of eroded lava became part of the possession of the half-tribe of Manasseh. Within it grows enormous oak trees.

Isaiah prophesied that the judgment of Christ would extend to all parts of the world including the oaks of Bashan.

References: II Nephi 8:28-32 (Isaiah 2:13-16); Numbers 21:32-35; Deuteronomy 3:14; Zechariah 11:2.

BATH—See Measure

BATS—Animals

Bats are the only mammals that fly, though others have the capacity to glide. Their wings are skin webs between the fingers of their hands. Their fingers are elongated to make the wings large enough to support their weight in flight. Only the thumb is not elongated. It is fitted with a claw to help the bat cling to surfaces. Bats spend their resting hours in dark caves. They fly out at night in hoards to eat, surviving mostly on insects; though some species suck blood, others prefer to eat fruit. Because of their nocturnal instincts they do not depend on sight but have been given a special radar system. Reflections of emitted sound direct the bat to prey or around obstacles.

When Isaiah prophesied that in the latter days men would throw their idols to the bats, he meant that they would be secreted in tombs or in caves. With the fall of each empire, its pagan worship ended with the burial of its idols in the rubble left behind. The invasion in A.D. 70 of the Roman general Titus sent Jewish survivors into the desert into the caves and rocks. Little was left of the idols and wealth the Jews had worshiped when the war was over.

References: II Nephi 8:36-37; Isaiah 2:20-21.

BEAR—*Animal*

Bears are carnivorous mammals. They lumber about flat-footed at a four mile an hour gait, but can reach speeds ten times that for short distances when enraged. When hungry, most bears prefer meat. They can attack a cow and break its neck with one whack from a powerful paw. Long claws and sharp teeth help the bear shred the victim.

The bear is part of the prophetic sign given for peace in the last days, to indicate that the cow and the bear, who are natural enemies, will coexist in peace.

References: II Nephi 9:120-124; 12:91-95; Isaiah 11:5-9.

BEES—*Animals*

Bees are social insects living in colonies called swarms. They build nests or hives in hollow trees, clefts of rocks, or ravines.

When bees are disturbed they attack with fury in great numbers, chasing their attackers until they die or are driven out of the bees' territory. They use nectar and pollen to produce wax for combs or chambers to be filled with honey for food or with eggs to produce more bees. The honey is sweet to the taste of man, so he robs the hive of its riches, often under attack from the bees.

The Jaredites, as they left the tower of Babel, spent some time in preparing food for their journey. Among the animals they brought were the honeybees in portable hives or deserets, to provide themselves with honey and with pollenizers for their crops in the New World.

The bee is also mentioned in prophecy to represent the warriors of Assyria that would come in swarms to Israel to hide in the ravines and rocks.

References: Ether 1:23-24; II Nephi 9:31; Isaiah 7:18.

BELLOWS—Tool

Bellows consist of a collapsible bag filled with a leather flap valve that opens to take air in when the bellows are opened but prevent the leaking of air when the bag is compressed. The air from the collapsing bag is forced through a small opening so that it can be directed under a flame to increase the heat of the fire. Temperatures for melting and molding of metals can be obtained from open fires in this way.

The invention of the bellows is generally credited to Anacharsis of Scythia in about 600 B.C. Nephi, son of Lehi the merchant and a worker of metals, understood their construction and use. When he was called upon to prepare from ore the tools he needed for shipbuilding, he first made a bellows to speed up the refining process.

References: I Nephi 5:70-74.

BENJAMIN—Nephite King (c. 130 B.C.)

King Benjamin was the son of Mosiah and father

of Mosiah. He drove the Lamanites from Zarahemla so that there was peace. Amaleki, the recorder, having no sons, gave the keeping of the plates of Nephi to King Benjamin's charge. He also had the sword of Laban and used it in the defense of the Nephites.

King Benjamin had three sons—Mosiah, Helaman, and Helorum. They were all taught reformed Egyptian so that they could read the plates of brass and the plates of Nephi, to preserve the beliefs and understanding of the Scriptures to teach the Nephites. Benjamin called Mosiah to be king after he was retired.

When the kingdom was conferred upon Mosiah, King Benjamin had a tower built from which to speak, so that the multitude gathered to hear his speech might see him at the same time. His message was written down by scribes and distributed among the people, also, so that none missed this ministry. He spoke to them of humility and the love of God for them. When he called them to repentance, Benjamin obtained an oath of the Nephites to take upon themselves the name of Christ and to live in righteousness and peace.

After the kingdom was conferred upon Mosiah, King Benjamin lived in peace three more years before he died. His words were taught for many generations among the Nephites.

References: Omni 1:40-43; Words of Mormon 1:4-5, 14-15, 18-27; Mosiah 1:1-4:7; 5:55; 11:105; Helaman 2:71; Ether 1:94-95.

BETHABARA—Old World City

Nephi wrote that his father, Lehi, told him that in about 600 years from the time they left Jerusalem, John the Baptist would baptize at Bethabara. John the Beloved reported that John the Baptist did baptize at Bethabara.

Bethabara is a town on the Jordan near the main ford northeast of Bethshean near the present town of Abara. It lies on the border between the lots of Benjamin and Reuben.

References: I Nephi 3:11; John 1:28-29; Judges 7:24.

BITTERN—Animal

A bittern is a bird of the heron family. It is a slender wading bird that prefers tall-grassed marshy ooze with floating grass stems for its nesting material. It is especially adept at concealing itself in the reeds by imitating a bunch of leaning stalks.

Isaiah prophesied that the Lord would cut off Babylon and prepare it for a habitat of the bittern. This meant that the once proud city would be reduced to rubbish covered by muddy pools and soggy marshes.

References: II Nephi 10:44, 45; Isaiah 14:22, 23.

BOATS—See Barges or Ships

BOAZ—City

In A.D. 375, during the last wars between the Lamanites and the Nephites, the Nephites were driven to the city of Boaz. There they boldly fought the Lamanites and were not driven out until the

Lamanites came against them the second time.

When they were driven out, the slaughter of the Nephites was great. Many women and children were offered by the Lamanites to their idols. The city was probably located north of Desolation.
References: Mormon 2:18-24.

BOUNTIFUL—City

In the great war of 66 B.C. between the Nephites and the Lamanites, the Nephites began from their eastern stronghold, the city Bountiful, to retake their lands from the Lamanite invaders. Working with that city as a base of operation, they retook Mulek and took their Lamanite prisoners to fortify their own prison with a wall of timber and earth.

Coriantumr, in 51 B.C., brought another invading army of Lamanites into the land with intentions of taking the city Bountiful, but he was repulsed before he was fully successful.

The sons of Helaman began their ministry at the city Bountiful in their attempt in 30 B.C. to re-establish and strengthen the church among the Nephites.
References: Alma 24:19-57; 25:52; Helaman 1:25-31; 2:77-78.

BOUNTIFUL—Old World Land

As the family of Lehi journeyed toward their land of promise, they came to a land rich in fruit and honey. It lay near the ocean, eight years' strenuous travel east-southeast from Jerusalem, Israel.

In Bountiful, the Lehites built a ship to carry

them and their possessions across the ocean to their destination.
Reference: I Nephi 5:62-181.

BOUNTIFUL—Nephite Land

Bountiful was a land filled with wild animals that had been driven there by the great drought of the times of the Jaredites. It bordered Desolation on its north, Zarahemla on its south, Nephi on its west, and the Lamanite seashore area on its east. The border between Desolation and Bountiful was a day-and-a-half journey by foot.

Many battles occurred in the land Bountiful over the years, as the Nephites fought the Lamanites and various groups of Nephite dissenters. In A.D. 34 the people gathered in the land Bountiful and there they were visited by Christ.
References: Alma 13:72-80; Helaman 1:30-31; 2:38-40; III Nephi 2:32-33; 5:1-3.

BOW—Weapon

A bow consists of a strip of wood or metal with a string drawn from end to end to make the strip bend into a slight arch. When not in use the bowstring is released and held limply by the straightened bow. When the bow is needed, the archer sets the string in the lower notch at the end of the bow and braces that end against the side of his foot. The bow is then pulled back with one hand while the other slides the upper loop of the string into the upper notch.

To shoot an arrow, the notch at the feather end

of the arrow is set in the string with one hand, while the other hand steadies the bow and the arrow is pulled back in the string. Releasing the string pushes the arrow forward by the force of the spring of the bow. When a bow has lost its spring, it will not straighten when the arrow is released.

As Lehi's family traveled toward the land of promise, they used their bows and arrows to obtain food. When Nephi's bow broke it made his two older brothers angry with him for the seventh time. This bow was made of fine steel. The bows of the brothers had lost their spring, so for awhile they could get no meat for the migrating family.

After much bickering, Nephi went out and cut for himself a new bow from wood and sharpened straight sticks for arrows. Using these simple weapons, he obtained the needed meat.

As the Nephites separated themselves from the Lamanites in the promised land after Lehi died, they began to prosper in the land. They fashioned bows and arrows to use as weapons of war to protect themselves from their ruthless brothers. The Lamanites in turn armed themselves with bows and arrows. After that, only occasionally was the bow and arrow mentioned as a means for obtaining food.

When an army surrendered, they handed over their bows and arrows as a sign of peace.

Bows and arrows were not mentioned as weapons used by the Jaredites.

References: I Nephi 5:17-41; II Nephi 8:96-98 (Isaiah 5:26-28); 9:37 (Isaiah 7:24); 10:18 (Isaiah 13:18); 12:10-13;

20:23, 74-75; 21:150-179; 22:4; Helaman 1:15; 5:111-119;
Mormon 3:11.

BRASS—Metal

Brass is an alloy of copper and zinc. Chemically,
the two metals produce a very durable surface, the
zinc retarding the corrosion of the copper. Because
it is cheap, abundant, and durable, it was used for
the keeping of permanent records. Laban kept
records on plates of brass. These were taken by
Nephi for the instruction of the Lehites in the promised land.

To direct the Lehites in their long journey from
Jerusalem to the promised land half the world
away, God gave Lehi a compass, or Liahona, made
of brass.

When the Lehites and the Jaredites arrived in the
New World they found an abundance of the ore
from which they could make brass. The Jaredites
fashioned breastplates for armor of brass. The Nephites used it for ornaments. King Noah was noted
for the brass ornamentation he had placed on the
buildings and temple at Nephi. The Lamanites
taxed the Nephites of their brass when they conquered them.

In a prophecy of the latter days, the Indians are
among the covenant people who will be given
hooves of brass to beat in pieces many people.
Isaiah symbolizes the stubbornness of people by a
brow of brass.

References: I Nephi 5:11; 6:11-12; II Nephi 4:21; Jarom
1:19-21; Mosiah 5:65; 7:6, 11-15; III Nephi 9:54; Ether 4:71.

BRASS PLATES—See Plates—Brass

BREASTPLATES—*Weapons*

The breastplates were shields that were worn over the shoulders and down to the thighs of the soldiers. They protected the most vital organs of the soldiers.

Breastplates of brass were worn by the Jaredites in the last struggle that eventually exterminated the race.

In a war between the Lamanites and the Nephites, Moroni, the Nephite war chief, armed his men with breastplates, probably of quilted leather, and so frightened the invading army that the Lamanites refused to fight. Zarahemnah, the Lamanite general, credited the breastplates and other advanced weaponry for the Nephites' success in overcoming his army.

The Lamanites began to arm themselves with breastplates like those of the Nephites.

References: Mosiah 5:65; Alma 20:21-24, 39-49, 77; 21:42-45, 154-179; Helaman 1:15; Ether 6:87.

BRIERS—*Plants*

Briers are short, spiney plants that grow together in patches of unkept soil and bear prickly fruit. They were planted around orchards and vineyards to act as barbed wire fences to keep out predators.

Isaiah prophesied that briers, or gentile heathen, would come up in the orchards, or holy places, of Jerusalem after the inhabitants were taken into captivity and scattered. After the overthrow of

Jerusalem in A.D. 70 by the Romans under the leadership of Titus, daily sacrifices ceased and the synagogues that remained were used for idol worship.

Later when the Jews come to reclaim the land and be gathered in the latter day, the briers will be burned (or their enemies destroyed) in one day (or year).

References: II Nephi 8:75-76 (Isaiah 5:5-6); 9:36-38 (Isaiah 7:23-25), 78 (Isaiah 9:18), 98-99 (Isaiah 10:17-18).

BROTHER OF JARED—Prophet (Ether)

Jared, at the time of the confounding of languages at the tower of Babel, called upon his brother to pray to God that the language of his family and friends be not changed. He recognized that his brother was favored of the Lord for his faithfulness. His brother was described as large and mighty in stature.

When the prayers of the brother of Jared were answered and their language was not confounded, Jared sent his brother to inquire of the Lord where they should go. The brother of Jared was told to gather his friends and their possessions to go to a choice land where they could remain as long as they were faithful in their service to God.

In their travels, the Lord went before them and talked to the brother of Jared as he would later lead Israel and talk to Moses.

The Lord gave the brother of Jared the plans needed to build eight barges to transport the Jaredites and their possessions to the New World.

The ships were to be built like submarines. Since they could have no fires in them, the brother of Jared prepared sixteen stones for light. He asked God to touch them so that they might glow during the journey to provide light for the pilgrims. Because of his great faith the brother of Jared saw the finger of God as He touched the stones.

When the brother of Jared saw that the finger was like the finger of man, he fell down in fear. Then God showed him the rest of the body he would assume in the meridian of time when he came to earth to be judged as Christ. The brother of Jared was the first man of faith great enough to return to the presence of God and see his likeness. God showed the brother of Jared all the history of man. He commanded him to write what he saw and seal up the record with the Urim and Thummim until the Lord should reveal them to man. These things were shown to the Lehites at the time Christ visited them after A.D. 34 but were sealed again by Moroni until man again is ready to receive them. This revelation has not yet taken place.

When the ships were prepared, the Jaredites gathered animals of every kind, including fish, cattle, birds, and bees, then entered the ship and proceeded on their journey across the ocean. During the journey the brother of Jared led in singing praises to God night and day. When they reached the promised land they spread out upon the New World.

As the brother of Jared grew old, he asked that the Jaredites be gathered, numbered, and allowed to make of him a last request. When this was done, the Jaredites asked for a king. The brother of Jared told them that this would lead to the eventual destruction of the Jaredites, but they persisted.

They were told to elect their king. When the majority called first one then another of the sons of the brother of Jared, none would accept the job nor would the brother of Jared coerce them to accept. Only Orihah, son of Jared, would accept. After Orihah began to reign, the brother of Jared died.

References: Ether 1:7-101; 3:1-35; 4:44, 109; 5:20-21, 25, 30-31.

BUCKLERS—Weapons

A buckler is a small shield worn on the arm of the warrior to protect his body. It is lighter and more easily shifted about as the soldier fights than a shield.

Gidgiddoni, the Nephite war chief, taught his people to arm themselves with bucklers in addition to other armor to protect themselves in a war with the Gadianton robbers.

References: III Nephi 2:38.

BUILDINGS

Lehi, the patriarch of the Lehites, saw in a vision a great and spacious building filled with people pointing and laughing at the repentant. This building was interpreted to Nephi to be the pride of the world.

Nephi, son of Lehi, in a prophetic parable told of a tower in the midst of the vineyard of the Lord. It represented the temple in the midst of the children of Israel. As the watchtower of a vineyard guards the fruit from thieves, the temple of Israel is to guard the faithful from Satan's forces.

A model of Solomon's temple was built under the direction of Nephi, son of Lehi, in the land of Nephi. Not having the same materials available to Solomon, Nephi made many substitutions in its construction.

In the peaceful days of Jarom, son of Enos, after the separation of the Nephites from the Lamanites, many buildings were constructed by the Nephites. In a land near Nephi was found a wilderness covered with the ruins of buildings built by the Jaredites during their several periods of prosperity.

The buildings constructed under the orders of King Noah, king of the Nephites who had returned to the Land of Nephi, were described as elegant and spacious, ornamented with fine work of wood, gold, silver, iron, brass, ziff, and copper. Noah built a palace, a tower near the temple, a tower on the hill north of Shilom, and many other buildings.

The Nephites built temples, sanctuaries, and synagogues after the Jewish mode. Later the Lamanites built similar structures. Both groups built many prisons.

The Zoramites built synagogues which had in the center high platforms for prideful prayer called the Rameumpton or Holy Stand.

Moroni, the war chief, taught his Nephite people

to build forts for the protection of every Nephite city.

When timber was scarce in the desolate north lands, the people built with cement. Instead of removing what little timber was there in construction, they had lumber shipped in from the south.

At the time of the death of Christ upon the cross in Jerusalem, there was a calamitous earthquake which caused nearly all the buildings to be cast to ruin, sunk and buried. After Christ appeared and taught the survivors, the people rebuilt the cities that were shaken down but not those that were sunk. By A.D. 322 the whole face of the land was again covered with cities.

In the last days, Mormon prophesied that a perfect city will be built into which a remnant of Lamanites will be gathered who will prepare for Zion. A temple will be built in the midst of the city for the endowment.

References: I Nephi 2:71-83; 3:89-94, 124-126; II Nephi 4:21-25; 8:71-72 (Isaiah 5:1-2); 11:65-69; Jarom 1:19-21; Mosiah 5:60-63; 6:11; 7:11-21; 11:5, 156-157; Alma 4:8; 11:22; 13:2, 24, 39; 16:88-89; 21:128-130, 162-165; 22:1-6, 16; 24:53-59; Helaman 2:7-14; III Nephi 2:18; 3:8; 4:6-17; 10:1-3; IV Nephi 1:8-10; Mormon 1:7; Ether 4:25, 46, 48, 56, 68; Moroni 7:1.

BULL—Animal

Bulls are male oxen or cattle. Undisturbed bulls are nervous. When disturbed they snort a warning then charge the disruption, whether it is a fluttering cloth, leaf, or an attacker. If a net is thrown over them, bulls struggle violently to tear the net with their horns which only further entangles the bull. The maddened bull becomes a ferocious, churning mass of horn and muscle until all his energy is spent.

Isaiah compares two prophets of the Lord sent to rebuke the inhabitants in a rebuilt Jerusalem as wild bulls caught in a net. These two bulls are two sons, or tribes, of Israel who will rebuke the enemies of Judah and Israel.

References: II Nephi 5:104-106; Isaiah 51:19-20.

C

CAIN—Murderer (Old Testament)

Cain believed Satan when he was told that if he murdered his brother Abel, it would not be known. Satan bought Cain's soul with that lie. He established secret combinations and oaths with Cain that have caused trouble in all generations as they have been passed down.

References: Helaman 2:150-152; Ether 3:89; Genesis 5.

CALNO—Old World City

Calno or Calneh was located near Arpad in Assyria. It was built by Nimrod of the lineage of Japheth, son of Noah. Calno, with the other Assyrian cities, was to be punished because of the pride of their king and their own idolatry.

It was destroyed by the Babylonian and Mede armies between 612 and 609 B.C.

References: II Nephi 9:86-95; Isaiah 10:5-14; II Kings 18:9-37; 19:9-37.

CARCHEMISH—Old World City

Carchemish was located northeast of Calno and Arpad in Assyria on the east bank of the Euphrates. It was renamed Europus by the Romans and was on the eastern boundary of the Roman Empire of A.D. 65. Carchemish with other Assyrian cities was punished because of the pride of their king and their own idolatry.

It was attacked by the Babylonians and Medes between 612 and 609 B.C.

References: II Nephi 9:86-95; Isaiah 10:5-14; II Kings 18:9-37; 19:9-37.

CATACLYSM

A cataclysm is a period of short duration during which a number of devastating natural events occur singly or in combination such as earthquakes, volcanos, avalanches, tidal waves, or meteoric falls. When the destructive force subsides, the surface of the earth is drastically changed. Whole towns are erased, buried, burned, sunk, or shattered to rubble. Millions of people are left destitute; millions more are dead.

A cataclysm was prophesied for the destruction of the cities of Sodom and Gomorrah. There were five cities in all believed to be buried at that time.

At the death of Christ on the cross in Jerusalem, a cataclysm involving earthquakes, storms, avalanches, and volcanoes struck the New World for three hours. Dust from the cataclysm remained heavy in the air for three days, preventing light from the sun or even candles to shine through.

Tremors were heard from this quake in Jerusalem half a world away. It opened graves and tore the curtain of the temple from bottom to top in that old city.

References: I Nephi 5:245-248; 3:102-111; Helaman 5:75-82; III Nephi 4:6-40.

CATTLE—Animal

Cattle were raised by the Jaredites and Lehites for food. It is a general term referring to domesticated animals.

References: II Nephi 9:38 (Isaiah 7:25); Enos 1:34; Mosiah 7:117 - 118; III Nephi 2:29-31, 42-45; 3:1, 31; Ether 4:18-21.

CEDARS—Plants

The cedars of Lebanon grew to great heights and were well known for the high quality of wood that could be produced from them. The wood is very durable and can take on a strong, shiny finish. Cedars were more valued than the wood of the sycamores which are similar but less durable.

In prophecy, Isaiah used the cedars of Lebanon to represent church leaders of long standing.

References: II Nephi 8:28-33; 9:69-70; 10:30; Isaiah 2:12-17; 9:9-10; 14:8.

CEMENT—Building Material

Cement is produced from gypsum or limestone. The mineral is heated to reduce its water content, ground, and mixed with sand or gravel. When the cement is needed it is mixed with water, formed by putting it in molds or applying it to the surface of other materials, and left to set. When the material sets it regains its rock form and characteristics.

When the Nephites spread northward into the land where trees were sparse, they built with cement supported by imported wood. Peoples of the southwestern United States and Central and South America continue to use this type of structure in many traditional buildings, particularly in arid, treeless areas.

References: Helaman 2:7-10.

CEZORAM—Judge (c. 31 B.C.)

Nephi, son of Helaman, delivered up the judgment seat of the Nephites to Cezoram so that he could go to preach among the people. Cezoram was murdered by a Gadianton robber as he sat in judgment.

References: Helaman 2:63-66, 136, 143.

CHALDEANS—Old World People

The Chaldeans conquered Babylon shortly before Lehi left Jerusalem. Later, led by Nebuchadrezzar II, they overthrew Jerusalem and took the Israelites into captivity.

Isaiah prophesied that God would have his way with them when the time came to redeem the children of Israel. After seventy years of captivity, the Jews were freed to return to Jerusalem by the Persian rulers who had defeated the Chaldeans. The Chaldean armies were finally scattered in about 478 B.C. by Xerxes.

References: I Nephi 6:21, 27; Isaiah 48:14, 20.

CHALDEE—Old World Land

Chaldee or Chaldea is the land from which Abraham came. It is the land of the Chaldeans. It lay between and included the Tigris and Euphrates valleys. Isaiah prophesied that the center of Chaldee, Babylon, would be utterly destroyed. See the article on Babylon for more details.

References: II Nephi 10:19; Isaiah 13:19.

CHARIOTS

Chariots were wheeled vehicles drawn behind a fast-paced horse as a means of transportation for the royal family or war leaders and their associates. They also were used to carry the war chiefs into battle. Egypt was famous for its many chariots. The children of Israel spent 600 years in Egypt, learning there of their construction and use.

The Lehites were displaced Israelites, so knowledge of chariots was with them. As they prospered, they built and used chariots.

King Lamoni, a Lamanite, traveled about his realm in chariots drawn by fine horses as early as 90 B.C. In A.D. 16 Lachoneus, the governor of the Nephites, had the people gather their chariots to form an army to fight the Gadianton robbers to drive them from the land.

In prophecy, Isaiah describes Assyria as a land full of chariots. Jesus tells us that unless the gentiles repent, all their horses and chariots, or means of transportation, will be cut off.

References: II Nephi 8:23-25; Isaiah 2:7-9; Alma 12:76-85; III Nephi 2:29-31; 9:101-104.

CHEMISH—Recorder (c. 280 B.C.)

Amaron delivered the records of the Nephites to his brother, Chemish. Chemish witnessed what Amaron wrote, then later passed the plates on to Abinadom, his son.

References: Omni 1:10-13.

CHICKEN—Animal

The chicken is well known for its protection of its young. A hen on a nest will viciously attack a predator until it sees that it must fly or die. When the chicks are hatched, they are cared for constantly by the hen. When predators near, the sun beats down, night falls, or a storm hits, the hen gathers her chicks under her strong wings and draws them close to her soft warm body until harm passes. She will furiously cackle at a stray chick and peck it to punish it. Chicks remain with the hen until fully feathered and independent.

When God called to the remnant who survived the cataclysm that struck the New World at the time of the crucifixion of Christ at Jerusalem, he told them of his desire to gather them as a hen gathers her chicks.

References: III Nephi 4:55-58.

CHRIST IN JERUSALEM—Redeemer (c. A.D. 1)

Lehi was driven from Jerusalem because he preached repentance and that the Messiah should come. He told of Christ's baptism by John and of Christ's death at the hands of the Jews he had come to save. Lehi told his family that Christ would come 600 years after they left Jerusalem.

Nephi, son of Lehi, saw that Christ would be born of a virgin after the manner of the flesh, be baptized, minister to the multitudes, be cast out from among the Jews, select twelve followers as special witnesses, heal the sick, be judged by his peers, be slain on the cross for the sins of the world, and remain in the grave three days before he would again arise. He tells us that Christ is God who has taken on the body of flesh to be judged of man. He reported that the same knowledge was given to and taught by Zenock, Neum, Isaiah, and Zenos.

Jacob, son of Lehi, continued to exhort the Nephites concerning the coming of God among the people, that God would become subject to man in the flesh and die that all men might become subject to God. While in the flesh, he would suffer the pains of all men in order that resurrection might pass upon all. He had to come to the Jews because no other nation would have crucified him.

King Benjamin proclaimed the coming of Christ, his miracles, temptations, anguish, name, mother's name, death, resurrection, and atonement. Benjamin recognized Christ as God who took upon himself the image of man to come and dwell among men.

Abinadi, the prophet to King Noah, told the citizens of Nephi that God himself would come down among men to bring forth the resurrection. He related particularly Christ's trial and death. Abinadi told them that Christ would be called the Son of God because he is God in the flesh.

Alma preached that Christ would be born of Mary at Jerusalem (Bethlehem is a suburb of Jerusalem), suffer pain and temptation, heal, take upon himself the sins of the people, and declare salvation.

Ammon, son of Mosiah and friend of Alma, taught that Christ would be born of a woman to redeem the believers.

Samuel, the Lamanite prophet to the Nephites, came in 5 B.C. to declare the sign of the birth of Christ, the star, and the sign of the death of Christ, three days of darkness.

References: I Nephi 3:4-15, 23-27, 58-62, 73-87; 5:233-248; 6:23-24; II Nephi 1:116; 6:7-10, 45-47; 7:5-9; 8:7-14; 9:66-67; 11:21-23, 34-36, 45-48; Mosiah 1:97-107; 2:7-17; 5:43-46; 8:13-37, 79-83; Alma 3:81-83; 5:13-23; 7:39-40; 11:29-30; 12:120, 142-143; 14:75; 16:207-210; 19:21-23; Helaman 5:54-62, 75-82.

CHRIST IN AMERICA—Redeemer (c. A.D. 34)

Nephi, son of Lehi, saw in a vision that at the time of Christ's death on the cross in Jerusalem, a great earthquake would occur in the New World that would change the face of the land and destroy all but a remnant of the people. The dust created by this cataclysm would cause three days of darkness during the time Christ would be in the grave. After that, Christ would come to the descendants of Lehi and ordain twelve disciples to follow him and minister to the people.

Nephi, son of Helaman, wrote that all the signs of Christ, given by Samuel, the prophet five years before, had occurred. The day before the coming of

God in the flesh, God himself spoke to Nephi, revealing his coming, to quiet the fears of Nephi for the righteous few who had been threatened with death if the signs did not come on schedule.

Thirty-three years later, the cataclysm predicted by Samuel as a sign of the crucifixion of Christ occurred. As the darkness hovered over the land, a voice was heard to call the people remaining after the cataclysm to repent. After three days of smothering darkness, dawn broke on a glorious day. Multitudes of those who survived gathered at Bountiful. Again, three times, the voice from heaven was heard. As the multitude watched, Christ descended from heaven and came to stand among them.

He taught them as he had taught the Jews in Judea. He selected twelve disciples to become the chief teachers after he returned to heaven. He healed the sick, blessed the children, endowed the twelve with the Holy Ghost, and ascended.

On the next day, he returned to teach prayer, observe communion, prophesy; then he ascended again.

The third day he appeared to the disciples to bless and transfigure them.

He appeared to the Lehites in the same body in which he appeared to the brother of Jared centuries before near the tower of Babel. All things were revealed to the brother of Jared and recorded on sealed plates. This message was unsealed and taught to the Lehite finders of the plates after Christ came to them. As the Lehites dwindled in unbelief, the plates were again sealed by Mormon, not to be unsealed until the world is ready to receive the message again.

References: I Nephi 3:102-113; II Nephi 11:58-73; Alma 11:31; Helaman 5:55-82; III Nephi 1:10-24; 4:3-13:28; Ether 1:68-81.

CIMETER—Weapon

The cimeter probably refers to a scimeter, or a curve-bladed short sword used now in Turkey. It was listed among the weapons of the Nephites and often with the sword. It was first mentioned in use as early as 420 B.C.

The Jaredites did not mention the use of the cimeter, though swords were their chief weapons.

References: Enos 1:31-32; Mosiah 6:19-21, 37-38; Alma 1:64-67; 15:32-34; 20:20, 23, 39-41, 74-75; 27:14-15; Helaman 1:15.

CLOTH

Cloth is woven from thread obtained from stems of plants or hair of animals. The thread is stretched on a frame in neat rows. A long strand is threaded in and out through the rows, then tamped to make it tight. By running the strand back and forth many times, cloth is obtained. By changing the colors of the thread or the pattern of the weave, designs are formed.

The strength of the cloth depends on the tightness of the weave and the type of fiber used. Fine twined fabric is made of thread twisted many times from long fine fibers.

Linen comes from the stem of the flax plant, silk

from the cocoons of special worms, and wool from sheep hair.

Both the Lehites and the Jaredites were reported to weave fine twined linen and silk. Archaeologists in Central America have found remains of these and other fabrics in the ruins there.

References: Mosiah 6:32-33; Alma 1:43-44; 2:8-10; Helaman 2:133; Ether 4:18-21, 73.

CLUBS—Weapons

Clubs were used by Zeniff, the leader of the emigrants who returned to reinhabit Nephi, against the Lamanites. The Lamanites often used clubs when attacking the Nephites. They were simply branches of trees cut to use like bats. Some were ornately carved to add superstitious taboo to the weapon. Some of the carving made the weapon more lethal. The carving also identified the owner. When branches of trees were unavailable the horns of various animals were used to make clubs.

References: Mosiah 6:19-21; Alma 12:52-58; 26:86-88.

COCKATRICE—Animal

The cockatrice, or basilisk, is a symbolic lizard-like serpent used in prophecy to represent a deadly, fiery, flying enemy. It is also used in the symbol of peace to represent the extent to which the deadly will be tamed.

References: II Nephi 9:120-123; 10:51; 12:91-95; Isaiah 11:5-9; 14:29.

COHOR—Son of Corihor (Ether)

Cohor, the Jaredite, joined his brother Noah to

rebel against Shule, the king. They overthrew Shule to obtain part of their inheritance. Noah took the kingship, leaving Cohor in obscurity.
Reference: Ether 3:53.

COHOR—Son of Noah (Ether)

When Noah obtained the kingdom from Shule, his father, and was about to put him to death, the sons of Shule slew Noah. Cohor took over the part of the inheritance left by his father; the other part was retained by Shule. He gathered an army to battle Shule but was defeated and slain. His son, Nimrod, returned Cohor's portion of the kingdom to Shule.

Later the descendants of Cohor refused to repent when preached to by Ether. In a final battle, all the descendants of Cohor were slain.
References: Ether 3:53-61; 6:18.

COM—Father of Heth (Ether)

Com reigned in the stead of his father Coriantum. During his reign, the secret societies began to flourish. Heth, his son, joined the secret societies, dethroned Com, and slew his father with his own sword.
References: Ether 1:6; 4:29-31.

COM—Father of Shiblom (Ether)

Com, son of Coriantum who lived in captivity, drew away half the kingdom of King Amgid. He ruled over his half-kingdom for forty-two years. He went to battle with Amgid and won the rest of the kingdom.

During his reign, robbers adopted the old secret plans and sought to destroy his kingdom. Com fought the robbers and defended the prophets who called for repentance and had been rejected by the people.

Com lived in peace to a good old age, and his son, Shiblom, took over the kingdom after him.

References: Ether 1:6; 4:85-92.

COMNOR—Hill

Toward the end of the Jaredite civilization, Shiz fought Coriantumr. Coriantumr pitched his tents in the valley of Shurr and gathered his armies on the nearby hill Comnor. He sounded the trumpets to call Shiz to battle with him. Shiz drove his army off the hill.

References: Ether 6:65-67.

COMPASS—See Liahona

COPPER—Metal

Copper is an element obtained by refining ore by roasting it at high temperatures. The surface of a piece of copper turns green with long exposure to oxygen or black with exposure to sulfur. Its strength and durability are improved by alloying it with zinc or tin.

Both the Lehites and the Jaredites found copper in abundance in the new world. The Lehites used the copper for many things including ornaments, machinery, and weapons. The Jaredites made breastplates and brass from their copper.

References: I Nephi 5:217; II Nephi 4:21; Jarom 1:19-21; Mosiah 5:65; 7:6, 11-15; Ether 4:71.

CORIANTON—Son of Alma (c. 74 B.C.)

Corianton went with his father, Alma son of Alma, to preach to the Zoramites. He failed at this, succumbing to pride in his own strength. He went to Siron where he fell in love with Isabel, a harlot. Instead of establishing the church as he was commissioned, he worked against it by his conduct.

His father was ashamed of him and pleaded with Corianton to repent. Apparently Corianton did repent, because his ministry to the Nephites was later acclaimed by his older brother, Helaman.

Later Corianton gathered people and took them to the land northward in a ship carrying supplies to those who had gone on ahead in order to establish new Nephite colonies.

References: Alma 16:84; 19; 21:185; 30:14-15.

CORIANTOR—Son of Mormon (Ether)

Coriantor was born and lived in captivity all his life. A leader of the growing band of robbers ruled in his stead. During his lifetime the Jaredites grew exceedingly wicked. Many prophets arose to call them to repent, but were rejected. Coriantor was the father of Ether, last recorder for the Jaredites.

References: Ether 1:6; 4:110-115.

CORIANTUM—Son of Emer (Ether)

Coriantum took over the kingdom of the Jaredites from Emer, his father. He reigned in peace and righteousness, and many cities were built during those prosperous times. He had no children by his first wife. When she died, he married a young maid who bore him many children. Among them was Com who reigned in his stead.

References: Ether 1:6; 4:23-29.

CORIANTUM—Son of Amnigaddah (Ether)

Coriantum lived all his life in captivity as did his father before him. He was the father of Com who regained the Jaredite kingdom from Amgid in battle.

References: Ether 1:6; 4:85-87.

CORIANTUMR—Son of Omer (Ether)

Coriantumr and Esrom were angry with their brother, Jared, who had placed their father Omer in captivity. They fought Jared until he agreed to give up the kingdom and his army was destroyed.

References: Ether 3:73-75.

CORIANTUMR—Last Jaredite (Ether)

Coriantumr was the king of the Jaredites in the days when Ether was prophet. The secret society that had developed sought to destroy Coriantumr. Coriantumr drew up an army and fought back. Among the leaders of the armies Coriantumr fought were Shared, Lib, and Shiz. In these wars all the Jaredites became divided between the two armies. The armies clashed to the death until only Shiz, Coriantumr, and Ether remained. Coriantumr killed Shiz and left the country not knowing that Ether was yet alive. Ether hid the records he kept and disappeared.

Coriantumr was discovered in Zarahemla by the Mulekites who had by that time arrived from Jerusalem. He lived with the Mulekites nine months, during which time he told the people the history of the Jaredites and of their end.

References: Ether 5:1-2; 6:16-106; Omni 1:36-37.

CORIANTUMR—Dissenter (c. 51 B.C.)

Coriantumr, a large and mighty Mulekite, was a descendant of Zarahemla. He was chosen to lead the army of Lamanites against the Nephites. He armed his warriors well and led them boldly into the center of the Nephite lands. The Nephites did not have time to draw together in defense so they fell before Coriantumr's army.

When Moronihah, the Nephite war leader, discovered that Coriantumr had captured cities in Zarahemla, he sent Lehi's army to head Coriantumr off before he got to Bountiful. The army of Coriantumr was surrounded and defeated in a bloody battle. Coriantumr was slain and his army sent out of the land in rout.

References: Helaman 1:16-34.

CORIHOR—Son of Kib (Ether)

Corihor rebelled against his father, the Jaredite king, and went to live in Nehor. He had many fair children there. Using flattery, Corihor drew away many people, then formed an army and overthrew his father in Moron near Desolation of the Nehors in the time of the Nephites.

While Corihor reigned by keeping his father in captivity, his brother Shule became angry and gathered an army. Shule fought Corihor and set his father back on the throne. For this act, Shule was awarded the kingdom when Kib died.

Corihor repented of his evil ways, so Shule gave him power in the kingdom.

Noah and Cohor, sons of Corihor, rebelled against Corihor and Shule. Later descendants of Corihor rebelled with Coriantumr against God and were destroyed in the last war of the Jaredites.
References: Ether 3:40-53; 6:18.

CORIHOR—Land

Coriantumr in the last war of the Jaredites fought Shiz. Shiz fled before the armies of Coriantumr to the land of Corihor, destroying and slaying the Jaredites in their path who refused to join them against Coriantumr. This land was not far from the sea and the valley of Shurr.
References: Ether 6:63-65.

CORIHOR—Valley

As the Jaredite army of Shiz waited for another battle with the Jaredite army of Coriantumr in the last war of that civilization, Shiz had his army pitch their tents in the valley of Corihor.

From this camp Shiz and his army marched out against Coriantumr at hill Comnor. Three times they battled. Twice Shiz was driven back. In the third battle Shiz wounded Coriantumr so that he was carried off the field as if dead. Shiz returned his army to camp in the valley of Corihor rather than chase Coriantumr's fleeing warriors.

As Coriantumr recovered, he began to see what he had done and he repented. He sent a letter to Shiz in the valley of Corihor, offering to surrender to him the kingdom.

Shiz replied that he wanted Coriantumr's life as well. This stirred both armies to anger, so Shiz pursued the army of Coriantumr to Ripliancum.

The valley of Corihor was not far from the land the Nephites would later call Desolation.
References: Ether 6:62-80.

CORN—Plant

Corn was a general term referring to wheat, barley, vetch, fitches, millet, beans, lentils, pulse, rye, or oats in the books of Nephi. Mosiah later listed corn as a specific crop.

According to legend, the Indians were given corn by an angel who taught them how to grow it and use it. There is not a wild corn plant from which domestic crops were derived. Tame corn will come up volunteer for only a few seasons even in cultivated fields.
References: I Nephi 2:40; 5:175-178; Mosiah 5:35-36; 6:12, 17.

COROM—Son of Levi (Ether)

Corum or Corom was the son of a Jaredite king. Corom was anointed king by his father and reigned in righteousness. When he died, Kish, his son, reigned in his stead.
References: Ether 1:6; 4:62-63.

COW—Animal

A cow is a female bovine—a horned, even-toed, cud-chewing creature. Cows were brought to the New World by the Jaredites when they left the tower of Babel and were raised for food. When the Jaredites were destroyed by a long civil war, the cows roamed free in the wilderness.

When they came to the New World the Lehites rounded up the cows, domesticated them, and maintained them for food.

The calf, or young cow, is used in prophecy in the symbol for peace of the last days.

References: I Nephi 5:216; II Nephi 9:120-124; 12:91-95 (Isaiah 11:5-9); Enos 1:34; III Nephi 2:29-31, 42-45; 3:1; Ether 1:22-24; 4:18-21.

CROPS

Both the Jaredites and the Lehites brought seeds with them to the New World. The seeds were planted and crops cultivated for use for food and to feed their domesticated stock.

Among the seeds mentioned were corn, barley, wheat, neas, sheum, and grapes. See these articles for specific information.

References: I Nephi 2:40; 5:13-14, 175-178; Mosiah 5:35-36; 6:12, 17; 7:21; Ether 1:22-24.

CROSS

The Jaredites and the Lehites were fully aware of the cross on which Christ was to be crucified. The brother of Jared saw Christ and was told about the cross. He taught the Jaredites. Lehi, Nephi, Jacob,

King Benjamin, and Alma knew Christ and taught the Lehites of the cross.

Christ himself came to the remnant of the people to tell of his cross after the cataclysm following his death in Jerusalem.

Archaeological evidence from ancient ruins indicates that the cross was important to the ancient inhabitants.

References: I Nephi 3:87; II Nephi 6:42; Jacob 1:8; III Nephi 5:78; 12:25-28; Ether 1:94-95.

CUMENI—City

Cumeni was a Nephite city in the land of Manti. It was conquered by the Lamanites in the war of 66 B.C. To release the city of Cumeni from the Lamanites, Helaman brought up the band of Ammonite youths who were converted Lamanites. He surrounded the city and kept the Lamanites from leaving and provisions from entering until the Lamanites within the city surrendered.

The Ammonites took the Lamanites captive, but found that they couldn't keep them in the city because they constantly struggled for freedom and required too much food for support. Helaman sent the prisoners to Zarahemla with a guard selected from the Ammonite warriors.

The guard conducted the prisoners away from the city but never made it to Zarahemla because of a battle with the escaping prisoners and another army that was about to invade Cumeni. They returned to Cumeni just in time to aid in the defense of the city.

Though many of the Ammonite warriors were wounded, none were slain in that battle. The city was maintained as a stronghold from which the Nephite army recovered the other cities of Manti from the Lamanite invaders.

References: Alma 26:15, 77-113.

CUMENIHAH—War Chief (c. A.D. 385)

Cumenihah was listed among the Nephite army leaders during their last war with the Lamanites. His ten thousand soldiers were completely destroyed by the Lamanites. Their bodies were left on the battlefield to decay.

References: Mormon 3:15-17.

CUMOMS—Animals

Cumoms were listed among the animals domesticated by the Jaredites. They were probably brought to extinction by the terrible famine and serpent infestation in the days of Heth. Many bones from now extinct animals are found by archaeologists in association with many ancient ruins in the New World.

References: Ether 4:18-21.

CUMORAH—Hill

For the last war of the Jaredites, the last army was gathered upon the hill Ramah which would later be called hill Cumorah by the Nephites.

It seems a coincidence that many centuries later the Nephites, under Mormon's leadership, would gather their last army upon the same hill. It was a hill well suited for an army camp, having an abundance of water available.

Mormon hid the records of the Nephites in the hill Cumorah to preserve them from falling into the hands of the Lamanites. Later Moroni dug up the abridgment made by Mormon and continued the record until he too was forced to bury the plates in another hill.

The Nephites moved out from the hill to battle and returned, having lost many tens of thousands of their best warriors in one battle. Those left were hunted down by the Lamanites until Moroni, son of Mormon, alone of the Nephites remained alive.

Contrary to popular belief, the hill in which Moroni hid the records was probably not the same hill as the one in which Mormon hid his records. Moroni left Cumorah pursued by the Lamanites and wandered about for nearly twenty years before he buried his record.

References: Mormon 3:3-14; 4:2-6; Ether 6:83; Moroni 10:1-2.

CUMORAH—Land

Cumorah was a land that surrounded hill Cumorah. Upon that land the Nephites met and were destroyed by the Lamanites in the last war between them. The bodies of the dead Nephites lay upon the land until their bodies moldered to dust.

References: Mormon 3:3-23.

CURELOMS—Animals

Cureloms were animals probably found here by the Jaredites. They were domesticated because of

their usefulness. They probably fell to extinction because of the famine that began in the time of Neth. Archaeologists find many bones of extinct animals in their digging.
References: Ether 4:18-21.

CUSH—*Old World Land*

Cush, now known as Ethiopia, is a region of Africa established by Cush, son of Ham, son of Noah. Isaiah prophesied that the Lord will gather his remnant people from Cush in the last days. They considered their kings to be "Lions of Judah" since Sheba, their ancient queen, was supposed to have had a child by Solomon, king of Israel.
References: II Nephi 9:126; Isaiah 11:11; Genesis 2:15, 10:4; I Kings 10:1-13.

D

DAMASCUS—*Old World City*

Damascus is the capital of Syria. It was founded by Uz, son of Shem, and is the oldest city having continuous habitation. It is surrounded by the Anti-Lebanon Mountains on the west, Mount Hermon on the southwest, Ghuta plain on the south and east, and on the east by the Syrian-Arabian desert.

Isaiah, in the days of Ahaz, called Damascus the head or capital of Syria and Rezin the head or king of Damascus. Isaiah told Ahaz that in 65 years Ephraim was to be broken, or defeated and scattered, by Pekah. The Syrians, Samaritans, and Ephraimites allied to destroy Judah. Because of this

God sent the king of Assyria, Shalmaneser, in 732 B.C., to Samaria and to Damascus to loot, destroy, and scatter the inhabitants.

References: II Nephi 9:21-95; Isaiah 7:8 - 10:14; II Kings 14:9; 18:9-37; 19:9-37.

DART—Weapon

A dart consisted of a shaft, head, and tail like an arrow. The shaft was shorter and thicker, the head smaller, and the tail thicker than that of the arrow. A dart was thrown at the target rather than shot from a bow. Sometimes the dart had a porous head and was soaked in flammable liquids to be lit and thrown to start fires.

Nephi, son of Nehi, warned his brothers of the fiery darts of the adversary, or the temptations of Satan. Jarom, son of Enos, mentions the making of darts for Nephite weapons that they might defend themselves against the Lamanites.

References: I Nephi 4:39-40; Jarom 1:19-21.

DAUGHTER OF JARED—Ether

The beautiful daughter of Jared felt sorry for her inconsolable father who had recently lost the kingdom of the Jaredites to its rightful king, Omer. Jared had won it by flattery and lost it by evil. Nevertheless, he mourned for the glory of being king.

His daughter, seeing him so disconsolate, looked into the records containing plans for obtaining the kingdom by secret combinations. She proposed to send for Akish, a gullible friend of King Omer. She would entice Akish to make him desire her for a wife. Then her father could ask the head of the king for a dowry.

Akish fell for the trap. Before he was told of the dowry, Jared administered the secret oath to Akish. Akish, using the same oath, established a secret combination among his family and went after the head of the king. Omer escaped before the deed was accomplished. Having abandoned the kingdom, Omer relinquished the throne to Jared. Jared gave his daughter's hand in marriage to Akish.
References: Ether 3:78-91; 4:1-5.

DAVID—King of Israel (Old Testament)

David was told of the treachery of Ephraim who conspired with Syria, and he was upset by this.

David was the first of a long line of kings to rule Israel. Ahaz and Christ were descendants in this line. David was known for his desire for many wives. We are told not to use David's sin as an excuse to commit the same sin. David's polygamy was considered an abomination to God.
References: II Nephi 9:15, 26 (Isaiah 7:2, 13), 67 (Isaiah 9:7); Jacob 1:15-17; 2:32-34; II Samuel 5; 12.

DAVID—Land

In the last war of the Nephites, the people under the leadership of Mormon were driven from the land of David. Angola was the capital city of David. The land of Joshua lay nearby.
References: Mormon 1:25-27.

DESERET—Animal

The deseret is a honeybee brought over to the

New World by the Jaredites both for food and to help in pollenizing the crops.

References: Ether 1:23-24.

DESOLATION—City

In A.D. 361 the Lamanites came to attack the city of Desolation but were repelled. They came again the next year but were again defeated, and the bodies of the slain were tossed into the sea. The inhabitants of the city became proud of their accomplishment and swore vengeance upon the Lamanites who had slain a few of the Nephites in the battle. Because of this, Mormon, their leader, refused to direct the armies of the Nephites for many years.

The next year, A.D. 363, the army of the Lamanites came again, but without the leadership of Mormon the Nephites were driven out of the city of Desolation to nearby Teancum which was by the seashore.

When in A.D. 364 the Lamanites drove the Nephites out of Teancum, the Nephites regrouped and fought the Lamanites with renewed vigor and drove the Lamanites from the city of Desolation. In this battle thousands from both sides were slain. The battle continued with the two armies exchanging possession of the city many times until A.D. 375, when the Lamanites came in such fury that the Nephites were completely driven out and many were slaughtered.

References: Mormon 1:71-76; 2:3, 4, 10-21.

DESOLATION—Land

Desolation was a north land, bordering Bountiful. It was covered by ruins from the Jaredite civilization. The same land was called Mormon by the Jaredites. The length of the border between Desolation and Bountiful was a journey of a day and a half by foot, and it extended from sea to sea.

Mormon, in 73 B.C., prayed that the land might be dedicated to liberty, particularly freedom of religion.

Morianton, a Nephite dissenter, was stopped in his flight by Moroni at the border of Desolation in 68 B.C. when he tried to lead dissenters out of the land of Morianton.

Hagoth launched his expeditions to establish new colonies from the sea on the borders of Desolation.

In A.D. 360 a long and arduous battle began between the Nephites and the Lamanites which lasted until A.D. 375, when the Nephites, nearly destroyed by then, were driven farther northward.

References: Alma 13:74-77; 21:46; 22:35; 30:6; III Nephi 2:32-33; Mormon 1:69; 2:1-21; Ether 3:43.

DESOLATION OF THE NEHORS—See Ammonihah—Land

DISCIPLES—New World Twelve (c. A.D. 34)

Jesus came among the people in the New World who had repented. The disciples were chosen, ordained, baptized by Nephi with water, and baptized by Christ with the Holy Ghost.

Jesus called Nephi, Timothy, Jonas, Mathoni,

Mathonihah, Kumen, Kumenonhi, Jeremiah, Shemnon, Jonas, Zedekiah, and Isaiah to be special witnesses to the people of Christ and his gospel.

When Jesus returned the second time to speak to the remnant in the New World, he found the disciples faithfully teaching the message he had given them. He prayed for the Father's forgiveness for them. The twelve were so completely cleansed that their garments glowed with pure whiteness.

With Jesus in charge, the disciples served to the multitude the Communion of bread and wine prepared by Jesus. Then they sat to listen to further teachings of Christ concerning their responsibilities, futures, promises, and warnings.

Jesus came to them to answer any questions the twelve might have. They asked for a name for the church and were told to name it after Christ. He then asked the twelve to tell him what they desired of him. Nine asked to live to the age of man and come speedily into the kingdom of God. Three asked to remain and continue their ministry through the ages until Zion came. Their desires were granted. Then they were transfigured and endowed for the fullness of ministry. All the gifts to be given believers were given them. They were freed completely from the power of Satan.

The twelve continued their ministry in perfection as they had been taught so that a perfect

society was established that lasted for 250 years.
References: III Nephi 9:4-46; 12:14-13:53.

DOG—Animal

A dog is an omniverous animal surviving on anything it can find. It does not refuse carrion flesh, even if partly rotted. When tamed, a dog can be trained to be useful to man in many ways.

The dog mentioned in the prophecy of Abinadi concerning the end of the priests of Noah, king of Nephi, is the wild dog. The wild dog consumed the bodies of the priests of Noah slain by both the Nephites and the Lamanites because they had committed so much evil against both nations.
References: Mosiah 7:48-49; Alma 1:97.

DOVE—Animals

Doves are soft, sleek, full-bodied birds. They mate for life. The hen lays one or two immaculate white or buff eggs in a soft, loose nest of feathers, straw, and twigs. Doves can be domesticated for racing or eating.

They are the only birds acceptable for a sacrifice, according to the Jewish law. When young, the doves were sacrificed for peace offerings or sin offerings.

It was a dove that brought the olive branch to Noah, signifying the end of the flood, from which act it became the symbol of peace. Each year the appearance of the dove heralds the coming of spring to Israel.

111

It was in the form of a dove that the Holy Spirit settled upon the freshly baptized body of Christ.

References: I Nephi 3:73-74; II Nephi 13:9-10; Genesis 8:52-56; Leviticus 12.

E

EDEN—Old World Land

Eden was a place described in ancient literature as a pleasant and delightful place where every tree was good for food and pleasant to the sight. The area contained an abundance of rich· minerals and plenty of fresh water.

God promised that the desert of the New World will become a garden and the wilderness like Eden in the last days.

References: II Nephi 5:72-74; Genesis 2:8-14; Isaiah 51:3.

EDON—Old World Land

Edon extended from south of the Dead Sea to the Gulf of Aquabah. Mount Seir was located within its borders. The land was inhabited by the descendants of Esau. When the Israelites were returning to the promised land from Egypt, Edon denied them safe passage. Because of this, in the latter days Judah and Ephraim (Israel and the United States) will unite to spoil Edon.

References: II Nephi 9:128-129; Numbers 20:14-21; Isaiah 11:13-14.

EGYPT—Old World Land

Egypt is a very ancient land still on the maps today. It was there that Joseph, son of Jacob, went to prepare a place for his family during the famine. It was there that Moses grew up and led Israel out of Egypt.

According to Isaiah, Egypt will be called upon to war with Israel. Later the Jews will be gathered out of Egypt again to gather into Israel. References: I Nephi 1:164-166; 5:132-137; II Nephi 2:5, 16; 3:1-2; 9:31 (Isaiah 7:18), 105, 107 (Isaiah 10:24, 27), 126, 131 (Isaiah 11:11, 16); 11:37-39; Mosiah 5:28-29; 7:94-95; Alma 8:3; 17:25-28; Ether 6:6.

EGYPTIANS—Old World People

Egyptians were the highly civilized inhabitants of ancient Egypt. Their language was relatively pure and easily written. The Israelites lived in Egypt from the time of Joseph to Moses, and thus learned their language, culture, engineering skills, and techniques for building pyramids and temples.

The Egyptian language was reformed by the Hebrews and used by Nephi to begin writing the record of the Lehites. The language was taught to Nephi by his father. Each succeeding generation learned it from their fathers to continue the record. The Lamanites gave up the records to the Nephites and for many generations lost their abilities in the Egyptian language. They were retaught by the priests of Noah who had become apostate Nephites.

The power of God was illustrated by Nephi

113

and others by the telling of the exodus of Israel from Egypt.

References: I Nephi 1:1, 102; 5:103, 109; II Nephi 9:130 (Isaiah 11:15); Mosiah 1:6; Alma 15:64; 17:25-28; Helaman 3:44; Mormon 4:98.

ELAM—Old World Land

Elam is an ancient land on the north of the Persian gulf. It may have been established by Elam, son of Shem. Elam lies on the eastern edge of old Babylonia and became a part of Persia after its defeat by Cyrus.

In the last days the Jews who are still in Elam are to be gathered by Israel, according to Isaiah.

References: II Nephi 9:126; Isaiah 11:11.

ELEPHANTS—Animals

Elephants are the largest living land mammals. They have tough, thick skin sparsely covered with coarse hair. Elephants move slowly on columnar legs, standing on thick flat pads behind spread toes. They use their muscular trunks and long tusks to uproot trees; thicker trees they push over by pressing their foreheads against the trees and shoving bulldozer fashion with their tonnage.

The trunk functions as a hand and curling arm. On the tip is a prehensile extension acting as a flexible finger for bunching straw or grass and holding it while the curling, snake-like trunk uproots it and stuffs the sweet morsel between massive jaws.

Elephants were found in the New World by the Jaredites when they arrived from the tower of Babel. They were said to be especially useful animals.

The Lehites did not find the elephants when they landed. It may well be that by that time they had become extinct due to predators and extended periods of drought. Bones of extinct elephants called mastodons are found in many parts of the New World by paleontologists. Recently a skeleton was found with an arrow embedded in its rib.

References: Ether 4:21.

ELIJAH—Prophet (Old Testament)

Elijah lived in the northern kingdom of Israel and prophesied during the ninth century B.C. for Ahab and Ahaziah. Elijah personally led the fight against idolatry in Israel. Because of his righteousness he conversed with God face-to-face. When his mission on earth was finished he was carried to heaven instead of suffering the usual ignominious death accorded other prophets.

Elijah came to Christ at the transfiguration and is to be sent again before the coming of judgment to reestablish love in families.

References: III Nephi 11:26-27; Malachi 4:5, 6; I Kings 17-II Kings 2:11.

EMER—Jaredite King (Ether)

Emer was the son of Omer. He reigned in righteousness and prosperity. Many rich

products such as silk, linen, gold, and silver ornaments were prepared during his reign. When he grew old he anointed Coriantum, his son, to reign in his place.
References: Ether 1:6; 4:15-24.

EMRON—Nephite Warrior (c. A.D. 421)

Emron was listed as one of the choice men of the Nephites. He was killed by the Lamanites in battle during the last war of the Nephites.
References: Moroni 9:2.

ENOS—Son of Jacob (c. 544 B.C.)

Enos prayed that his people might live in righteousness and have someone to teach them to repent. Because of his fervent prayers, Enos was told that the record he was keeping would be used to bring the Lamanites to belief in God. During his time the Nephites and Lamanites became more separated. The Nephites prospered and had to be prodded constantly to keep them from being carried away in pride. The Lamanites became as ravenous animals. The two nations warred frequently, the Lamanites to take and the Nephites to preserve.

Enos turned the records over to his son, Jarom, when he grew too old to keep them.
References: Jacob 5:45, 46; Enos 1; Jarom 1:1.

EPHAH—See Measure

EPHRAIM—Tribe of Israel

Ephraim was the younger son of Joseph, the

son of Israel. His children were blessed by Israel as a separate tribe, even though he was a grandson rather than a son of Israel.

Ahaz, a king of Judah, was told that Ephraim was about to ally with Syria and Samaria to fight Judah. For this, Ephraim would be cut off for a while after five years. Later Manasseh and Ephraim would join to fight against Judah. Still later Ephraim and Judah would join to fight the enemies of Judah.

In 732 B.C. the king of Assyria, Shalmaneser, fought the confederacy of Syria, Samaria, and Ephraim. As a result Ephraim was scattered.

References: II Nephi 9:15 (Isaiah 7:2), 21-22 (Isaiah 7:8-9), 30 (Isaiah 7:17), 69-70 (Isaiah 9:9-10), 80-81 (Isaiah 9:20-21), 128-129 (Isaiah 11:13-14).

EPHRAIM—Hill

Ephraim was located in the Jaredite kingdom near Nehor. It contained the ores needed to produce steel. Schule went there in anger because his brother, Corihor, held their father, Kib, in captivity. There Shule made swords from steel smeltered from ores to arm himself and his army to fight Corihor. He defeated Corihor and restored the kingdom to his father.

References: Ether 3:44-46.

ESROM—Brother of Jared (Ether)

Esrom and his brother Coriantumr became angry with the evil acts of their brother Jared, who had made himself king by exiling their father Omer. Esrom and Coriantumr gathered

117

an army loyal to Omer. They dethroned Jared and restored the kingdom to Omer.
References: Ether 3:73-76.

ETHEM—Descendant of Ahah (Ether)

Ethem was a Jaredite descendant of Ahah who took over the kingdom after Ahah and followed in his evil ways. In the days of Ethem many prophets came to tell the people of their sins and to call for their repentance, while warning them of the Lord's vengeance. Ethem refused to change his ways. His son Moron reigned after Ethem.
References: Ether 1:6; 4:102-106.

ETHER—Last Jaredite Recorder (Ether)

Ether was the son of Coriantor. He was born in captivity and never took his rightful place as king of the Jaredites. He prophesied to the people of the degree of wickedness to which they had fallen. He warned them that unless they repented the Lord would allow them to destroy themselves and their entire civilization with them. He explained that the new world in which they lived had been dedicated to freedom and worship of God, and that the new Jerusalem would be established there by a remnant of the seed of Joseph, son of Israel.

His prophecies and teachings were ignored. He was forced to go into hiding in a cave because of oppression, going out at night to see how the people fared, and to finish the record of the Jaredites.

Ether was saddened and frustrated as he watched the secret combinations build and begin to divide the kingdom between Coriantumr, the king, and Shared, leader of the secret society. Ether told Coriantumr what would happen if he did not repent. Ether continued his silent watch as the two armies fought to the last man, Coriantumr.

Ether then left his cave, finished the record, hid it so that the people of Limhi would find it many years later, then rested from his labors until the end of his days.

References: Ether 4:115; 5:1-5; 6:2-109.

EVE—First Woman (Old Testament)

Eve was the first woman and was given to Adam to establish the first family. She was beguiled by Satan, disguised as a serpent, into disobedience to God, then enticed Adam to join her in that sin. Because of this, Adam and Eve were separated from the face of God, driven from the Garden of Eden, and brought forth children to till the earth.

References: I Nephi 1:160; II Nephi 1:104-106; Genesis 3:6-4:3.

EZAIAS—Prophet (Old Testament)

Ezaias is listed by Nephi, son of Helaman, as a prophet who testified of the coming of Christ, or God in the flesh. Like most of his fellow prophets, he refused to remain silent when threatened by his Jewish peers, but continued to forewarn the Jews that they would mercilessly slay their own Messiah. He, like the rest of the prophets of doom, died because of his testimony. Because he was said to have blasphemed, his prophecies were not retained in the old Jewish records.

Laban, in his zeal to keep a perfect record, must have included them in the plates of brass he kept for the priests. When Nephi took the plates of brass in obedience to God, he had the now lost prophecies of Ezaias and took them to his father Lehi.

References: Helaman 3:54.

F

FATHER OF LAMONI—Lamanite King (c. 80 B.C.)

The father of Lamoni was the very proud and powerful king of all the civilized Lamanites. He called a feast commanding all his sons and the minor kings under him to appear. When his son, Lamoni, failed to appear, he went to look for him.

The father of Lamoni found his son traveling on the way to Middoni in the company of a despicable Nephite. He ordered his son to immediately slay this enemy of the people. When his son refused, he jumped off his own chariot determined to slay first Lamoni and then the Nephite.

To his amazement, the Nephite jumped between the slashing sword and his son. He turned on the Nephite in full fury. In the combat he was wounded so that he could not fight, but to his astonishment he was not slain. Instead he heard the Nephite ask for the life of his son and the freedom of the minor land he ruled. He did what he had to: he agreed, then stood quietly and watched his son drive away.

The father of Lamoni returned to his own realm and fell into confused depression. While he was in the midst of this black mood there appeared before his throne Nephites claiming to be the brothers of the bold one who had defended his son. They offered to be his servants, but he refused, desiring instead to be taught as his son had been taught.

Using the knowledge of the Great Spirit already accepted by the father of Lamoni, Aaron taught him of the ways of God and called on him to repent. When the king bowed before God, he fell into a trance.

The queen came in and, seeing the king fallen, assumed that Aaron had killed him. She ordered the servants to slay Aaron, but the servants, knowing what had happened, refused. The queen then sent for the people to come and slay Aaron and the disobedient servants.

Aaron, noting the stubbornness of the queen, raised the king from his trance. The father of Lamoni stood on his feet and began to tell the queen and his subjects of the marvelous things he had learned. Further, he sent a proclamation throughout the land that the sons of Mosiah were to be allowed to teach unmolested.

The sons of Mosiah preached under the protection of the father of Lamoni until all the civilized Lamanites were converted. The people were renamed Anti-Nephi-Lehies after the name of the son of the father of Lamoni. Anti-Nephi-Lehi took the throne when his father died.

References: Alma 12:77-78, 189-215; 13:30-82; 14:1-24.

FISH—Animals

Fish are cold-blooded vertebrates that generally have scales and breathe through gills. They require water to live in. Isaiah reminded the Israelites that it was God who had the power to dry up the sea and the fish would die and stink. In explaining the good gifts that God has for his followers, Christ said that if we were asked for a fish we would not offer a serpent.

The Jaredites gathered fish and placed them in a vessel of water to keep them as they traveled from the tower of Babel to the New World. The fish that survived the trip uneaten were probably loosed in the rivers when the Jaredites arrived in the New World.

References: II Nephi 5:53-54 (Isaiah 50:3); III Nephi 6:22; Ether 1:23-24.

FLAG

Moroni, chief commander of the Nephite

armies, became distressed because Amalickiah had desired to be king and had divided the people. He tore his coat and used a piece of it to make a flag. He wrote upon it, "In memory of our God, our religion, and freedom, and our peace, our wives, and our children," and fastened it to a pole.

Calling this the title of liberty, he held it as he knelt in prayer to God for protection of the Christians. Moroni then rallied the Christians around his flag and prepared an army to fight the Amalickiahites.

A little later as the Lamanites descended upon the Nephites for war, the king-men, probably remnants of Amalickiahites who had not fully repented, refused to fight. Moroni again hoisted his flag to rally the people to destroy the king-men or compel them to serve the country. This time the nobility were forced to repent, be slain, or be imprisoned.

Teancum, a captain of the Nephite army, used the flag to gather an army to go out to Gideon and retake the Nephite cities from the Lamanite invaders.

References: Alma 21:41-60, 71; 23:21-26; 29:4.

FLY—Animal

A fly is an insect having one pair of wings. Flies live in nearly all parts of the world. They are known to be well adapted for biting as well as carrying germs and viruses which cause human diseases and death. Many flies develop in swarms, attacking a single victim or group of victims in unison.

The fly was used in prophecy to represent the swarm of Egyptians that would one day invade Israel.

References: II Nephi 9:31; Isaiah 7:18.

FORTS—Buildings

In about 72 B.C. Moroni began to build forts for the protection of the Nephite cities against the invading Lamanites.

The forts first were banks of earth and walls of stone. Later ditches were added around the outside of the walls. Next, works of timber were built to top the walls to the height of a man. Picket frames were built on the timbers, then towers on the timbers to overlook the picket fence.

During the earthquakes preceding the coming of Christ to the New World, these forts were destroyed.

In about A.D. 327 Mormon began again to build forts to protect the Nephites against the Lamanite armies. They did not work, and the Nephites were eventually destroyed by the Lamanites.

Nephi, son of Lehi, prophesied that long after the fall of the Nephites the gentiles would come into the land and build forts to fight and subdue the Lamanites.

References: II Nephi 11:81-85; Alma 21:128-130, 150-152, 162-165, 170, 171; 22:1-6, 10-12; 24:2, 5-7, 11-12, 19-20; 25:51-52; 29:52; III Nephi 2:18, 34-37; Mormon 1:26, 49, 70.

FOWL—Animals

Fowl refers to birds of any kind, particularly domesticated edible species. They eat a variety of foods from seeds to carrion. Waterfowl are especially adapted by oily feathers and hollow bones to sit high on the water when they float.

Nephi reminded the Lehites that the fowl were created by God. Alma reminded the Zoramites that the last sacrifice would not be a fowl. When Christ preached to the remnant of the Lehites when he came to the New World, he reminded them that birds are not required to sow to have food but have what they need provided by God.

The Jaredites who left the tower of Babel snared fowl to bring with them to the New World. They built barges light like waterfowl in which to travel.

References: II Nephi 1:94-99; Alma 16:207-210; III Nephi 6:4; Ether 1:22-24, 45-46; 3:4.

FULLER'S FIELD—Old World Place

A fuller is an artisan in cleaning and bleaching cloth in preparation for dyeing. The cloth was trampled on a stone submerged in water. When the cloth was cleaned of its oils and gums it was spread carefully to dry on the grass in a field in order that it be bleached by the sun. The field in which the cloth was spread was called the fullers field. It always lay near a plentiful supply of water not far from a large town. Fuller's soap was used

to help cleanse the cloth.
References: II Nephi 9:16; Isaiah 7:3.

G

GAD—City

Gad was one of the cities built before the coming of Christ that was burned with fire during the earthquake that shook the New World at the death of Christ in Jerusalem. This destruction occurred because the inhabitants had cast out their righteous citizens and had stoned their prophets.
References: III Nephi 4:38-40.

GADIANDI—City

Gadiandi was one of the cities built before the coming of Christ. It was so filled with iniquity that during the cataclysm that preceded the coming of Christ to the New World, it was sunk and destroyed.
References: III Nephi 4:34-35.

GADIANTON—Robber (c. 50 B.C.)

Gadianton was exceedingly expert in organizing secret combinations and using secret oaths to commit murder. He became the leader of the devious band of robbers formed by Kishkumen.

He sent Kishkumen to kill Helaman so that he could obtain the judgment seat and thus issue decrees in favor of the robbers. When the plan failed, Gadianton gathered his band and hid them in the wilderness away from the wrath of Helaman.

Gadianton's band of robbers remained hidden, occasionally coming into cities to murder and rob, then hiding again in their secret places. The numbers in the band increased, including both Nephites and Lamanites. The Lamanites repented and sought continually to destroy the band, but the Nephites in their pride joined in greater numbers and protected the band. The leaders among the Nephites joined the band, so that the wicked went unpunished for their crimes while the righteous were condemned for their goodness.

Nephi condemned the people openly for harboring such a band. Gadianton riled the people to try to make them destroy Nephi. Nephi, son of Helaman, testified to the people of the acts that the robbers were committing against them, prophesying of the very death of their chief judge. The Nephites would not listen, but sought to kill Nephi, so the Lord removed him from their midst.

Nephi, son of Nephi, asked the Lord to allow famine and the sword to come among the Nephites to destroy them in hopes that some of them would repent. For three years the famine raged and the invasions came, before the Nephites repented and rid themselves of the Gadiantons.

Four years later the robbers' band was reestablished. The band grew to infest the Nephites almost totally. Samuel, the Lamanite prophet, came among them to prophesy of the coming of Christ. When the signs came as given to herald the birth of Christ, the Nephites were stirred to repent again. The Gadianton band was driven back into the wilderness for only a short while before it began to thrive again.

In A.D. 16, Lachoneus, the chief judge of the Nephites, raised an army to fight the Gadiantons now led by Giddianhi. The battle continued until the robbers were completely overthrown.

After Christ came and ministered to the people in the New World, they lived in peace and prosperity for 244 years. But again the people began to be filled with pride and began to reestablish the secret societies. Their wickedness continued from that time until the Nephites were completely destroyed.

References: Helaman 1:38-51; 2:21, 38:168; 3:3-5, 28, 32-132; 4:2-19, 31-47; III Nephi 1:33-37, 48-50, 54-56; 2:11, 19-20, 39-89; 3:4; IV Nephi 1:50-54.

GADIOMNAH—City

Gadiomnah was one of the cities built before the coming of Christ to the New World. It was so filled with iniquity that God caused it to be sunk and buried during the cataclysm that occurred at the time of the crucifixion of Christ.

References: III Nephi 4:34-35.

GALILEE—Old World City

Galilee is the name of the mountainous northernmost region of Israel west of the Jordan

River. It was divided between Ashur in the northwest, Zebulun in the southwest, Naphtali in the east, and Issachar in the southeast. Galilee was annexed by David to his kingdom.

When Israel was divided, Galilee became part of the northern kingdom. Tiglath-pileser III conquered it in 723 B.C., along with the rest of Israel, and turned it into the Assyrian province of Magiddu or Megiddo.

Isaiah prophesied that the people of Galilee would not understand the truth given to them when Christ came. In fact, this is just what happened. Though Jesus spent his boyhood there and preached by the sea, Galilee remained relatively unaffected by Christianity, maintaining its Jewish culture through the centuries of changing conquests.

References: II Nephi 9:61-67; Isaiah 9:1-7; Gospels.

GALLIM—Old World Place

Gallim, the place in Palestine of the springs near Jerusalem, is not exactly located. Some authorities believe it is situated north of Jerusalem, others south. It was listed among the cities to be attacked by the Assyrian, according to the prophecy of Isaiah.

References: II Nephi 9:111; Isaiah 10:30.

GAZELEM—Servant (Uncertain)

Gazelem, a servant of the Lord, is to be given a stone by which the secret works of darkness will be made known to all people.

In the latter days, Gazelem has been designated as Joseph Smith, Jr.

References: Alma 17:55; Doctrine and Covenants 101:8.

GEBA—Old World City

Geba or Jeba is a city of Benjamin located on the south side of a steep ravine facing Michmash which makes it an excellent location for military surveillance.

When the Assyrian was to come to attack Israel, he was to take up lodging at Geba, according to the prophecy of Isaiah.

References: II Nephi 9:110; Isaiah 10:29.

GEBIM—Old World City

According to Isaiah, the inhabitants of Gebim would flee before Assyria when that country attacked Israel. Gebim is a place in Palestine, the place of the cisterns.

References: II Nephi 9:112; Isaiah 10:31.

GIBEAH—Old World City

Gibeah was the capital established by Saul, the first king of Israel. It is located in the land of Benjamin, four miles north of Jerusalem.

According to Isaiah, when the Assyrian came to attack Israel, Gibeah of Saul would have fled. And so it was when the army of Sennacherib approached Jerusalem in 587 B.C.

References: II Nephi 9:110; Isaiah 10:29.

GID—Captain (c. 63 B.C.)

Gid was the captain of the band of Ammonite

soldiers who were sent by Helaman to take the Lamanite prisoners back from Cumeni to Zarahemla. He reported to Helaman that the prisoners attempted to escape and were slain or had run free. Gid ordered the band to return to Cumeni. They returned in time to aid the defense of the city against another Lamanite invasion and the city was saved for the Nephites.

Gid was placed in charge of another band to lie in wait to entrap the Lamanites as they came out of Manti. The trap was successful. Using the same strategy, Gid was able to help the Nephites regain their strongholds without losing one of his men.

References: Alma 26:105-117, 138-147.

GID—City

Gid was a fortified city of the Nephites located on the east border of Bountiful by the Sea. Amalickiah, a dissenter and king of the Lamanites, took possession of Gid in about 67 B.C. The Lamanites used the city to keep their Nephite captives.

When Amalickiah was slain by Teancum, Ammoron, his brother, took his place as Lamanite king and war chief. Since Ammoron refused a prisoner exchange, Moroni, the Nephite war chief, decided to take the prisoners by subterfuge. He sent the Lamanite guards of Gid a gift of drugged wine. While the guards slept, Moroni passed weapons over the wall to the Nephite captives. When the guards awoke, the prisoners rioted. The Lamanites surrendered themselves and the city of Gid to Moroni.

The Lamanite prisoners were forced to increase the fortification of Gid. They were then moved to Bountiful.

In 30 B.C., Nephi, son of Helaman, preached to the inhabitants of Gid to bring them to repentance and reestablish peace among them.

References: Alma 23:31-33; 25:33-60; Helaman 2:77-78.

GIDDIANHI—Leader of Robbers (c. 16 B.C.)

Giddianhi wrote a letter to Lachoneus, governor of the Nephites, asking for the surrender of the government to him and his band of robbers. Instead of bending to Giddianhi's request, Lachonius drew the righteous Nephites together, with all their possessions, for protection. They forced Giddianhi, who survived by making short raids on unsuspecting Nephites, to come out of hiding and fight openly.

The army of Giddianhi wore loincloths of lambskin, dyed their bodies red in blood, shaved their heads, and wore helmets. Their appearance caused the Nephites to tremble and fall on their knees to ask the Lord for strength and deliverance. The robbers thought they fell in fear and boldly rode into battle to mow down the supplicants. To their surprise, the Nephites rose up and faced them, well armed and ready for battle.

The battle that followed was great and terrible.

Giddianhi was overtaken and slain. So many of the robbers were slain that it was two years before they dared come out against the Nephites again.

References: III Nephi 2:1-60.

GIDDONAH—Son of Ishmael (c. 74 B.C.)

Giddonah, high priest in Gideon, was the father of Amulek, the second witness of God for Alma. Korihor, the antichrist who had come to Gideon to preach, was bound by the Nephites who lived there and brought to Giddonah for judgment. Giddonah had Korihor taken, still bound, to Alma, son of Alma, for sentencing.

References: Alma 8:1-2; 16:23-37.

GIDEON—Man of Valor (c. 145 B.C.)

Gideon tried to slay King Noah because the king had demonstrated his wickedness by evicting Alma from the land of Nephi and having Abinadi, the prophet, burned at the stake. Gideon chased the king onto the tower near the temple and was about to accomplish his mission when the king shouted that a Lamanite invasion was upon them. Gideon's attention was turned against the Lamanites. King Noah fled the tower and the land of Nephi, taking his priests with him and leaving the women and children behind to plead for them with the Lamanites.

With King Noah gone, the kingdom was left to Limhi, his son. Those Nephites who had been left behind surrendered to the Lamanites. Gideon secretly sent men into the wilderness to search for Noah and his priests to slay them. They found that the king had already been slain by his disenchanted companions. When Limhi heard what had happened to his father, he was angry and sought to execute those who had slain his father. Gideon intervened and told Limhi to explain to the king of the Lamanites that it was his father and his priests who had wronged them. This helped make their captivity easier.

Later when Ammon and his brothers arrived from Zarahemla, Gideon led the people out of the city by night to safety. They followed Ammon on to Zarahemla and to freedom.

Nehor began to preach apostasy among the Nephites at Zarahemla. Gideon, by then an old man, heard this and sought Nehor out to debate with him. When Nehor found that Gideon was revealing his sins before the people, he slew Gideon.

References: Mosiah 9:77-102, 128-134; 10:5-17; Alma 1:10-15, 53, 76; 10:59.

GIDEON—City

Gideon was located in the valley of Gideon named for the man of valor. Alma came there to preach and to establish the church. Later the people of the city returned to their wickedness and the city was cursed.

References: Alma 4:8; Helaman 5:17-22.

GIDEON—Land

The land of Gideon surrounded the city and valley of Gideon. The church was established there by Alma. It lay north of Manti.

When Korihor came into the land to preach apostasy and priestcraft, he was bound and brought to Giddonah, high priest in the land, who sent him on to Alma, son of Alma, to be judged.

Later Pahoran fled to Gideon when the king-men of Pachus sought to take the judgment seat from him and fill it with evil men. Pahoran gathered an army of freemen from Gideon and sent for Moroni, who was busy fighting Lamanite invaders, for help in quelling the internal rebellion. Moroni came as bidden, put down the rebellion, executed or imprisoned the king-men, and slew Pachus. The men of Gideon returned home.

References: Alma 6:1; 12:1; 16:23-38; 28:6-27; 29:3-11.

GIDEON—Valley

Gideon was a valley which lay on the east of the river Sidon. In pursuing the Amlicites, Alma rested his army in the valley of Gideon. While there, spies were sent out to watch the Amlicites. They returned to report that the Lamanites were coming. The Nephites under Alma quickly returned to Zarahemla.

When peace was established in the land, Alma returned to Gideon to preach.

References: Alma 1:76-83; 4:7-8; 6:1-2.

GIDGIDDONI—War Chief (c. A.D. 16)

Gidgiddoni was appointed war commander because he was a great prophet and chief judge of the Nephites. He led the people against the Gadianton robbers who infested the land with terror. He armed his warriors so well that the robbers were beaten back and many were slain in the battle that ensued. Gidgiddoni pursued the robbers until the Gadiantons were nearly destroyed and their leader, Zemnarihah, was hung. Thus peace was established in the land of the Nephites.

References: III Nephi 2:23-74; 3:7.

GIDGIDDONAH—War Captain (c. A.D. 385)

Gidgiddonah was a valiant leader of a band of ten thousand Nephite soldiers who fought the Lamanites in the last war of the Nephites. He and all his men were slain in a single battle.

References: Mormon 3:15.

GILEAD—King (Ether)

Gilead was the brother of Shared, the leader of the wicked band trying to overthrow the Jaredite kingdom. After Coriantumr, king of the Jaredites, slew Shared in combat, Gilead took two years to gather an army by secret oaths to fight Coriantumr. He slew enough of Coriantumr's forces while they lay drunk to take over the throne. Two years later he was slain by his own high priest.

References: Ether 6:37-43.

GILGAH—Son of Jared (Ether)

Gilgah came over to the New World from Babel with his father. When the time came for Jared to die, an election was held to choose a king. When Gilgah was elected, he refused to serve and his father would not force him to serve.
References: Ether 3:16-33.

GILGAL—War Chief (c. A.D. 385)

In the last war of the Nephites Gilgal led his ten thousand warriors to battle against the Lamanites. He and all his soldiers were killed.
References: Mormon 3:15.

GILGAL—City

Gilgal was a city filled with such wicked inhabitants that when the cataclysm at the time of the crucifixion of Christ came, the city was sunk in an earthquake and all the inhabitants buried.
References: III Nephi 4:31.

GILGAL—Valley

Coriantumr, the Jaredite king, met Shared, leader of the rebels, in battle at the valley of Gilgal in the last war of the Jaredites. The battle lasted three days until Coriantumr beat Shared and pursued him to the nearby plains of Heshlon.

Shared regrouped his warriors and chased Coriantumr back to the valley of Gilgal after another battle. In this conflict, Shared was

killed after he wounded Coriantumr in the thigh so that he had to be carried from the field of battle. In the two years required for the gash to heal the battle was moved elsewhere.
References: Ether 6:29-34.

GIMGIMNO—City

Gimgimno was one of the wicked cities sunk by the earthquakes at the time of the crucifixion of Christ. In its place, hills and valleys were made.
References: III Nephi 4:34-35.

GIN—Weapon

A gin is a type of trap or snare to catch birds in trees. Isaiah compared the miracles of Christ in Jerusalem to a gin with its inhabitants.
References: II Nephi 9:52; Isaiah 8:14.

GOATS—Animals

Goats are small bovines. They are like sheep except that they are smaller and lighter, have straighter horns, shorter upturned tails, and a distinctive odor.

Goats and wild goats were found in the wilderness by the Lehites when they arrived in the New World. They probably came from the goats brought over by the Jaredites from the Old World when they left the tower of Babel. They roamed free after the Jaredites destroyed themselves in a great civil war.

The Lehites rounded up the goats and domesticated them for their hair, skins, meat, and milk.

References: I Nephi 5:216; Enos 1:34; Alma 10:85; Ether 4:18-21.

GOLD PLATES—See Plates of Gold

GOLD—Metal

Gold is a yellow element that does not degenerate with age. It is easily worked into ornaments and pounded into thin plates. It is soft enough to be etched and hard enough to hold the pattern etched into it.

When the Lehites reached the New World, they found gold in abundance. From the gold, plates were made on which a record of the people was kept. Ornaments and coins of gold were also made. As the Nephites grew rich from time to time, they became prideful and persecuted their poorer brethren until the Lord brought them to their knees.

Jaredites also found gold in the New World and suffered from the disease of lust for it.

References: I Nephi 5:217; II Nephi 4:21; Jacob 2:14-16; Mosiah 7:6-15; Helaman 2:130; Ether 4:18-29, 71.

GOMORRAH—Old World City

Gomorrah was one of five Old World cities buried under a volcanic eruption because of the great sins of the inhabitants. Its ruin is believed to lie beneath the south end of the Dead Sea.

Babylon had a similarly complete destruction as prophesied by Isaiah when Xerxes the Persian completed the destruction begun by Cyrus.

References: II Nephi 10:19; Isaiah 13:19; Genesis 18-19.

GRAPES—Plant

Grapes are the fruit of the true vine. They grow anywhere, producing fast-growing woody stems. The broad-lobed leaves grow opposite grasping tendrils that twist around twigs, branches, or bark to attach the vine for support against a less movable object. The fruit grows in clusters in a variety of colors from white to purple-black. Tame grapes are large and juicy with small seeds. Wild grapes are smaller and bitter with larger seeds.

Isaiah compared the righteous Israelites to the tame grapes and their prideful brothers to wild grapes. Christ compared the good grapes to the fruit of the thorn which is bitter and inedible.

References: II Nephi 8:71-74; III Nephi 6:28.

GRASS—Plant

Grass is a thin, spike-leafed plant having hollow stems and petalless flowers. It grows either from seed or extensions of the roots or both. Many cereal grains are the seed of grass plants. When the weather is too cold or too dry, the leaves of the grass turn brown. When the weather warms and the rain falls, the plants send up fresh green shoots among the yellowed straw. Nephi likened Christ's resurrection to the ability of the grass to take on newness of life after the rain. Christ reminded the Nephites that God is willing to care for men as he is to take care of the fragile grass.

References: I Nephi 5:92-96 (Isaiah 51:12-13); III Nephi 6:8.

GREAT SPIRIT

The Lamanites refused to accept the prophecies concerning the coming of God to the world in a body of flesh. Instead they built up belief in a Great Spirit who was their creator, all wisdom, and their protector. To him they prayed for rain, good harvests, family growth, guidance, and strength. The Lamanites believed that he would show favor to them whatever they did unless he was exceedingly angry. Then he would come among them in the form of an animal, man, an eagle, or thunderbird to wreak vengeance upon them before returning to heaven or the happy hunting ground.

King Lamoni and his servants were afraid of Ammon, the Nephite evangelist, because of his great strength. They supposed him to be the Great Spirit come to them in the form of a man. Because of this Ammon was able to convert those Lamanites to a belief in God.

References: Alma 12:64-73, 81, 92-93, 103-106, 164-167; 13:41-43.

H

HAGOTH—Ship Builder (c. 57 B.C.)

Hagoth was a curious Nephite who built a large ship and invited all who would come with him to colonize a new land. He launched his ship on the border between Bountiful and Desolation and the ship headed out across the west sea (Pacific) in a north direction.

The next year he built other ships to take more emigrants to the new lands. The first ship also returned for provisions and took more pilgrims back to the land northward. They did not return again.

Another ship left from the same port heading west. It is believed that this ship landed in Polynesia with its passengers.

References: Alma 30:6-13.

HAMATH—Old World City

Hamath is a town in the territory of Naphtali south of Arpad on the Orontes River east of the coastal mountain range. The Assyrian Sennacherib, as prophesied by Isaiah, boasted of the strength of Hamath and her idols, and his strength to overcome them with greater power.

In the last days, the Lord promised to recover the Israelites from Hamath where they were taken captive.

References: II Nephi 9:86-95, 126; Isaiah 10:5-14; 11:11; II Kings 18:9-37; 19:9-37.

HARP—Musical Instrument

The harp is made of a hollow bow of wood holding strings of different lengths and thicknesses. The strings are plucked to produce sweet music.

Isaiah warns the people that they must not spend their time in listening to the music of the harp and drinking wine while they forget to worship God.

References: II Nephi 8:81-82; Isaiah 5:11-12.

HEARTHOM—Jaredite King (Ether)

Hearthom was the son of Lib in the line of kings. He reigned for twenty-four years before the kingdom was taken from him. He then lived in captivity the remainder of his days and begat Heth.

References: Ether 1:6; 4:80-84.

HELAM—City - Land

Alma gathered out of Nephi the Nephites who had believed Abinadi's words; he led these people away from the wrath of the apostate King Noah. They journeyed eight days into the wilderness toward Zarahemla. There they found a very beautiful land, rich in soil and fresh water. They stopped there to pitch their tents. They then decided to live there and began to plant crops and build a city.

The Lamanites, who were searching for King Limhi and his people also fleeing from Nephi, came upon Helam. Alma surrendered the city to the Lamanites. The Lamanites made Alma's old enemy Amulon their governor. He treated the citizens of Helam very harshly.

The people of Helam cried to God for help. He made their burdens lighter and gave them strength to perform their tasks. Under God's direction, Alma gathered his people and their possessions. God caused a deep sleep to come upon the Lamanite guards and told Alma to lead the people to Zarahemla. The Amulonites then took possession of the city of Helam.

Later these Amulonites came against the Anti-Nephi-Lehies who had just been converted. When they found that the converts would not resist them but submitted themselves to the sword they went to Ammonihah and exterminated the Nephite inhabitants there.

References: Mosiah 11:1-43, 54-76, 174; Alma 14:21-22, 48-60.

HELAMAN—Son of King Benjamin (c. 130 B.C.)

Helaman was very carefully taught in the language of the Egyptians. He could read and write so that he could teach the Nephites the law and commandments.

References: Mosiah 1:2-14.

HELAMAN—Son of Alma (c. 74 B.C.)

Helaman was the son of Alma and grandson of Alma. He was left behind to keep watch on the church in Zarahemla, when his father and two brothers went to preach to the Zoramites.

His father gave him charge over the records of the Nephites, the directors (Urim and Thummim), sword of Laban, and the Liahona. Alma blessed Helaman, then departed to Melek, and was never heard from again.

Helaman took charge of the church as its high priest. His first contention was with Amalickiah who wanted to be king of the Nephites. Moroni, the war chief, put Amalickiah's followers to the sword and chased Amalickiah out of the land.

Helaman reestablished order in the church

so that they had peace for four years. During this time Moroni fortified all the cities of the Nephites and Amalickiah made himself king of the Lamanites.

When Amalickiah led the Lamanites to invade the Nephites and had taken possession of one town after another, Helaman went to the Ammonites, who had vowed never to take up arms even in their own defense, for help. Instead of allowing those who had taken the oath of peace to break it, he gathered an army of two thousand young men who had not made the vow. With this army, Helaman was able to recapture Antiparah and from that post many other cities until the Lamanites were driven from the land.

Following the war, Helaman began the work of rebuilding the church. When peace was established, Helaman died, and the records were given to Shiblon.

References: Alma 16:84; 17:1-84; 18:1; 21:3-8, 16-36, 73, 142, 185; 22:40-41; 24:63-78; 26:1-170; 27:1-3, 16, 44, 55; 29:13, 52-63; 30:1-2, 15.

HELAMAN—Son of Helaman (c. 50 B.C.)

Helaman received the records of the Nephites from his brother, Shiblon. He was made chief judge by the vote of the people. Kishkumen, a leader of the secret combinations, sought to kill him, but Helaman's servants killed Kishkumen instead and told Helaman of the plot. Before Helaman could capture the band of thieves, Gadianton took leadership and took the thieves into hiding.

Helaman retained his judgment seat and ruled justly until he died and his eldest son, Nephi, became judge in his stead.

References: Alma 30:15-21; Helaman 1:38-52; 2:17-18, 33, 66-76, 150-151; 3:1; 5:140; III Nephi 1:2.

HELEM—Companion of Ammon (c. 121 B.C.)

Helem is named as one of fifteen men chosen by King Mosiah to accompany Ammon on a journey to find out what had happened to those Nephites who returned to Nephi-Lehi. They wandered in the wilderness for forty days until they came to the land of Shiblom.

Leaving the rest behind, Helem and his brethren went with Ammon to Nephi. They met and were captured by King Limhi of that land. After two days in prison they were released and Ammon told Limhi who they were. Limhi was so overjoyed to meet his brethren that he called for a feast. After that, nothing more was heard of Helem.

References: Mosiah 5:1-24.

HELMETS—Weapons

The Nephites, Lamanites, and Jaredites were known to have headplates or helmets to defend their heads from wounds in battle.

References: Alma 20:21, 39-41, 47-49; 21:42, 179; Helaman 1:15; III Nephi 2:49-51; Ether 6:87.

HELORUM—Son of King Benjamin (c. 130 B.C.)

Helorum was very carefully taught to read, write, and understand the Egyptian language used to keep the records of the Nephites. He also learned the laws of God.

References: Mosiah 1:2-14.

HEM — Companion of Ammon (c. 121 B.C.)

Hem went with Ammon and fourteen other men to Nephi-Lehi. He was sent by King Mosiah to find out what had happened to the people who had left earlier to repossess the land of their first inheritance.

The group traveled for forty days, suffering hunger, thirst, and fatigue, until they came to Shiblom. There they were captured by King Limhi, put in prison for two days, and released to be tried before the king.

When King Limhi heard that they were from Zarahemla, he rejoiced because he was their brother, a descendant from those that Hem and his brethren were seeking. King Limhi prepared a feast and had the others at Shimlon brought down to it. No more is heard of Hem.

References: Mosiah 5:1-24.

HEN — See Chicken

HERMOUNTS — Wilderness

Hermounts was a wilderness area west across from the river Sidon and northwest of Zarahemla. In the battle of 87 B.C., the Nephites chased the Lamanites there. The area was filled with wild and vicious animals. The animals killed and wounded Lamanites in such great numbers that when the vultures had finished picking the corpses clean, the bones were piled in heaps upon the earth.

References: Alma 1:93-97.

HESHLON—*Plain*

Heshlon was a plain on which the Jaredites fought. Coriantumr chased the armies of Shared there. The battle that followed put Coriantumr in retreat toward the valley of Gilgal which was nearby.

References: Ether 6:31-32.

HETH—*Son of Com (Ether)*

Heth adopted the secret plans of Satan and slew his father with his own sword so that he could reign as king of the Jaredites.

Wickedness spread in the land. God sent prophets to the people to testify against them and to give warning that unless they repented a great drought would cover the land. At the bidding of King Heth, the prophets were slain or cast out of the land.

The promised drought came swiftly. The animals migrated southward toward the land called Zarahemla by the Nephites. Poisonous serpents were sent to further punish the people and trap them in the southland. All the animals migrated and many perished from famine and thirst. The Jaredites gobbled at their carcasses until only bleaching bones were left in the trails toward the south.

When the people saw that they had to repent or perish, they repented. When they were sufficiently humble, the Lord sent rain upon the land again. Many species of animals were brought to extinction. Heth and all his family had perished except Shez, who reigned in his father's stead.

References: Ether 1:6; 4:29-43.

HETH—Son of Hearthom (Ether)

Heth lived in captivity all his days. He was son of a Jaredite king and great-great-grandfather of King Com. His son Aaron lived in captivity as well.

References: Ether 1:6; 4:82-85.

HETH—Land

Jared, the evil king of the Jaredites, rebelled against his father and went to the land of Heth, where he plotted and flattered the people until he had gained the support of half the kingdom against his father, King Omer. With his army he went back to battle his father for the remainder of the kingdom.

References: Ether 3:69-71.

HIGHWAYS

Highways and roads in prophecy often refer to ways of life. Isaiah was sent to meet Ahaz in the highway near Jerusalem. A new highway is to be built on which the Jews are to travel to Israel in the last days.

The Nephites built an extensive highway system, both of the Macadam or improved dirt type and of concrete or fitted stone. Remnants of this highway system are found in many parts of the New World.

During the earthquake preceding the appearance of Christ in the New World, the highways were broken up. After the remnant of people had reestablished themselves, they rebuilt and constructed a new highway system between lands as the civilization expanded. Many of these roads are still in use in Central America.

References: I Nephi 2:81; 3:125; 6:41 (Isaiah 49:11); II Nephi 9:16 (Isaiah 7:3), 131 (Isaiah 11:16); Helaman 3:10-11; 5:80; III Nephi 3:8; 4:11.

HIMNI—Son of Mosiah (c. 100 B.C.)

Himni, along with his brothers, sought to destroy the church of Christ established by Alma. After the conversion of Alma, son of Alma, he too was converted because he witnessed the angel and heard Alma's testimony of a vision of hell. He, along with his brothers, began to testify to the church of the need for repentance and went throughout the land of Zarahemla to repair the damage they had done.

The Nephites sought Himni to be their king after his father, but he refused because of the greater mission he had. He pleaded with his father for permission to go to the Lamanites to convert them also. This request was granted.

With the protection of the Holy Spirit, Himni went to the Lamanites. After much suffering, the king of the Lamanites was converted. Under the king's protection, Himni went to preach in the land and many were converted because of his ministry. When the work was finished, he rejoiced in the success of their prayers and work.

The uncivilized Lamanites came upon the converts to destroy them. Together Himni and his brothers gathered the converts, called Anti-Nephi-Lehies, and conducted them to Zarahemla. Along the way they met Alma and rejoiced. Alma joined them, then took the sons of Mosiah to his own home while Ammon took care of the needs of the converts.

Himni's next mission was with Alma to the Zoramites, but few were converted. After returning to Zarahemla, and a war, Himni began again to reestablish the church in the land.

References: Mosiah 11:159-176, 203-206; 13:3-6; Alma 13; 14:1-12, 78; 16:83-121; 17:5; 21:185.

HOMER—See Measure

HOREB—Old World Mountain

Horeb is near Mount Sinai. It was there that Moses was given the law by God. Twice Moses spent forty days in communion with God on Mount Horeb, and Elijah spent forty days in communion with God there. When Christ came to the New World, he reminded the people that the law was given to Moses at Horeb.

References: III Nephi 11:25; Exodus 19:20; 24:18; 34:28; I Kings 19:8.

HORSES—Animals

Horses are mentioned in connection with

chariots, in use by the Lamanites and the Nephites. Ammon was respected by the Lamanites because of his obedience to King Lamoni in preparing his horses and chariots.

Lachoneous ordered the Nephites to gather their horses and chariots in defense against the Gadiantons. They returned to their lands in chariots after the defeat of the Gadiantons.

Christ uses the horse and chariots to warn men that if the gentiles are not converted, in the last days their means of transportation will be cut off.

References: II Nephi 8:23 (Isaiah 2:7); Alma 12:76-82, 188; III Nephi 2:29-31; 3:1; 9:101.

I

INSECTS—*Animals*

Insects have six jointed legs. Most have wings sometime in their lives. They are hatched from eggs. Most go through stages of development that are drastically different in shape and habit. Most are vegetarians, eating leaves, stems, roots, seeds, and sap from plants until they strip gardens to barren soil. Others sting, pinch, bite, and suck blood from animals, including men.

When Abinadi the prophet was condemned by the inhabitants of Nephi to burning at the stake before King Noah, he cursed them with calamities, including being pestered by insects.

References: Mosiah 7:53.

IRON—*Metal*

Both the Jaredites and the Lehites found iron in abundance in the New World. The metal is hard, dense, and easily worked into a variety of useful objects. If not cared for, it rusts into useless red flakes. Unlike copper that oxidizes only on the surface, iron oxidizes all the way through if it is not kept dry. Iron holds its shape in thinner plates than copper and is therefore more useful in making tools.

The Jaredites used iron for farm tools and weapons of war. The Nephites used the metal in a similar fashion and for ornamentation of buildings as well.

Because of its well known unique properties iron was used in prophecy. The rod of iron in Lehi's vision represents the unbending truth of God. The yoke of iron represents the heavy burden caused by apostasy due to the lies of Satan. The iron sinew of the neck represents the strong, unbreakable stubbornness of the Lehites. The thickets of the forest are to be cut down by God with iron which is the sharp edge of eternal truth. The iron horn represents the preaching of truth.

References: I Nephi 2:62-78; 3:68-69, 140; 4:38-40; 6:11-12 (Isaiah 48:4-5); II Nephi 4:21; 9:115 (Isaiah 10:34); Jarom 1:19-21; Mosiah 7:6, 11-12; III Nephi 9:54; Ether 4:71.

IRREANTUM—*Ocean*

Irreantum is the name the Lehites gave the ocean they crossed to the New World. It was a large ocean that took them many days of sailing to cross. Many authorities believe this to be the Indian Ocean.

References: I Nephi 5:64.

ISAAC—Patriarch (Old Testament)

Isaac was the son of Abraham who was taken to the mountains to be offered as a sacrifice to God. This was done in similitude of God's offering himself up in the flesh for our sins. Isaac continued all his life to demonstrate his faithfulness to God. For his faithfulness, Isaac was rewarded a place in the kingdom of God to go out no more. Isaac was one of the few men of the time before Moses to have only one wife, Rebekah, and no concubines. His life was full of peace and prosperity.

The God of the Nephites was identified with Isaac. The covenants between God and Isaac were recognized by the Nephites, that through his seed, the promises of God would be fulfilled and all the world be blessed. Both Jesus and Joseph Smith, Jr., were of his lineage.

References: I Nephi 2:4; 5:132-133, 240; Jacob 3:6; Mosiah 5:28-29; 11:26; Alma 3:44; 5:42; 15:63; 17:2; Helaman 2:25-26; III Nephi 2:77; Mormon 4:70; Genesis 21-26.

ISABEL—Harlot (c. 73 B.C.)

Isabel was a harlot in Siron who tempted Corianton, son of Alma, to follow her instead of continuing his mission to the Zoramites. Because of this, many of the Zoramites had the excuse they wanted to reject the teachings of Corianton's father.

References: Alma 19:5.

ISAIAH—Prophet (Old Testament)

Isaiah, the son of Amoz, was of noble descent. He served as prophet to Judah and Jerusalem from the year of the death of King Uzziah, about 740 B.C., until he was supposedly martyred by Manasseh by being trapped in a hollow tree and sawn asunder. He married the Prophetess, and had at least two sons, Shearjashub, and Mahershalal-hash-baz.

Copied from the plates of brass obtained from Laban, the prophecies of Isaiah concerning the houses of Ephraim and Manasseh, the city of Jerusalem, the New World, Zion, and the scattering and gathering of the Jews are recorded in Nephi's writings. Nephi selected and arranged these prophecies in chronological sequence in his lessons for his brothers.

Abinadi used the prophecies of Isaiah concerning the coming of God in the flesh to teach King Noah and his followers. Though King Noah did not believe him, Alma, one of Noah's priests, did and used Abinadi's words to gather out from the land of Nephi those Nephites who would listen.

Christ told the people who were in the New World to study the words of Isaiah because of the fullness of the prophecies he wrote.

Mormon repeats Christ's plea for all people to search Isaiah.

References: I Nephi 4:30-33; 6:3-5; II Nephi 5:9-15; 8:2-17 (Isaiah 6:1-8); 9:16 (Isaiah 7:3); 10:1 (Isaiah 13:1); 11:1-14; Mosiah 8:15-33; Helaman 3:54; III Nephi 7:43; 9:47; 10:27-29; Mormon 4:27; Isaiah.

ISAIAH—Disciple (c. A.D. 34)

Isaiah was called by Christ and ordained a disciple. As such he taught one twelfth of the multitude to worship and pray. Then after being baptized by Nephi, he baptized those of his people who desired to covenant with God. When all were baptized, the Holy Ghost was given to them.

See *Disciples* for the rest of the story.

References: III Nephi 9:4-15.

ISHMAEL—Father (c. 600 B.C.)

When the Lord gathered Lehi and his family out of Jerusalem, the sons of Lehi were not married. In order for the family to increase, the Lord sent Nephi and his brothers back to Jerusalem for Ishmael and his family of daughters and sons. After much persuasion the family agreed to come so that wives were provided for the Lehites.

They had not gone far when Laman, Lemuel, and two daughters and two sons of Ishmael decided to return to the gay, secure life of Jerusalem. Using all the courage he could gather, Nephi withstood them and convinced them of their error, but not before he had been bound with rope. By the power of God he broke his bonds before them.

Along the way, the sons of Lehi and Zoram, who had come from the house of Laban, took the daughters of Ishmael for wives, fulfilling the desires of the Lord. Ishmael died, leaving his daughters grief stricken and ready to give up and return to Jerusalem. Only chastening by the voice of the Lord returned the rebellious wives and sons to obedience to their father, Lehi.

References: I Nephi 2:7-39; 5:7, 44-54.

ISHMAEL—Father of Giddonah (Unknown)

Ishmael was a descendant of Aminadi and grandfather of Amulek, the second witness for Alma.

References: Alma 8:1.

ISHMAEL—Land

The sons of Ishmael joined with Laman and Lemuel to become Lamanites. They inhabited a land they called Ishmael after their father. Ammon came there to preach to them and convert them to the love of God.

They carried Ammon, bound, before their king, Lamoni. When the king asked Ammon if he wished to live there, he agreed, and rather than live in a palace took a place as a shepherd servant. Through the efforts of Ammon to demonstrate the life of a Christian, the attention of the Ishmaelites was obtained and they were converted to Christianity. They became the Anti-Nephi-Lehies, later called the Ammonites.

References: Alma 12:29-32, 197-200; 13:23-35; 14:13-26, 73-74.

ISHMAELITES—Descendants

The Ishmaelites came out of Jerusalem shortly after Lehi left to join Lehi's family and intermarry with them. Two sons and two daughters of Ishmael joined Laman and Lemuel to form the rebellious Lamanites. During the journey to the New World the Ishmaelites argued with Nephi many times.

Before he died Lehi exhorted the Ishmaelites to be subject to Nephi. However, soon after his death the Ishmaelites separated themselves, with the Lamanites and Lemuelites, from Nephi, Sam, Jacob, Joseph, and Zoram and their families.

The Ishmaelites, like the Lamanites, shaved their heads, were naked except for a loincloth, had dark skins, believed that Lehi had lied to them, and did not keep a record of their people. Thus they lost the language and Scriptures to keep them civilized.

Ammon came to the Ishmaelites to convert them to correct beliefs in God. He succeeded in turning them so completely from their uncivilized ways that they never fell away from the truth. They became the Anti-Nephi-Lehies, or Ammonites.

Some of the Ishmaelites refused to come to the truth and remained with the Lamanites in rebellion, coming many times against the Nephites in an attempt to destroy them and take their possessions.

After Christ came all believed the truth for two hundred years. Then, because of pride, the people broke up again into tribes. The Ishmaelites rejected the truth and willfully rebelled against God.

Later the Nephites became even more sinful than the Lamanites and the Ishmaelites joined in a war that was concluded only when the Nephites were completely destroyed.

References: I Nephi 2:12, 31-35; 5:25, 33, 48-49, 180-210; II Nephi 1:52-54; 3:17, 24-27; Jacob 1:13-14; Alma 1:103-106; 12:29, 117; 20:15; 21:116-120; IV Nephi 1:42-43; Mormon 1:8-9.

ISRAEL—Patriarch (Old Testament)

Israel, first named Jacob, was a twin to Esau and was born of Isaac and Rebekah. He was taught by Rebekah to be gentle yet strong. He was a farmer and shepherd while his brother was a hunter.

Israel bought his brother's birthright with a bowl of soup and his blessing with a bowl of boiled spicy meat.

Sent away by his father to marry in Haran, Jacob was cheated of his first choice, Rachel, and forced to marry Leah, her older sister. He worked for and married Rachel, anyway. There was constant rivalry between his wives for his affection.

Jacob had twelve sons by his wives and their two handmaids. These sons were the heads of the twelve tribes of Israel. The twelve apostles whom Christ appointed in Israel and ordained in Jerusalem on Pentecost are to be the judges of the twelve tribes at judgment.

Nephi, son of Lehi, quotes Isaiah's warning for the Lehites who came from Judah across the sea and are of the house of Israel. He exhorted them to remain faithful to God.

Christ is known as the mighty one of Israel because he is an Israelite by birth.

Jacob, son of Lehi, continues admonishing the house of Israel to which the Lehites belong.

The law was given to Moses for all Israel. Moses led the Israelites through the Red Sea. The Israelites were scattered, yet each tribe received a visit from Christ. Eventually all the twelve tribes of Israel are to be gathered again.

References: I Nephi 1:164-165; 2:1-2; 3:115; 6:1 - II Nephi 11; Mosiah 5:63; Alma 14:126; Helaman 3:44; III Nephi 4:55-59; 7:6; 11:25 (Malachi 4:4); 13:41-44; Mormon 1:82-83.

J

JACOB—Israel (Old Testament)

Jacob was renamed Israel when God covenanted with him to be a father of nations and to bless all the world through his seed. Before he died, Jacob blessed his sons and especially blessed Joseph and the two sons of Joseph, prophesying of the family of Lehi. Jacob was rewarded for his faithfulness by being given a place in the kingdom of God to go out no more.

Jacob's name is used by the Nephites to define their God. Christ was known as the mighty one of Jacob.

The seed of Jacob were scattered to all the world by invading armies from Assyria, Babylonia, and Rome, and by the separation of groups before the invasions by the direction of God. In the latter days the seed of Jacob is to be gathered from the world to Israel and Zion. If by then the gentiles have refused to repent after receiving the truth, the remnant of the seed of Jacob will go forth to wreak vengeance on the unrepentant.

References: I Nephi 2:4; 5:132-133; 6:56 (Isaiah 49:26); II Nephi 5:45 (Isaiah 49:26); 8:19-22 (Isaiah 2:3-6); 9:68 (Isaiah 9:8), 101-105 (Isaiah 10:20-24); 10:23 (Isaiah 14:1); 11:158 (Isaiah 29:32); Mosiah 5:28-29; 11:25-26; Alma 3:44; 5:42; 15:63; 17:2; 21:54-59; Helaman 2:26; III Nephi 2:77, 104-109; 4:72; 9:51-58, 99; 10:1-3; 11:9 (Malachi 3:6); Mormon 2:54; 3:32-33; 4:70.

JACOB—Son of Lehi (c. 589 B.C.)

Jacob never saw Jerusalem; he was born on the journey from Jerusalem to the ocean before the Lehites crossed to the New World. Aboard the ship crossing the ocean, while Jacob was yet very young, his older brothers, Laman and Lemuel, bound Nephi, nearly causing his parents to die of grief because of their constant battling. Only when the compass failed and they saw that the storm was about to sink the ship did they repent, release Nephi, and establish peaceful coexistence.

Jacob's father, Lehi, blessed Jacob before he died, telling him to be subject to Nephi and to God. After Lehi died, the peaceful coexistence suddenly ceased as Laman demanded his right as oldest son to determine the destiny of the family. From that time Laman and Lemuel sought to destroy Nephi and all his family and followers. Nephi was forced to take his family and Zoram, Sam, Jacob, and Joseph into the wilderness for safety.

Jacob was ordained a high priest at the hands of Nephi in 569 B.C. Ten years later Nephi called upon him to preach to the people. He prophesied of the scattering of the Jews, the gathering of Israel, the coming of Christ, restoration of the church, affliction of the Lamanites by the gentiles, and establishment of Zion.

Nephi testified that Jacob saw and knew Christ. He gave Jacob the plates and commanded him to maintain the history of the Lehites on them.

During Jacob's time of leadership the people began to prosper exceedingly. Jacob was called upon by God to warn his people of the pit of pride they were about to fall into. Because they knew good from evil, their unrighteousness would lead to their complete destruction at the hands of the Lamanites.

Toward the end of his life Jacob contended with Sherem, who did not believe in the coming of Christ. Sherem asked Jacob for a sign of the truth; Jacob gave him death.

Before he died Jacob passed the plates on to his son, Enos.

References: I Nephi 5:179, 188-208; II Nephi 1:59-128; 4:1-13, 42; 5 - 8:4; 13:2; Jacob 1-5; Words of Mormon 1:4-5; Alma 1:104.

JACOB—Lamanite Leader (c. 66 B.C.)

Jacob was a Zoramite who joined the Lamanites in a war against the Nephites. He was put in charge of the soldiers left to guard the city of Mulek. Moroni sent a letter to Jacob, asking him to meet the Nephites in battle on the plains near the city, but Jacob refused.

Moroni took his army west of the city and concealed them in the wilderness. He sent Teancum with a small force down to the seashore in plain sight of the city of Mulek. When Jacob learned of the small force of Teancum, he sent his army out to destroy them. When Teancum saw Jacob's army coming he retreated with his soldiers along the seashore northward, leading the guard away from the city.

When the armies of Teancum and Jacob were out of the way, Moroni took his forces in and recaptured the city of Mulek. Meanwhile Teancum led Jacob's army into the army of Lehi near Bountiful. Jacob saw Lehi's army and hastily retreated to Mulek. With Lehi's army behind, Moroni's army in front, and Teancum's small force at the side, the army of Jacob was trapped. Jacob's army fought furiously; nevertheless he was killed and his army captured.

References: Alma 24:24-44.

JACOB—King of Robbers (c. 30 B.C.)

Just six years after the Nephites had turned to righteousness and had rid themselves of the secret combinations, they returned to those wicked ways. A new secret order was established with Jacob as leader and king. He was one of the chief disbelievers to condemn the prophets for teaching about the coming of Christ.

Jacob saw that the Nephites who opposed him, though not united, were more numerous than his band, so he took his followers to the land northward. There they established a kingdom and were joined by dissenters who were flattered away from the tribes by Jacob. When the numbers in Jacob's kingdom were great enough, they drew up an army to fight with the tribes of the Nephites.

The Jacobites were destroyed about A.D. 34 by the cataclysm that came at the time of the crucifixion of Christ. This catastrophe removed the evil of the Jacobites before it could overcome all the people in the New World.

References: III Nephi 3:43-50.

JACOB—City

The city of Jacob was one of the cities sunk during the earthquakes that preceded the coming of Christ to the New World. This catastrophe removed from sight the evil in that city.

References: III Nephi 4:34-35.

JACOBITES—Descendants of Jacob

Following the death of Lehi the Lehites

separated into tribes named after the sons of Lehi. The Jacobites of the family of Jacob joined with the division called Nephites.

After the coming of Christ, the people again divided themselves into tribes, one tribe calling themselves Jacobites. The Jacobites were among the true believers of Christ.

About A.D. 322 the war began between the Nephites, among them the Jacobites, and the Lamanites. By the end of the battle the Jacobites were no more.

References: Jacob 1:13; IV Nephi 1:40-41; Mormon 1:8.

JACOBUGATH—City

Jacobugath was established by the king of Jacob. The inhabitants became a very wicked people who used secret combinations to commit murder. They worked continually to destroy the Nephite government and peace in the country. The prophets who tried to call them to repentance were slain. For this continual and complete wickedness, God burned the city of Jacobugath, and the inhabitants with it, during the cataclysm that preceded the appearance of Christ in the New World.

References: III Nephi 4:36-37.

JACOM—Son of Jared (Ether)

Jacom came with his father and others from the tower of Babel. When the Jaredites desired a king, and Jacom was elected, he refused, nor would his father coerce him to accept.

References: Ether 3:16-32.

JARED—*Leader of the Jaredites (Ether)*

Jared was the head of a family living at Babel when the tower was built. He recognized his brother for his great faith and used him as spokesman before God. When Jared realized that God was about to confound the language of all the people and scatter the people over the world, he asked his brother to petition God to allow his family and friends to maintain their pure language and be sent together wherever God willed.

On the direction of God, Jared led their families and friends to the New World in eight barges, taking with them seeds and animals from the Old World.

The Jaredites thrived in the new land, finding an abundance of materials with which to prosper. When Jared and his brother were old they gathered all the Jaredites together to ask them what they needed before their leaders died. The Jaredites asked for a king.

After trying to dissuade them but failing, Jared told the Jaredites to vote for a king. When they elected his sons, the sons refused to serve. Only Orihah would accept.

After Orihah took over leadership, Jared and his brother died.

References: Ether 1:6-29; 3:1-35; 4:44.

JARED—*Son of Omer (Ether)*

Jared rebelled against his father, King Omer, and went to live in Heth. While there, he

166

flattered the Jaredites until half the kingdom followed him. He gathered an army and fought his own father, taking the kingdom and placing his father in captivity.

Later, the brothers of Jared, Esrom and Coriantumr, raised an army to recover the kingdom for their father. They fought Jared by night and destroyed his army. Jared pleaded for his own life and was spared when he agreed to return the kingdom to his father's rule.

Still yearning for the kingdom, Jared sulked. His daughter, to please herself and her father, devised a scheme whereby she trapped Akish, a gullible friend of King Omer, into killing the king to return the rule to Jared. The reward was Jared's daughter's hand in marriage. Before the plan could be fully accomplished, Omer, warned by God, fled, abandoning the kingdom to Jared.

Now Akish, seeing how well the conspiracy worked, used the same plan to rid himself of Jared. Jared was murdered and Akish became king.

References: Ether 3:68-85; 4:4-7.

JAREDITES—Followers of Jared

When the language was confounded and the people scattered from the tower of Babel, Jared asked his brother to pray to God that the language of Jared, his friends, and their families be not confounded, and to learn where the group was to go in the scattering that followed.

The Jaredites were allowed to keep their pure language and were sent to the New World. They were warned, however, that if they did not remain faithful, they would be destroyed from off the face of the land.

Twenty-two people boarded the eight barges prepared by the Jaredites, along with seeds, food, and a variety of domestic animals. They remained aboard the barges for nearly a year.

When they arrived at the New World, they discovered a choice land with an abundance of materials to build a prosperous nation. They spread out on the land and began to thrive.

Before they died, Jared and his brothers gathered the people to number them and to ask them what they needed. They asked for a king. After warning them that this would lead to their eventual destruction, Jared conceded. Of the sons of Jared and his brother, only Orihah, son of Jared, would accept. He reigned in righteousness, followed by Kib.

Corihor, the next king, began to bring down the civilization by putting his father in captivity. Shule returned the kingdom to Kib by fighting Corihor.

The Jaredites fluctuated between periods of righteousness and prosperity and periods of pride and wickedness which eventually led to destruction. They suffered periods of famine, one lasting several generations. Finally they became so divided that righteousness disappeared from among them except for their last prophet,

Ether. The Jaredites divided themselves into two great armies under Shared and Coriantumr. Those who refused to take sides were slain. The two armies fought until only Coriantumr remained alive; Ether was hidden in a cave watching the battle.

Ether hid the records of the Jaredites near the field of their last battle and disappeared. Coriantumr stumbled to the city of Zarahemla where the Mulekites had settled. He lived with them nine months, telling them of his background.

Much later the Nephites under King Limhi found the Jaredite records and took them to Mosiah to translate.

References: Omni 1:36-39; Mosiah 9:166-169; 12:16-26; Ether; Moroni 9:24.

JAROM—Recorder (c. 420 B.C.)

Jarom was the son of Enos who gave him charge of the plates of Nephi. In his day he saw many wars between the Nephites and the Lamanites. While the Lamanites became more animalistic, the Nephites prospered, building and fashioning machinery and weapons for defense. Many prophets and church leaders kept the Nephites in obedience to the Law of Moses.

When Jarom grew too old to keep the records any longer, he gave them to his son, Omni.

References: Jarom 1:1-19; Omni 1:1.

JASHON—City - Land

In the last war between the Nephites and the Lamanites, the Nephites fled to the city of Jashon. They stopped their retreat long enough to draw together to prepare a defense and to rest. Later they were driven on by the Lamanites.

It was near the city of Jashon that Ammoron buried the records of the Lehites. Mormon dug them up later and continued the record.
References: Mormon 1:43-47.

JAVELIN—Weapon

The javelin was among the first weapons prepared by the Nephites for defense against the murderous Lamanites. It was constructed of a large sharpened stone attached to a long slender rod by a strap or thong.

Teancum used a javelin to kill Amalickiah, the dissenter who became king of the Lamanites, in a war between the Lamanites and the Nephites. Teancum slew Ammoron, the brother of Amalickiah, in a similar manner to end the war.
References: Jarom 1:19-21; Alma 23:41; 29:43.

JEBERECHIAH—Father of Zechariah (Old Testament)

Jeberechiah was the father of Zechariah, who was a witness for Isaiah concerning the coming of Maher-shalal-hash-baz.
References: II Nephi 9:39-40; Isaiah 8:1-2.

JENEUM—War Chief (c. A.D. 385)

Jeneum led his ten thousand Nephite warriors

into battle against the Lamanites in the last war with the Nephites. He and all his soldiers were slain.

References: Mormon 3:15.

JEREMIAH—Prophet (Old Testament)

Jeremiah was born at Anathoth, in northern Israel, of a rich priestly family of Hilkiah around 645 B.C. He was the contemporary of Zephaniah, beginning his prophesying in the thirteenth year of the reign of Josiah and into the time of the Babylonian captivity. He remained a bachelor all his life.

Shortly before Lehi and his family left for the New World, Jeremiah, at that time in the court of Zedekiah, was put in prison. His prophecies had been recorded on the plates of Laban but were as yet untested.

He testified of the destruction of Jerusalem, the seventy-year captivity of its inhabitants in Babylonia, the return to Jerusalem, the coming of Christ, the scattering of the Israelites, and the eventual gathering of the Jews.

Jeremiah died in Egypt where he had been taken against his will shortly after the Babylonian captivity. The manner of his death is uncertain.

References: I Nephi 1:163; 2:21-22; Helaman 3:54-58.

JEREMIAH—Disciple (c. A.D. 34)

Jeremiah was called out by Christ and ordained a disciple to the remnant of the Lehites surviving the cataclysm. As such, he taught a portion of the multitude to worship and pray and reinforced the message of Christ. After being baptized by Nephi, he baptized those who desired to covenant with God. When all were baptized the Holy Ghost was given to the covenant people.

See *Disciples* for the rest of the story.

References: III Nephi 9:4-15.

JERSHON—Land

Jershon was a land by the sea on the south border of Bountiful. It was a possession of the Nephites. When Ammon brought the Anti-Nephi-Lehies to the chief judge of the Nephites, the people voted to accept the Anti-Nephi-Lehies and give them Jershon in which to dwell. From that time they were called the Ammonites.

Since the Ammonites refused to take up arms in their own defense, the Nephites set a guard of their own men, supported by taxes from the Ammonites, around Jershon to protect it.

Korihor entered Jershon to preach wickedness to the Ammonites, but he was bound and cast out of the land.

The Zoramites opened a land called Antionum which was south of Jershon. When Alma and his companions went to Antionum to convert the Zoramites, the converts were cast out followed shortly by Alma and Amulek. They all fled to Jershon where they were taken in by the Ammonites. This angered the Zoramites, who sought revenge against the Ammonites by plotting with the Lamanites to destroy them.

The Ammonites left Jershon for Melek so that the Nephites would have room to withstand the invasion. With Moroni as their leader, the Nephites armed themselves well and stood prepared to meet the Lamanites when they arrived.

Zerahemnah led the Lamanites into Antionum. When he saw the preparations of the Nephites at the border of Jershon, he was frightened and departed with his army to Manti in anticipation of surprising the Nephites there.

References: Alma 15:23-43; 16:1, 20-22, 80, 240-252; 20:4, 17-29.

JERUSALEM—Old World City

At first Jerusalem was called Salem under Prince Melchisedec. Many centuries later David conquered the Jebusites who lived there when he was clearing Canaan for Israel occupation. Solomon built a temple there to take the place of the worn tabernacle of Moses.

After this followed years of kings who permitted wanton lusts to go on unchecked in the city, while instigating most of the wickedness themselves. Worship declined in spite of the prophets sent to call the people to repentance from time to time.

Jerusalem remained the capital of the people of the tribes of Judah and Benjamin. The other ten tribes were scattered because of their worship of the golden calf.

In about 600 B.C., Lehi was told to prophesy

to the city concerning their wickedness and coming destruction. When they sought his life, God told Lehi to take his family and depart from Jerusalem. Lehi also took Zoram, the servant of Laban, and Ishmael and his family of daughters. They took the record of the priests from Laban containing their genealogy, the Scriptures, and the prophecies.

When the Lehites were well on their way to the New World, Lehi saw the destruction of Jerusalem in a vision. Prophecies concerning the rebuilding of Jerusalem, the coming of Christ, later destruction, scattering of its inhabitants, and the eventual gathering of the Jews and renewal of Jerusalem were given to the descendants of Lehi.

Laman and Lemuel, the older sons of Lehi, never forgave their father for taking them away from Jerusalem. Their descendants fought with the Nephites until the Nephites were eventually destroyed.

References: I Nephi 1:3, 11-28, 40-145; 2:7-11, 19-24; 3:2-4, 52; 5:47, 95-96; II Nephi 1:4-5; 5:100-114 (Isaiah 51:17 - 52:2); 8:17-73 (Isaiah 2:1 - 5:3); 9:14-115 (Isaiah 7 - 10); 11:6-24; 12:81; Jacob 5:43-44; Omni 1:26; Mosiah 7:79; 8:86; Isaiah 52:9; III Nephi 1:2-3; 4:73; 7:44; 9:71-85; 10:5; 11:4-9 (Malachi 3:1-6); IV Nephi 1:34-35.

JERUSALEM—Lamanite City

Near the borders of Mormon, in the land of Amulon, the Lamanites built a great city they called Jerusalem after the city of Laman's birth.

Aaron came to that city to preach in the synagogues built there by the Amalekites and Amulonites. They believed, like the Nehors, that all men would be saved, no matter what they did in life. When Aaron tried to teach them the truth, they spurned him because they did not believe in prophecy or redemption. Aaron left them and went on to Ani-anti.

When the Lamanites were converted and became the Anti-Nephi-Lehies, the citizens of Jerusalem roused themselves to try to destroy the converts. But Ammon, aware of their plot, removed the converts from the land into the protection of the Nephites.

The great city of Jerusalem was sunk during the cataclysm that changed the face of the New World, and water covered the ruins in A.D. 34.

References: Alma 13:1-16; 14:21-22; III Nephi 4:31-33.

JESSE—*Father of David (Old Testament)*

Jesse, the grandson of Boaz of the house of Judah, lived in Beth-lehem. He was a landowner, a man of standing. He kept sheep, using his sons as shepherds.

Samuel came to Jesse to ordain his son, David, to be the second king of Israel and first of a long line of kings. Jesse encouraged David to kill Goliath to save Saul, the Benjamite.

Christ himself was of the lineage of David and Jesse, being referred to as the rod out of the stem and root of Jesse.

References: II Nephi 9:116-119 (Isaiah 11:1-4), 125 (Isaiah 11:10); I Samuel 16, 17.

JOHN THE BAPTIST—Prophet (c. A.D. 30)

John the Baptist was the son of Zechariah of the house of Aaron. He was called before he was born to prepare the way for the coming of Christ to Jerusalem.

Lehi prophesied of a prophet who should come before and prepare the way for the coming of Christ to Jerusalem. He was to cry repentance to the Jews and baptize in Bethabara the covenant people, including Christ. When he baptized Christ, he was to witness that he had baptized the Lamb of God.

Nephi also saw John in a vision as well as his works to prepare for and baptize Christ.

John the Baptist lived in the wilderness and worked exactly as had been prophesied. Later he was beheaded on the orders of Herod at the request of his wife as a favor for the dancing of her daughter, Salome, for the governor.

References: I Nephi 3:7-12, 71-74; II Nephi 13:6-10; Luke 1:1-25; 3:1-29; Matthew 14:1-12.

JOHN THE REVELATOR—Prophet (c. A.D. 30)

John was one of the apostles of Christ at Jerusalem. He was chosen to write prophecies concerning the last days and the end of the world. He wrote in prophetic language so that only those who seek the truth will find it. He was never to taste of death until the fulfillment of the revelations.

John was the son of Zebedee, a fisherman. He was called from his tasks by Christ to be an apostle. He became a constant companion of Christ and was therefore present at the transfiguration, as well as other major events in Christ's ministry, death, and resurrection. John was given responsibility for Mary, the mother of Christ, at the crucifixion.

John wrote two books that give us special insight into the life and nature of Christ and the future of the world. He was exiled to the island of Patmos where he presumably wrote his prophecies into books to preserve them for the world. There is no record of his death.

References: I Nephi 3:238-251; III Nephi 13:15-19; Ether 1:111-113; Gospels of the New Testament, especially John; Acts; Revelation.

JONAS—Disciple (c. A.D. 34)

There were two men named Jonas (one was the son of Timothy) who were called by Christ in the New World to be special witnesses of the gospel to the Lehites. They were baptized by Nephi, then helped others covenant by baptizing them. They taught a portion of the multitude to worship God and to pray while waiting for the second appearance of Christ among them. For the rest of their story see *Disciples.*

References: III Nephi 9:4-15.

JORDAN—Old World River

The Jordan flows from spring-fed Lake Huleh in the Anti-Lebanon Mountains to the Dead

Sea, 1,290 feet below sea level. It follows the lowest depression known to exist on earth. Since it is the largest river of continual flow in the land promised to Abraham, it has much biblical significance.

It was the river Jordan that Jacob crossed on his way to obtain a bride in Haran. Here Joshua stopped the flow to take the Israelites across to conquer Jericho. It acted in the healing of Naaman. It stopped flowing to allow Elijah to cross before being taken to heaven and Elisha to return back across carrying Elijah's mantle. For centuries it served as a boundary between nations.

Lehi told his family that John the Baptist would baptize the people, including the Messiah, in its water.

Nephi, son of Lehi, reminded the people that God, beginning at the Jordan, had driven the inhabitants from the promised land before the children of Israel.

References: I Nephi 3:11; 5:117; II Nephi 9:61; Isaiah 9:1.

JORDAN—City

As the Nephites fled from the Lamanites in their last war, they came to the city of Jordan. For a while they were able to maintain that city, but were again driven before the Lamanites.

Reference: Mormon 2:28-33.

JOSEPH—Son of Jacob (Old Testament)

Joseph, youngest son of Jacob and Rachel

born at Paddanaram, was a tattletale. Because of this he was loved by his father but hated by his jealous brothers. When occasion arose they sold him to traders who were on their way to Egypt. Potiphar, the steward of the Pharaoh, bought him.

In the midst of good fortune and responsible power, Joseph fell into trouble through no fault of his own; yet even in prison he prospered. Brought out through his gift of prophecy, he prospered again, obtaining a position through which he helped his family survive a severe drought.

It was important to Lehi and his descendants to know that they were of the house and lineage of Joseph. They obtained and kept the plates of brass on which were printed the genealogy and records of the prophets.

Because the Lehites were of the tribe of Joseph, the promises made by God to Joseph were theirs. They were to be part of a righteous branch broken off and grown over the sea. To this branch Christ came to bring light and freedom. A book to be written of the Lehites was to be joined with the book or testaments of the people who remained in Jerusalem, to confound false doctrine. From them a choice seer would come who would convince his brothers of the knowledge of the covenants. This, because he was to be Joseph, son of Joseph, has been interpreted to be Joseph Smith, Jr.

He would translate the book and reestablish the church among them.

Amulek, the second witness for Alma, traced his lineage to Joseph, son of Jacob. Moroni, the Nephite war chief, reminded the people that a remnant of the tribe of Joseph would always be preserved. The new Jerusalem to be built in the New World is to be for the gathering of the tribe of Joseph.

References: I Nephi 1:165-168; 2:2; II Nephi 2:5-31; 3:1-6; 11:40; Jacob 2:33-34; Alma 8:1-3; 21:54-60; III Nephi 2:104-106; 4:72; 7:13; Ether 6:6-10; Genesis 37, 39-50.

JOSEPH—Son of Lehi (c. 588 B.C.)

Joseph was the last son born to Lehi. He was born in the wilderness after the Lehites left Jerusalem and was still quite young when Lehi died.

Lehi, in his patriarchal blessing of Joseph, promised that his seed would not utterly be destroyed as would the other Nephite tribes. Joseph was to be blessed over his brothers because of the covenant Jacob gave Joseph. From the lineage of Joseph, the son of Lehi, was to be born one mighty among them who would be an instrument for God to work wonders and help in the restoration of Israel.

Joseph was taken by Nephi into safety when he led his family away from Laman who had become so angry as to try to slay them. Joseph was ordained by Nephi to be a high priest to the Nephites. He was later described by Alma as a just and holy man.

References: I Nephi 5:179-208; II Nephi 2:1-5, 44-50; 4:8, 42; Jacob 1:18; Alma 1:104.

JOSEPHITES—Descendants

The descendants of Joseph, son of Lehi, joined the Nephite civilization. They shared in Nephite history. After the coming of Christ, and 230 years of peace, the Josephites reformed a tribe of true believers. When the Lamanites and the Nephites warred until the Nephites were destroyed, some of the Josephites survived to maintain a needed remnant.

References: II Nephi 2:44-50; Jacob 1:13; IV Nephi 1:40-41; Mormon 1:8.

JOSEPH SMITH, JR.—Prophet (c. A.D. 1830)

Lehi repeated the promise given to Joseph, son of Jacob, to Joseph, his son. He told Joseph that someday a choice seer or possessor of the Urim and Thummim was to be raised up from the house of Joseph, son of Jacob. This seer was to be honored by the Indians. His calling was to translate the records written by the Nephites and abridged by Mormon. He was to be like Moses, to bring the testimony to the Indians and have no other occupation. Those who tried to force him to give them the plates of the record were to be condemned by God. Anyone who tried to keep him from his work was also condemned.

Joseph was not to be a great speaker, but would be given a spokesman and a scribe as Moses was given Aaron.

The name of this man was to be Joseph, son of a man named Joseph, of the tribe of Joseph, son of Lehi.

Joseph Smith, Jr., fulfilled all these prophecies. Joseph was called of God when he was fourteen years old, as he inquired of God which church he should join. He had no occupation at that time, though he knew how to labor beside his father in the field. He knew how to read and write but could not be considered a learned man. He was taught by Moroni what he should do as his life progressed.

Joseph began the job of translation in 1827 and finished in 1829 with the help of Oliver Cowdery who became both scribe and spokesman for him. During that time the plates had to be carefully guarded. They were lost once when Joseph submitted to the pleading of Martin Harris to show the translation to his wife, so Moroni reclaimed them for a while. When Joseph prepared himself, the plates were returned and the work of the translation completed. None who sought the record for the value of the gold were successful.

In 1830 the move westward was begun, and the message was carried to the Indians who were delighted to receive it.

In 1844, Joseph Smith, Jr., was martyred by a mob in Carthage, Illinois, but not before he had ordained his son, Joseph, to be his successor.

References: II Nephi 2:10-49; Genesis 50:26-33; Mormon 4: 18-21; Church History, Volumes 1 and 2.

JOSH—War Chief (c. A.D. 385)

Josh led his ten thousand Nephite warriors into battle against the Lamanites during the last war of the Nephites. All of his men perished in a single confrontation.

References: Mormon 3:15.

JOSH—City

The city of Josh was among those buried during the cataclysm preceding the coming of Christ to the New World. This was done to prepare the way for a righteous civilization that lasted for 230 years.

References: III Nephi 4:38-40.

JOSHUA—Land

Mormon, the war chief of the Nephites, led the people out of David to Joshua during the last war of the Nephites. Joshua was a land in the west near the beach. There the Nephites gathered and stayed for fourteen years because they had begun to repent. When they were stirred up in pride, the Lamanites came upon them again and drove them to Jashon.

References: Mormon 1:27-42.

JOTHAM—King of Judah (Old Testament)

Jotham was the father of Ahaz, the king served by Isaiah the prophet.

References: II Nephi 9:14; Isaiah 7:1.

JUDAH—Old World Land

The inhabitants of Judah, the land surrounding Jerusalem, were to write a testimony of the Lehites in the last days for refuting false doctrine and establishing peace.

Prophecies concerning the removal of the inhabitants from Judah and the scattering of the people were well known to the Lehites. Later the people were to be gathered to the promised land. After that the enemies of Judah were to be destroyed with the help of Ephraim and Manasseh. When Christ comes in judgment, Judah will return to righteousness.

References: I Nephi 1:3, 161; 6:8 (Isaiah 48:1); II Nephi 2:19-24 (Genesis 50:31); 8:17 (Isaiah 2:2), 39-77 (Isaiah 3:1 - 5:7); 9:14-81 (Isaiah 7:1 - 9:21), 127-129 (Isaiah 11:12-14); III Nephi 11:7 (Malachi 3:4).

JUDEA—City

Judea was a city of Manti. In the wars of 66-64 B.C., it had been captured by the Lamanites under Ammoron and retaken by the Nephites under Antipus.

Helaman brought his two thousand young Ammonites to join Antipus there, hoping to recapture the cities of Manti. From Judea, Helaman and Antipus worked strategies that eventually repulsed the enemies from the land. Supplies, captives, and warriors were moved back and forth between the armies and Judea until the land of the Nephites was again free.

References: Alma 26:10-84.

K

KIB—King (Ether)

Kib, the son of Orihah, was the second king of the Jaredites. Corihor, his son, took the kingdom from him by flattery and battle because of rebellion and jealousy. He kept his father in captivity until Shule, his younger brother, fought Corihor and regained the kingdom for his father, taking his father out of captivity. Because of Shule's loyalty, Kib bestowed the rule of the Jaredites upon Shule before he died.

References: Ether 1:6; 3:39-46.

KIM—King (Ether)

Kim, son of Morianton, was the king of the Jaredites. Kim ruled unrighteously; therefore his brother overthrew him and held him in captivity the remainder of his life. He was the father of Levi.

References: Ether 1:6; 4:57-59.

KIMNOR—Father of Akish (Ether)

Kimnor was the father of Akish, who reestablished the secret oaths on the advice of the daughter of Jared whom he later married.

References: Ether 3:82.

KISH—King (Ether)

Kish was the son of the good King Corom. He reigned until he died and his son Lib reigned in his stead.

References: Ether 1:6; 4:63-64.

KISHKUMEN—Murderer (c. 52 B.C.)

Kishkumen murdered Pahoran as he sat upon the judgment seat of the Nephites. He had worked under the orders of Paanchi, the brother of Pahoran. To keep from being discovered, Kishkumen disguised himself and established a secret order to help him.

Later Kishkumen tried to murder Helaman. However, a servant of Helaman discovered the plot. When Kishkumen came to accomplish the murderous deed, the servant of Helaman led him into a trap and stabbed him to death. The servant then ran to Helaman to tell him of the plot and its outcome. Gadianton took over Kishkumen's band and secreted them in the wilderness.

References: Helaman 1:9-12, 38-49; 2:141, 147-148.

KISHKUMEN—City

The city of Kishkumen was filled with unrighteous people. When God sent prophets and preachers to them to call them to repent, they stoned the preachers and cast out the prophets from among them. For this wickedness the city was burned and all its inhabitants were destroyed during the cataclysm that preceded the coming of Christ to the New World.

References: III Nephi 4:38-40.

KORIHOR—Antichrist (c. 74 B.C.)

Satan appeared to Korihor in the form of an angel and told him that the Nephites had gone astray. He taught Korihor that there was no God and how to live a materialistic life.

Korihor followed the beliefs given him by Satan. As he did, Korihor began to believe the lies he taught. He went among the Nephites at Zarahemla teaching his lies. No one could stop him because it was against the law to persecute a man for his beliefs.

He denied prophecy and the coming of Christ. He preached against atonement, sin, guilt, and life after death.

When he went to Jershon, among the Ammonites, he was cast out of the land. He went into Gideon but was bound and taken before the high priest and the chief judge. The chief judge sent Korihor to Alma, chief judge of the Nephites.

Korihor continued to blaspheme before Alma and would not recant. Then he asked Alma for a sign that God existed. Alma gave him dumbness.

When Korihor was struck dumb, he realized that all his work as an antichrist was useless as he had been deceived. He repented of his sins, but Alma left his dumbness with him.

When the Nephites saw the judgment of Korihor and were told that if they continued in the ways of Korihor his judgment would fall upon them, they repented. The hold of Satan upon them was broken. Later, a people called the Zoramites "ran upon" Korihor until he died.

References: Alma 16:7-79.

KUMEN—Disciples (c. A.D. 34)

Kumen was one of the twelve men called by Christ in the New World to be special witnesses of the gospel. He was baptized by Nephi, then helped to baptize those who would covenant to obey the commandments and worship God in holiness. He taught a portion of the multitude to worship and pray while they awaited the second appearance of Christ among them. For the rest of the story see *Disciples.*

References: III Nephi 9:4-15.

KUMENONHI—Disciple (c. A.D. 34)

Kumenonhi was one of the twelve men called by Christ to be a special witness to the people of the New World. He was baptized by Nephi, then helped to baptize those who covenanted to obey the laws of God. He taught a portion of the multitude to worship and pray while they waited for the second coming of Christ among them. For the rest of his story, see *Disciples.*

References: III Nephi 9:4-15.

L

LABAN—High Priest (c. 600 B.C.)

While Lehi was settling his family in the wilderness awaiting direction concerning which way to travel, the Lord told him to send his sons back into Jerusalem to Laban to obtain the records of the family.

As usual, Laman and Lemuel balked because they were afraid of Laban. Nephi agreed to go because he knew that the Lord would give them no commandment without means to accomplish it. And so they went.

When they came near the city, the brothers cast lots to see who would go to bargain with Laban. The lot fell to Laman. When he went, he asked Laban for the records, but Laban called him a robber and had him thrown out. He hurried back to his brothers and reported.

Next, at Nephi's bidding, they tried to buy the records. When Laban saw the treasure he took it and chased them out, sending his servants after them to slay the brothers. The sons of Lehi fled before the servants and hid in the wilderness.

In anger, Laman and Lemuel began to flog Nephi and Sam. An angel appeared to them and stopped the beating. They were told to go once more and the records would be theirs. Though the brothers withdrew their lashes, they seethed and murmured with fear.

Nephi told them that if they would go to the walls of the city and hide, he would go to Laban and get the records. The brothers followed unwillingly.

Nephi crept into the city and neared the house of Laban. He found Laban stretched upon the ground drunk. In a sheath beside Laban lay a beautiful sword of steel with a pure gold hilt. Nephi drew the weapon and was told by the Lord to kill him. Nephi hesitated. He was told by the Lord that Laban's death was necessary to obtain the records to save the future generations of Lehites from falling into ignorance and unbelief. Therefore Nephi obeyed the Spirit and cut off the head of Laban. He put on the clothes of Laban and moved toward the house.

Entering the house, he found the treasury and the servant in charge of the key. Imitating Laban and using the servant to help, Nephi obtained the records and took them, the sword, and Zoram the servant of the treasury out of the house, city, and eventually out of the land.

References: I Nephi 1:60-126; 2:17; II Nephi 1:55.

LACHONEUS—Chief Judge (c. A.D. 1)

Lachoneus received a letter from Giddianhi, the leader of the secret combination of robbers, asking him to surrender authority to him. Instead of surrendering, Lachoneus called the Nephites to pray for strength and gather together for defense.

The people did as Lachoneus ordered them. They brought with them their animals and provisions so that the land was empty of food except where they gathered in Zarahemla. This made it necessary for the robbers to make open war on the Nephites to keep from starving.

Lachoneus preached repentance to the people so that they repented and prayed for help from the Lord against their enemies. Lachoneus appointed Gidgiddoni, a prophet, to lead them in battle. When the battle was over, peace was established among the Nephites.

Lachoneus turned the judgment seat over to his son, Lachoneus, when he was too old to continue to serve.

References: III Nephi 1:1; 2:1-89; 3:1-9, 21.

LACHONEUS—Son of Lachoneus (c. A.D. 29)

Lachoneus took over the judgment seat from his father. The lesser judges in the land were wicked. They condemned to death the prophets and preachers of repentance without consulting Lachoneus according to the law. Only after the execution of the servants of God was Lachoneus made aware of the judgments.

When Lachoneus received the complaints against the lesser judges, he set about to arrest them. The judges formed a secret order to overthrow Lachoneus and establish a kingdom to bring the people into submission. When Lachoneus was slain, the people divided into tribes or families and refused to be subject to a king.

References: III Nephi 3:21-37.

LADDERS

Moroni, the war chief, taught the people in about 61 B.C. to make ladders to go over the walls and defenses of the Lamanites. The ladders were made of strong cords and were used extensively as archaeology will testify.

References: Alma 29:25-27.

LAISH—Old World City

Laish, later known as Dan, lay east in the valley of the springs that feed Lake Huleh in Israel. It was an isolated, independent city. After it was overthrown by the Danites, it was rebuilt, expanded, and renamed Dan.

Laish is listed by Isaiah as one of the cities to cry because of the destruction by the Assyrian.

References: II Nephi 9:111; Judges 18:7-31; Isaiah 10:30.

LAMA—War Chief (c. A.D. 385)

Lama led his ten thousand warriors to battle during the last war of the Nephites against the Lamanites, and all, including Lama, were slain.

References: Mormon 3:15.

LAMAN—Son of Lehi (c. 600 B.C.)

Laman was the oldest son of Lehi. When his father took the family away from Jerusalem because it was about to be destroyed, Laman went reluctantly. Laman loved the rich life of a bachelor in Jerusalem and could not forgive his father for tearing him away. He could never believe that God could speak to his father. Since he was not there when Jerusalem was conquered, he did not believe that his father spoke the truth. Leaving their treasures behind was almost too much for Laman.

When the brothers were sent back to Jerusalem for the records of Laban, Laman was chosen to make the overtures to obtain them. Using all his flattery, he begged Laban for the plates, but was thrown out for all his eloquence. From that bitter experience, he never recovered. When all their treasure was seized by Laban the bitterness increased. Even his younger brother Nephi's acquiring of the records by violence added to his frustration.

Ten times before the family reached the New World, Laman, with the help of his brother Lemuel, lashed out at Nephi with tongue and whip. Each time these fights caused a setback in the family's progress and a delay in the journey. Only the appearance of an angel and the voice of God could temporarily quiet the feud.

Laman married one of the daughters of Ishmael, a chosen servant whose daughters were to wed the sons of Lehi. Laman's wife helped him to contend with Nephi. As long as Lehi lived Laman had to respect him because of the Law of Moses under which they lived. Even then the quarreling reached such a crescendo on the boats built to carry the Lehites to the New World that Lehi and his wife became sick unto death. The knowledge of this did not stop Laman from his cruelty toward Nephi. Only the storm and loss of direction that would have buried him in the sea held him back from killing his brother.

Soon after his father's death, the anger in Laman grew again. The contentions with Nephi grew harsher until he again sought Nephi's life. Without his father to stop him from his evil intent, Laman tried to carry out the threat he had so long set on Nephi's head. The Lord warned Nephi to take his family and all who would go with him and flee into the wilderness for safety.

When Laman died, he left for his children's legacy a hatred for the family of his brothers who sided with Nephi and a curse that would for many generations separate them from God and turn them into a savage race.

References: I Nephi 1:29-45, 54-104, 131-134; 2:12-14, 26-40, 85-92; 5:22-27, 48-54, 85-102, 153-168, 180-210; II Nephi 1:52-54; 3:24-25; 4:1-7; Alma 1:105-106; 12:117; 14:57; 20:14-15.

LAMAN—King of Lamanites (c. 187 B.C.)

King Laman gave Zeniff, the Nephite, possession of the land of Lehi-Nephi in order to bring the more industrious Nephites into subjection. He allowed the Nephites to possess the land in peace until they had used their strength to make the land prosperous. Then he began to stir up the hearts of the Lamanites to war against them.

But the craftiness of Laman was not sufficient to overcome Zeniff and his people at that time. When the war between them ended, Laman's warriors were driven back and Zeniff's people lived in peace for twenty-two years, building and prospering until King Laman died.

References: Mosiah 5:32-37; 6:13-34, 54.

LAMAN—*Son of King Laman* (c. 187 B.C.)

When King Laman died, his son Laman reigned in his stead. He began to stir up the Lamanites, as his father did, against the Nephites in Lehi-Nephi. After Zeniff had conferred the kingdom upon Noah, who was ambitious and held the people in subservience, Laman was more successful in his battles against the Nephites. Under Limhi, who followed Noah as king of the Nephites, King Laman took complete control over the Nephites. He continued to tax them heavily until Ammon and Gideon led the people out of Lehi-Nephi.

In search of the escaped people, Laman found the Amulonites and took them as teachers to the Lamanites. He also found Alma and those who had escaped from King Noah and set Amulon over them as governor until they also escaped to Zarahemla.

References: Mosiah 6:34-35; 9:89-90; 10:14-16; 11:43-56.

LAMAN—*Servant* (c. 73 B.C.)

Laman was a servant to the king of the Lamanites when Amalickiah dissented from the Nephites and slew the king of the Lamanites in an ambitious move for power. Amalickiah, seeing Laman and his fellows flee, blamed the death dealt by his own servant on them. Laman fled to the Ammonites.

When Amalickiah brought his troops to war with the Nephites, they succeeded in capturing many cities. Moroni, Nephite war chief, called upon Laman for help in recapturing Gid. He gave Laman drugged wine to give to the Lamanite guards of the city.

Laman went with a small force to Gid and hailed the guards. He told them he had escaped from the Nephites and taken some of their wine with him. The guards received him openly, then begged for his wine. He warned them against drinking it. Nevertheless they drank deeply because it was pleasant to the taste. They became merry and then dropped into a deep sleep.

While they slept Laman returned to the Nephites to report the success of Moroni's plan. Moroni's men returned to Gid, armed the prisoners, awaited the guards' return to wakefulness, and captured the city.

References: Alma 21:103-112; 25:30-50.

LAMAN—City

Laman was a city inhabited by very wicked people. When prophets were sent among them, they were cast out. When preachers came among them to cry repentance, they were stoned.

At the time of the death of Christ, this city among others was burned and all its inhabitants with it.

References: III Nephi 4:38-40.

LAMAN—Old World River

When Lehi took his family out of Jerusalem as he was instructed by God, he went into the wilderness to the shores of the Red Sea. He camped near a river which flowed into the Red Sea which he called the Laman. He compared his son to that river, desiring that his son be as steady in his ways as the river in its continuous flow.

References: I Nephi 1:33-36; 5:15.

LAMANITES—*Darkskinned Lehites*

The Lamanites were the descendants of Laman, Lemuel, the sons of Ishmael, and all who dissented from the Nephites because of apostasy.

They were told by Lehi that as long as they kept the commandments they would prosper in the land. They would not perish from the land, but in the end would be blessed.

After Lehi died, a severe hatred developed because of Laman's jealousy for his brother Nephi. Because of this passion to kill Nephi, the Lamanites were cut off from the presence of God and were cursed with dark skins so that the children of the Lamanites and the Nephites would not readily intermarry.

The Lamanites began to be an idle people, no longer farming but hunting wild beasts for food. Nevertheless they maintained their family relationships and did not resort to polygamy. They lived in tents, wore loincloths of skins, shaved their heads, ate raw meat, and sought continually to destroy the Nephites. The Nephites tried to convert them from time to time, but they refused to learn. They began

197

to enjoy murder, especially of the Nephites, drank blood of animals in their rituals, painted their foreheads red, and worshiped idols.

In about 110 B.C., Ammon went to the Lamanites with the express purpose of converting them to righteousness. By his perseverance he was able to establish a church among them, whose people never did fall away from righteousness. These people, later called the Ammonites, went to Zarahemla and were given the land of Jershon in which to dwell.

Later Nephi and Lehi went to the Lamanites and converted many so that the Lamanites became more righteous than the Nephites at that time. The Lamanites came to the Nephites to preach repentance to them.

Samuel was a Lamanite prophet sent to the Nephites to tell them of their impending judgment and the coming of Christ.

When the Lamanites continued in righteousness, the curse of the dark skin was removed from them.

After Christ came there were no more Lamanites and Nephites until A.D. 322, when dissenters from the church established by Christ began to call themselves Lamanites and to reestablish the traditions of the original civilization. They became as vicious and bloodthirsty as their former counterparts, reverting to the same customs of dress and style of living. It was these Lamanites who eventually destroyed the Nephites from off the land by about A.D. 421.

It is to the Lamanites that the records of

the Nephites are dedicated for their conversions, after it lay hidden in the earth awaiting the day of its translation.

References: II Nephi 3:6-17; 4:19-20, 31-41; Jacob 1:13-14; 2:45, 54-59; 5:39-41; Enos 1:19-33; Jarom 1:2, 14-18, 21; Omni 1:14-41; Words of Mormon 1:23-25; Mosiah 5:20; 6:13-23, 28-29, 45-54; 7:22-24; 9:80-163; 10:3-14; 11:33-87; Alma 1:84-120; 7:17-36; 11:9-12, 20; 12:6 - 15:45; 16:1-5, 81, 251-255; 20:3-96; 21:1-128, 158-180; 22:7-8, 23; 23:27 - 29:47; 30:18; Helaman 1:15-35; 2:11, 35, 54-61, 78-128, 164; 3:25-29; 4:26, 30-31; 5:120; III Nephi 1:35-37, 48-50, 52-53; IV Nephi 1:22-23, 39-45; Mormon 1:8-71; 2:3-33; 3:2-17; 4:8-12; Ether 1:97; 5:15-16; Moroni 1:1-4; 9:2-26; 10:1.

LAMONI—*Lamanite King (c. 90 B.C.)*

Lamoni was a descendant of Ishmael who had become king of the Lamanites in the land of Ishmael under his father's rule over all Lamanites. When Ammon came to their land hoping to convert the Lamanites, Lamoni offered him the hand of his daughter in marriage and a place in the king's house to live. When Ammon, a Nephite, refused, Lamoni was startled. Most Nephites came as ambitious dissenters and made good war chiefs, but this man desired only to be a servant.

Lamoni sent Ammon to tend the sheep and, upon his return from the pastures, to care for his horses. When the servants returned from tending the sheep, there was much excitement among them, for they had returned carrying the arms of their enemies. The king sent for the servants to determine the cause of the excitement.

The servants told the king how Ammon had dealt with their enemies, hacking off the arms of those who dared attempt to slay him, yet receiving no wounds. They reasoned that he must be the Great Spirit who had come among them.

When the king asked them where Ammon was, they told him that he was tending the horses. Lamoni was amazed to hear of a servant so obedient, since he had always had to remind his servants of their chores. Lamoni was ready to send for Ammon when he appeared, having finished his duties and coming to inquire of his king for his next assignment.

Seeing the king in a puzzled state of mind, Ammon was about to leave but was told to remain. Ammon faced the king and asked for his next assignment, but the king only sat silently and gazed at Ammon in astonishment.

Finally the Spirit of God revealed to Ammon what had the king so perplexed. Ammon began gently to explain to the king who he was and what he had done. This only increased the king's amazement because Ammon had read his thoughts. The king asked Ammon outright if he were the Great Spirit. From that question a conversation continued between Lamoni and Ammon that eventually led to a strong bond of friendship and to Lamoni's conversion to righteousness.

As he was converted, he fell into a trance of ecstasy where he was further instructed by the Holy Spirit. Lamoni's servants, thinking him dead, wished to bury him. His wife, refusing to believe that, called upon Ammon who assured her that the king only slept and on the next day should awake.

As the queen watched by his bedside, the king awoke just as Ammon had predicted. Lamoni prophesied to his wife of the many marvelous things he had seen. Together Lamoni, the queen, the servants, and Ammon sank in joy.

Akish, a maidservant who witnessed the scene, called for the people to come and see the marvelous event. The people, misinterpreting what they saw, were about to slay Ammon for mass murder when Akish roused the queen who in turn roused the king.

Through the testimony of King Lamoni and the queen, many were converted, baptized, and organized into a church.

Lamoni asked Ammon to accompany him to a feast prepared by his father. Ammon refused because he had been directed to go instead to Muloki to free his brothers from prison. Lamoni decided to go with Ammon, since the king of Muloki was his friend.

Along the way they met Lamoni's father who demanded that Lamoni kill Ammon. When Lamoni refused, his father decided to slay Lamoni then Ammon. Ammon defended Lamoni. This shocked Lamoni's father into listening to

Ammon. Because of Ammon's entreaty, Lamoni was given full power in Ishmael, no more to be subject to his father.

Lamoni and Ammon continued to Muloki, saw the release and recovery of the brothers, then returned to Ishmael. There Lamoni had synagogues built in which Ammon could teach the people the ways of righteousness.

Lamoni conferred the kingdom on his son, Anti-Nephi-Lehi, and died as the Lamanites were preparing to destroy the converts in Ishmael.
References: Alma 12:30-37, 60-221; 13:19, 23-24; 14:23-27.

LEBANON—Old World Land

Lebanon is a land which includes a mountain range north of Israel. The mountains, because of their good rainfall, produce excellent cedar. From this timber, the temples at Jerusalem were built by Solomon and rebuilt by Ezra.

Lebanon was first to be hewn down to fall to a mighty one, Rome, then Christ came to the world. For many years Lebanon was left alone to redevelop on its own. Then in the latter days, Lebanon is to be again a fruitful field. Lebanon is regaining its prosperity at the present time.

The leaders of the people are to follow the same course as Lebanon—first humbled, fallen, ignored, then fruitful in bringing to pass God's work.
References: II Nephi 8:28-29 (Isaiah 2:12-13); 9:114-115 (Isaiah 10:33-34); 10:30 (Isaiah 14:8); 11:154 (Isaiah 29:29).

LEHI—Prophet (c. 600 B.C.)

Lehi was a resident of Jerusalem who, when the prophets cried repentance, listened and humbly prayed for the welfare of his people. As he prayed, the Lord appeared before him. He returned home and went to bed and there received a vision of the captivity of Jerusalem by Babylon and other revelations.

After that Lehi went to preach to the people to try to bring them to repentance, but they only mocked him. When they sought to kill him, the Lord told Lehi to leave all and take his family and provisions into the wilderness. Lehi went.

At the shores of the Red Sea they stopped, built an altar, and praised the Lord. There they remained until all preparations were made for further travel.

All along the way from Jerusalem to the New World, Laman and Lemuel murmured against their father. Lehi rebuked them constantly to keep them in the way.

Lehi sent his sons back to Jerusalem to obtain the family records kept by Laban. While they were gone his wife, Sariah, murmured against Lehi, fearing that their sons had been slain. The return of their sons with the records quieted her fears forever.

When Lehi took the plates and carefully read them, he saw that he was of the lineage of Joseph. He told his sons much concerning the plates of brass and his descendants.

Lehi sent his sons back to Jerusalem once more to convince the family of Ishmael to go with them so that there would be wives for his sons.

Later, Lehi in vision saw his own return to paradise where his wife, Nephi, and Sam joined him but Laman and Lemuel would not. He told his family of this dream and of his concerns for his wayward sons because of it. In addition he prophesied of the destruction of Jerusalem, the coming of Christ in 600 years, John the Baptist and his work, the dwindling of the Jews in unbelief, the scattering of the Jews, and the gathering of the Jews in the latter days.

When Lehi was told to move on with his family, at his tent door he found a compass, or Liahona, to guide him on his way by directions of the spindles or by words written on the ball. Eight years they traveled eastward with no fires to warm them or cook their food. At the sea at last Nephi built a ship to carry them to the New World. By that time Lehi had two more sons and some daughters.

On the way across the sea the squabbling between Laman and Nephi became so intense that Lehi and his wife were helpless to overcome it with reason. In utter despair they took to their beds and their health dwindled. That did not affect Laman who was intent on slaying Nephi. Only when the ship was about to be sunk did Laman relent. Lehi slowly regained his strength, and the family at last arrived at their destination in safety.

Before he died, Lehi begged his sons to submit themselves to Nephi and obey the commandments of God. He blessed each of his sons and their families before he died.

Time was measured from the time Lehi left Jerusalem. Lehi's commandments and blessings were continuously repeated among his descendants. References: I Nephi 1:1-66, 145-174; 2:1-8, 36-92; 3:1-27; 5:10-67, 175-217; II Nephi 2:1 - 3:23; Jacob 2:44; Enos 1:42; Mosiah 1:5, 77; 4:6; 13:2, 67; Alma 7:9-17; 12:115-118; 15:37; 17:19-20; 22:19-21; Helaman 3:58; III Nephi 1:1-3, 44; 2:56, 98-100, 102, 105; 4:73; Ether 6:4.

LEHI—Son of Zoram (c. 81 B.C.)

Lehi, went with his father, Zoram, in search of the Nephites taken captive by the Lamanites. Alma told them to go to Manti. There they found their brethren and guided them back to their own lands.
References: Alma 11:1-13.

LEHI—War Leader (c. 74 B.C.)

Moroni, in encircling an invading army of Lamanites, had Lehi conceal his forces on the south of hill Riplah. When the Lamanites came, the trap was swiftly closed. After a bloody battle, the Lamanites surrendered, gave an oath never to fight the Nephites again, and were sent home.

Two years later Lehi was called upon again by Moroni to lead an army to protect the city of Noah. His job was made easier by the high banks of dirt Moroni had built to surround and protect the city. The Lamanites feared Lehi greatly but fought anyway. When the battle was over, few Lamanites survived and they slunk off into the wilderness. Of the Nephites, only a few, exposed at the top of the embankments, were wounded; none were slain.

Lehi's army was then moved to Bountiful. When the Lamanites who came against it saw it was led by Lehi, they fled in confusion. Lehi knew that Moroni had an army waiting for them at Mulek and did not overtake the Lamanites as they fled but followed steadily. When the armies of the Lamanites and Nephites did clash, the Lamanites fought strongly with the army of Moroni, but surrendered or fled from Lehi until the Lamanite army was a boiling mass of confusion. Moroni, seeing that, called for complete surrender. The Lamanites readily agreed. Moroni ordered the Lamanites to bury the dead, then turned them and the city of Mulek over to Lehi.

Later Pahoran begged Moroni to leave the army in the charge of Lehi and Teancum while he came to Pahoran to settle a civil uprising. The king-men wished to rid themselves of a judge and establish themselves in places of power and prestige.

When the internal conflict was settled, Moroni returned to war. The army of the Lamanites had been pushed together into a small place, having fled before Lehi and Teancum. In a night attack, Teancum went alone and slew the Lamanite king but was slain by the servants afterward. The Lamanites were slaughtered or driven out of the land so that the long war finally was at an end.

In ignorance, Coriantumr walked his Lamanite army into the midst of the Nephite land seeking again to overthrow it ten years later. Lehi was sent against him, to head the Lamanites off. In dread, the Lamanites hastily retreated, waiting for them. The war was over in a single battle. The Lamanites straggled home in defeat.

References: Alma 20:38-95; 21:167-180; 24:35-52.

LEHI—Son of Helaman (c. 46 B.C.)

Lehi and his brother Nephi went to the Nephites to preach. When the church was in order, they extended their mission to the Lamanites.

In the land of Nephi, they were taken by a Lamanite army and cast into prison and left without food or water many days in the hope of weakening them. When the Lamanites came to the prison to slay them, they found Nephi and Lehi surrounded by fire so that they could not come near them. The Lamanites were frozen with fear.

Nephi and Lehi told the Lamanites not to be afraid. With earthquakes and the voice of God as their witness they called on the Lamanites to repent. A darkness surrounded them so that they could not escape. Aminadab, a Nephite dissenter, saw the faces of Nephi and Lehi glow through the darkness as they conversed with angels; he called to the Lamanites to look. When the Lamanites saw, they asked Aminadab what they should do. He told them to repent quickly and call upon Christ so that the darkness would be removed.

When they did, the Lamanites too were surrounded with fire as the darkness evaporated. Angels came and ministered to them until all were completely converted to righteousness. They left in joy to convert their brothers to righteousness that exceeded the righteousness of the Nephites.

Nephi and Lehi returned to work again among the Nephites.

References: Helaman 2:19, 47-50, 66-124; 4:23, 29.

LEHI—City - Land

Lehi was built by the Nephites about 72 B.C., on the north of Bountiful by the seashore bordering Morianton.

From 72 to 68 B.C., a conflict arose between the people of Morianton and Lehi over the border that separated their two lands. The conflict grew until the Nephites of Morianton armed themselves to slay their brothers. The Nephites of Lehi fled to Moroni for protection. Morianton, who led the people from Morianton, decided that rather than fight Moroni he would lead his people northward to a land covered with lakes.

Moroni, not wanting another group of dissenters to rouse the Lamanites to battle, headed them off and brought them back. He forced a treaty between Lehi and Morianton.

In 67 B.C. Amalickiah came to take possession of the land. It was released by the armies of Mormon after a long war.

In 29 B.C. the whole land was united and all borders erased. For convenience, the land south was called Lehi and the land north Mulek.

References: Alma 22:16, 26-39; 23:1, 30-32; 27:5-7; Helaman 2:126-133.

LEHI-NEPHI—City - Land

Lehi-Nephi is the name King Mosiah gave to the first city established by the Nephites when they separated themselves from the Lamanites. Elsewhere it is called the land of Nephi.

References: Mosiah 5:1-5; 6:9.

LEHONTI—War Leader (c. 72 B.C.)

Lehonti was the leader of the Lamanite army. The army had encamped at Antipas because they refused to obey the king's orders to fight with the Nephites. Amalickiah, a Nephite dissenter, was sent by the king with orders to compel the army to fight. Amalickiah sent for Lehonti to come down to meet him, but he feared for his life. Amalickiah sent a second time and was again refused. The third time Amalickiah promised that Lehonti could bring his guard with him, so Lehonti came.

Amalickiah conspired with Lehonti to have him capture his own army with the agreement that Amalickiah would become second in command. When the treaty was accomplished, Amalickiah had Lehonti slowly poisoned until he was dead; thus Amalickiah gained control of the Lamanite army.

References: Alma 21:89-100.

LEMUEL—Son of Lehi (c. 600 B.C.)

Lemuel was the second son of Lehi. He stubbornly followed Laman in all disputes and joined in the hatred of his brother for his blessings and leadership. He echoed Laman's gripes about having left his life of luxury in Jerusalem to follow his dream-struck father off into nowhere. Having not returned to the area, Lemuel never believed that the destruction of Jerusalem took place. He refused to call upon God for a personal witness.

When told by his father to return to Jerusalem to obtain the family records from Laban, Lemuel balked. Under stern command, he went.

When Laban would not give the records to Laman or sell the plates, Lemuel joined Laman in beating Nephi and Sam in anger and frustration. They were stopped by the appearance of an angel who reprimanded them. Even then Lemuel argued that they should rouse an army to obtain the records.

When Nephi agreed to go into Jerusalem alone,

Lemuel hid with his brothers and waited by the wall of the city. When Nephi returned with the records wearing Laban's clothes and leading Zoram, Laban's servant, Lemuel and his brothers ran off in terror. Nephi's call stopped them. When they had regained their composure, they returned to the camp of Lehi near the Red Sea.

Lemuel married one of the daughters of Ishmael, who had been called to join the exodus. He taught her to follow Laman as well. Throughout their journey to the New World, they opposed every turn and change that had to be made. Often they bound Nephi and abused him terribly.

In a vision, Lehi saw that Lemuel would not be obedient and obtain paradise. In his blessing of Lemuel's children, Lehi placed the sins of these children on Lemuel for not rearing them in an atmosphere of the love of God.

Shortly after the death of Lehi, Lemuel joined Laman in driving Nephi away by continually threatening him with death.

References: I Nephi 1:29, 35-46, 50-52, 62, 91-105, 131-133; 2:12-14, 26-40, 43, 59-61, 86-92; 5:25-27, 48-54, 85-102, 150-168, 182-209; II Nephi 1:52-54; 3:24-27; Alma 1:105-106; 12:117.

LEMUEL—City

Lemuel was a city of Lamanites in the land of Shemlon near Nephi, the first city built by the Nephites but later abandoned by them. Under the ministry of Ammon and his brothers, the Lamanites of that city were converted to righteousness and never did fall away.

References: Alma 14:11-14.

LEMUEL—*Old World Valley*

When the family of Lehi left Jerusalem, they stopped in a valley near the Red Sea through which flowed a river. Lehi called it Lemuel in comparing it to his stubborn son, trying to show him that he should convert his stubborn resistance to obedience into steadfast commitment.

There Lehi rebuked his sons for their disobedience. They stayed by the river Lemuel until all preparations were made for their journey to the New World.

References: I Nephi 1:37-44; 2:92; 3:22; 5:6.

LEMUELITES—*Descendants*

Lemuelites were the descendants of Lemuel who, like their father, subjected themselves to Laman and followed his deceitful ways, never moving out to initiate anything.

In Lehi's blessing they were told that eventually they would overcome the Nephites when the Nephites became more wicked than the Lamanites, and in the end would be blessed.

Although all were converted after the coming of Christ to them, the Lemuelites reformed in about A.D. 230 to eventually destroy the Nephites as they straggled along with the Lamanites in war.

References: II Nephi 3:14-16; Jacob 1:13; Alma 21:119-120; IV Nephi 1:42-43; Mormon 1:8-9.

LEOPARD—Animal

The leopard is a sleek short legged spotted cat that eats meat. It makes no distinction between the tame animals of men and the wild game of the woodlands. It will come into a village at night and with no provocation take a man to stave its hunger. It ranges through both Africa and Asia, using its beautiful coloration as camouflage.

Shepherds of Israel, before the wide use of the gun, often had to deal with leopards who sprang out of the woods to steal their kids or young goats.

Isaiah prophesied that the time would come that such complete peace would reign on the earth that the leopard would lie down with the kid without harming it.

References: II Nephi 9:120-124; 12:91-95; Isaiah 11:5-9.

LEVI—Son of Kim (Ether)

Levi began his life in captivity to his uncle. After forty-two years, he regained his kingdom, then reigned over the Jaredites in righteousness the remainder of his life. He turned the kingdom over to his son, Corom, when he died.

References: Ether 1:6; 4:59-62.

LEVI—Son of Israel (Old Testament)

Levi was a son of Israel whose children were called to be priests of Israel. Christ prophesied that in the latter days the sons of Levi, or the priesthood, will be purified to make offerings in righteousness to God.

References: III Nephi 11:6; Malachi 3:3.

213

LIAHONA—Compass

The liahona was also known as the ball, director, or compass. It was found by Lehi at his tent door on the morning that the family were to begin their long trek to the New World.

It was a ball of fine brass enclosing two spindles, one of which pointed the direction they were to travel. It appears to have been somewhat like a gyroscope energized by the power of God and regulated by faith. As bickering arose among the family members, the compass would fail them. When they were confounded and peace returned along with renewed faith in God, the liahona would regain its power.

After one early and severe quarrel, God chose to give the Lehites direction by writing a message on the ball. From that time the message would change from time to time as needed by the struggling family.

When the Lehites arrived in the New World, and after Lehi died, the family permanently split into two civilizations. Nephi took the liahona with him where it remained a possession of the Nephites. The liahona was passed along from recorder to recorder as generations passed, along with the plates of the records and the sword of Laban.

References: I Nephi 5:11-12, 32-37, 190-209; II Nephi 4:17; Mosiah 1:23-24; Alma 17:71-80.

LIB—Son of Kish (Ether)

Lib reigned over the Jaredites in the stead of his father, Kib. His righteousness and good reign led to the eventual destruction of the poisonous serpents that had plagued men and animals for many generations. This allowed the people to go farther southward to obtain food and Lib even helped with the hunting.

The Jaredites began to build cities on the narrow strip of land just north of the place where the Nephites would dwell centuries later. They continued in righteousness and peace, prospering in many ways under Lib's rule. When Lib died, Hearthom reigned in his stead.

References: Ether 1:6; 4:64-80.

LIB—King by Murder (Ether)

Lib murdered the high priest of Gilead to obtain the kingdom of the Jaredites. He maintained an army by secret combinations. Lib fought Coriantumr during the last long struggle of the Jaredites. After much battling back and forth, Coriantumr finally succeeded in killing Lib, so Lib's brother Shiz took charge of his army and war continued.

References: Ether 6:44-52.

LIMHAH—Captain (c. A.D. 385)

The ten thousand men led by Limhah, a Nephite captain, against the Lamanites in the last war of the Nephites were annihilated in a single battle near the hill Cumorah where the plates of Nephi and the relics were buried by Mormon.

References: Mormon 3:15.

LIMHER—Spy (c. 87 B.C.)

Limher was sent by Alma to spy on the Amlicites to bring back news of their movements. While watching, he and his companions saw the approach of the Lamanites and fled to warn Alma. Alma, because of this forewarning, was able to retreat with his army to safety and prepare for the Lamanite invasion.

References: Alma 1:77-86.

LIMHI—Son of Noah (c. 124 B.C.)

Limhi was the grandson of Zeniff, who left Zarahemla with a group to reinhabit their first land of inheritance, Nephi. Limhi was king of those Nephites who remained after his father Noah had caused such turmoil in the land that Alma left with his group of converts and the priests of Noah left with Noah. It was to Limhi that Ammon and his band of sixteen men came to give news of Zarahemla and inquire of their safety.

The news was shared during a great feast. Limhi told Ammon of the plates found by his scouts sent out to find a way to Zarahemla. The plates were written in a strange language and Limhi was anxious to have them interpreted.

Limhi gave Ammon a copy of their own history to read and told him of their struggles against suppression and bondage by the Lamanites. Ammon suggested that they all return to Zarahemla with him as guide.

The people of King Limhi had struggled

to maintain the land for many years and had fought desperately three times to rid themselves of their burdens imposed by the Lamanites. They, at last, had humbled themselves and had become submissive. With the coming of Ammon, their faith was renewed and as a body they became desirous of baptism. They asked Ammon to do this but he declined, feeling unworthy of such a task.

At last, with the help of Gideon, a back way was found out of the city. A huge tribute of wine was sent to the Lamanites. The Lamanites drank it, and while they slept, the followers of Limhi escaped in the night with all their possessions.

Once in Zarahemla the people turned over their own records and the records of the lost civilization to King Mosiah, who read them. Again Limhi asked for baptism for his people, and Alma, the high priest in Zarahemla, consented. The people of Limhi then melted back into the Nephite society.

References: Mosiah 5:12-86; 9:91-92, 103-107, 121-127, 135-181; 10; 11:34, 77-96.

LINEN—Cloth

Both the Jaredites and the Nephites in periods of prosperity were weavers of fine twined linen. It is produced from flax plants that are soaked and beaten to remove the fibers from the stems of the plants. After the fibers are stretched to increase their strength, they are twisted together to form thread. The fiber is worked between two spindles. Fine twined linen must be pulled and spun many times to insure thin thread. Weaving with the finer thread takes longer but produces a lighter, more flexible fabric for making clothes.

Nephi, son of Lehi, saw in his vision of the great and abominable church the furnishings draped with fine twined linen.

References: I Nephi 3:142-144; Mosiah 6:32-33; Alma 1:43-44; 2:8; Helaman 2:133; Ether 4:18-19.

LION—Animal

The lion is a tawny yellow cat, the male having a great mane of hair around its neck. It roams the grasslands of Africa in search of game for food. When angered, the lion will fight ferociously with its huge powerful paws with outstretched claws that slice flesh and snap bones. Fearlessly it pounces into the herds owned by men, slaughtering its victim in a single swipe of its paw, gathering the corpse in its huge jaws, and bounding back into hiding. When the lion roars, its deep-throated message carries great distances and strikes fear in the heart of any who hear it.

In describing for men the peace that is to come, Isaiah says that the lion, the calf, and fattling will lie down together and be led about by a child. The lion is the symbol of both England and Ethiopia; the child is Christ, according to some interpretations. Others ascribe the lion to Judah.

The Lord has promised an avenger among the

people who will not repent, who shall charge the unrepentant like a lion among them.

Mosiah compares the fighting of the people of Limhi against their Lamanite enemies to that of a lion.

When Alma and Amulek appeared from the rubble of the prison of Ammonihah which had held them, the people of Ammonihah fled from them as goats from lions.

Christ taught the remnant who heard him in the New World that if the gentiles did not repent, the Indians would go among them and tear them to pieces like lions.

References: II Nephi 8:98-99 (Isaiah 5:29); 9:120-124; 12:91-95 (Isaiah 11:5-9); Mosiah 9:117; Alma 10:85; III Nephi 9:51-52, 99; Mormon 2:54.

LURAM—Choice Warrior (c. A.D. 400)

Luram was a great warrior in Moroni's army in the last war of the Nephites as they were being exterminated by the Lamanites. Though he fought valiantly, he was slain.

Reference: Moroni 9:2.

M

MACHINERY

Both the Jaredites and the Nephites in periods of prosperity made machines and tools with which to work. Both emphasized that the machines were for two specific purposes, food production and war.

Archaeologists have found small models of what they now believe to be farm machines in their Central American diggings. These models were believed to be used as toys just as modern youth play with model airplanes and cars.
References: Jarom 1:19-21; Ether 4:75-77.

MADMENAH—Old World City

Madmenah is a town in the inheritance of Judah. It lies in the mountainous area of Judah north and very near to Jerusalem, on the slope of the mountains. It was removed before an invasion prophesied by Isaiah came from the north upon Jerusalem. The name means dung heap.
References: II Nephi 9:112; Isaiah 10:31.

MAHAH—Son of Jared (Ether)

When Jared became old, he had all the families of the Jaredites gathered together to take a census and ask them what blessing they wished before he passed on. They desired a king. After a discourse on the evils of a king, Jared agreed. The people elected Mahah but he refused. His brother Orihah became king.
References: Ether 3:16-33.

MAHERSHALAL-HASH-BAZ—Son of Isaiah (Old Testament)

The Lord told Isaiah to sire a son by his wife and call his name Mahershalal-hash-baz, as an omen concerning the invasion of the king of Assyria. The child was not to learn to talk until the beginning of the invasion.

The name means haste spoil, speed prey.
References: II Nephi 9:39-41; Isaiah 8:1-3.

MALACHI—Prophet (Old Testament)

Not much is known of Malachi, the man. He wrote the last book of prophecy included in the record of the Jews, probably after their return to Jerusalem, the rebuilding of the temple, and a decline in righteousness among the Jews.

Jesus told the remnant that met him in the New World to study Malachi for prophecies concerning the second coming of Christ to the world. A portion of his writings is quoted in the record of the Nephites.
References: III Nephi 11:2-27; Malachi 3-4.

MANASSEH—Son of Joseph (Old Testament)

Manasseh was born of an Egyptian mother, Asenath, in Egypt. Though he was the first-born, he received a lesser blessing than his younger brother, Ephraim, from their father and their grandfather, Israel. From Manasseh came the Lehites who traveled to the New World. From them came many of the people now called Indians.

Isaiah prophesied that Manasseh and Ephraim will join against Judah to bring them to submission.
References: II Nephi 9:80-81; Isaiah 9:20-21; Alma 8:3.

MANNA—Bread

Manna was given to the children of Israel as they wandered for forty years in the wilderness.

It appeared six days a week as dew on every surface. It was sweet like honey and could be gathered and used to prepare bread for the day.

The story of the appearance of manna to the Hebrews was used among the Lehites to impress upon the people the goodness of God.

References: I Nephi 5:110; Mosiah 5:28-29; Exodus 16.

MANTI—Spy (c. 87 B.C.)

Manti was sent by Alma with three others to spy on the Amlicite camp and relate their movements. He returned in haste to tell of the coming Lamanite invasion. Alma gathered his army and retreated to Zarahemla to prepare to meet them.

References: Alma 1:77-86.

MANTI—City

Manti was a city of Nephites captured by the Lamanites during the invasion of 66-63 B.C. Manti was near Cumeni. When Cumeni was recaptured by Helaman's Ammonite striplings, it was held against attack and the Lamanite warriors were sent back to Manti to be held for ransom.

After Cumeni was secured, Helaman elected to recapture Manti. This was done by drawing the Lamanites with a seemingly weak force. The city was retaken by a larger force while the Lamanites were gone.

References: Alma 26:15, 97, 118-165.

MANTI—Hill

Nehor, the apostate, was taken to the hill Manti and executed because he led people to disbelieve the word of God. This hill was located in the land of Zarahemla.

References: Alma 1:22-23.

MANTI—Land

Manti was a land of the Nephites that lay across the Sidon, south from Zarahemla. When escaping the army of Moroni at Jershon, Zarahemnah brought his Lamanite army into the wilderness around and back toward Zarahemla supposing to come into Manti in a surprise attack. But Moroni, having been forewarned by Alma, was ready with an ambush. The Lamanites were surrounded and, in a bloody battle, so thoroughly defeated, that they did not return to invade the Nephites for almost six years.

Under Amalickiah, they did return. Manti was captured by the Lamanites along with a good portion of the Nephite territory. Five years were required for the Nephites to drive the Lamanites out from this invasion.

References: Alma 11:9-11; 12:1; 13:68-69; 20:25-98; 26:15; 27:6.

MARTIN HARRIS—Philanthropist (c. A.D. 1830)

Though Martin Harris is not mentioned by name, many of the events that shaped his life are described. He was a rich man who became interested in Joseph Smith's work of translation of the records of Nephi. He financed much of the printing and work of Joseph. He acted as a scribe for a short while even though his wife and family were vehemently opposed to the work.

He was the man who took a copy of the first 116 pages and lost them by showing them or delivering them to another. He also took a copy of the writing from a page and Joseph's translation of that page to a professor, Mr. Anthon, who asked to see the plates, but Martin refused. Professor Anthon admitted that the language was some sort of reformed Egyptian and that he could not translate it himself. He conceded that Joseph's translation was probably quite accurate.

Martin also served as one of the three witnesses of the plates. To his dying day he continued to testify of the truth of Joseph's translation of the record from the plates, though he had become estranged from the church Joseph founded.
References: II Nephi 11:129-144; Church History, Volume 1.

MARY—Mother of Jesus (c. A.D. 1)

Nephi, son of Lehi, saw in a vision that a virgin from Nazareth, pure and white, would give birth to Christ after the manner of the flesh.

King Benjamin, son of Mosiah, declared that her name would be Mary in his proclamation to the Nephites in Zarahemla about 124 B.C.

Alma, son of Alma, told his brethren in Gideon of Mary giving birth at Jerusalem

(Bethlehem is a suburb of Jerusalem) and that she was a virgin who had conceived by the power of the Holy Ghost. She was to be told of the nature of her son, Christ, before he was born.

References: I Nephi 3:52-62; II Nephi 9:27 (Isaiah 7:14); Matthew 2:6; Mosiah 1:102; Alma 5:19.

MATHONI—Disciple (c. A.D. 34)

Mathoni was one of the twelve men called by Christ in the New World to be special witnesses of the gospel. He was baptized by Nephi, then he helped to baptize those who would covenant to obey the commandments and worship God in holiness. He taught a portion of the multitude to worship God in holiness, and to pray while they awaited the second appearance of Christ among them. For the rest of the story see *Disciples.*

References: III Nephi 9:4-15.

MATHONIHAH—Disciple (c. A.D. 34)

Mathonihah was one of the twelve men called by Christ to be a special witness to the people of the New World. He was baptized by Nephi, then helped to baptize those who would covenant to obey the laws of God. He taught a portion of the multitude to worship and pray while they awaited the second appearance of Christ among them. For the rest of the story see *Disciples.*

References: III Nephi 9:4-15.

MATTOCK—Weapon

The mattock was an iron blade fastened to a wooden handle as an ax. It was also used as a plow or hoe in peaceful times. The mattock is to be used to clear the land of Israel both from enemies and from weeds in the time of the gathering of the house of Israel.

References: II Nephi 9:38; Isaiah 7:25.

MEASURES

In Jerusalem the system of measures included the homer and ephah as dry measures. The basic unit was the homer, about 48 gallons. The ephah was one-tenth homer. The bath, equal in capacity to the ephah, was used as a liquid measure only.

In Isaiah's prophecy, the vineyard of ten acres was to yield one bath or about five gallons of grape juice which is poor production. If a homer full of seed produced only an ephah of crop then that describes an approaching famine.

When the Lehites left Jerusalem they rejected the Jewish system of measure. Their system changed from merchant to merchant and from time to time until King Mosiah, son of King Benjamin, established order in measure during his reign. The exact nature of this system is not given.

References: II Nephi 8:80; Isaiah 5:10; Alma 8:54-55.

MEDES—Old World People

The Medes were descendants of Japhetha

who settled north of Chaldea and south of the Black Sea. They were famous for their horses.

Isaiah prophesied that it would be the Medes who would overthrow Babylonia and destroy Babylon.

In 539 B.C., the Persians (Medes) under Cyrus slew Belshazzar and captured Babylon. Darius I was set on the throne. He returned the treasures of the Jews to Jerusalem, and eventually the Jews themselves, with Xerxes completing the task in about 478 B.C.

References: II Nephi 10:17, 18; Isaiah 13:17, 18; Daniel 5:30; Ezra; Nehemiah; Esther.

MELCHISEDEC—Prophet (Old Testament)

Melchisedec was a high priest and king in Salem. It was to him that Abraham went to pay tithes and receive communion and a blessing. Melchisedec preached repentance to his wicked people and brought them to righteousness. Thus he was known as the prince of peace. The Melchisedec order of the priesthood is named after him. In this priesthood are elders and high priests. Bishops, patriarch-evangelists, apostles, and prophets are high priests; the seventy are elders.

References: Alma 10:6-15; Genesis 14:16-40.

MELEK—Land

Melek lay west of the river Sidon, across from Zarahemla and east of the wilderness called Hermounts. Alma came to Melek to preach. The people repented under Alma's ministry.

Amulek and Zeezrom were there when Alma called them to further ministry.

References: Alma 6:4-7; 16:83.

METALS

In the land Bountiful in the Old World, Nephi was sent to find ore for metal from which he would prepare tools to build a ship to cross the ocean to the New World. He apparently knew how to work ores before he left Jerusalem.

When the Lehites reached the New World they prepared gold, silver, copper, iron, brass, steel, and ziff from ores. All these metals except ziff are still being mined and used today.

From these metals the Nephites prepared plates on which they engraved their records, and from which they made ornaments, machinery, tools, and weapons.

The Jaredites, before the Lehites came, found gold, silver, iron, brass, and copper. They produced the same kinds of things the Nephites did.

For further information see the specific kinds of metals.

References: I Nephi 5:71-74, 84, 217-218; II Nephi 4:21; Jacob 2:14; Jarom 1:19-21; Mosiah 5:64-66; 7:6, 11-15; 9:169; Helaman 2:130; Mormon 4:6; Ether 4:71.

MICHMASH—Old World Town

Michmash was a city among the inheritance of the tribe of Benjamin. It is located east of Bethel and north of Jerusalem. Isaiah prophesied of the overthrow of Michmash by the Assyrians, under

Shalmaneser, on their way to Jerusalem in about 722 B.C. Today the ruined village is known as Mukmas.

References: II Nephi 9:109; Isaiah 10:28.

MIDDONI—Land

Ammon's brothers, Aaron and Muleki, were in prison at Middoni, a land of the Lamanites, because of their preaching against wickedness. Lamoni, a king of the Lamanites at Ishmael, went with Ammon to free them because the king of Middoni was a friend of his. After their successful mission, Ammon and Lamoni returned to Ishmael. Aaron and Muleki went to Nephi to convert the father of Lamoni. Through the father of Lamoni, Aaron was allowed to preach unhindered so that the people of Middoni were eventually converted and joined the Anti-Nephi-Lehies.

References: Alma 12:183-189, 215-221; 13:16-23, 30-35; 14:13-14.

MIDIAN—Old World Land

The land of Midian was occupied by descendants of Midian, son of Abraham by Keturah, Abraham's second wife. The Midianites in cooperation with the king of Moab hired Balaam, a prophet, to curse Israel when they came near on their way back to Canaan from Egypt with Moses. For this and other wickedness, they were overthrown later by Gideon, the judge of Israel, at Oreb. God had sent Gideon's small army to overthrow the invading Midian hoard by confusion. In the same manner, Isaiah prophesied that the Assyrian would be overthrown.

References: II Nephi 9:107 (Isaiah 10:26); Judges 7.

MIGRON—Old World City

Migron is a town south of Michmash in a line with Madmenah and Jerusalem. It is north of Jerusalem and in the route of the Assyrian invasion prophesied by Isaiah that came in 722 B.C., led by Shalmaneser.

References: II Nephi 9:109; Isaiah 10:28.

MINON—Land

Minon was a land between Zarahemla and Nephi. Out of that land came the invasion of the Lamanites reported by the spies sent to watch the camp of the Amlicites.

References: Alma 1:80-81.

MOAB—Old World Land

Moab was inhabited by the descendants of Moab, son of Lot, Abraham's cousin. When Moses and the Israelites asked to cross the land on the way to the promised land the first time, they were refused passage. Because of this, they were excluded from worship with Israel. They became staunch enemies of Israel.

In Isaiah's prophecies of the latter days, Moab is one of the lands to be conquered when Ephraim and Judah join to put down the ancient enemies of Israel.

References: II Nephi 9:128-129; Isaiah 11:13-14.

MOCUM—City

Mocum, because of the evil people who lived

there, was sunk and covered with water during the great upheaval of the earth following the crucifixion of Christ and preceding his appearance in the New World.

References: III Nephi 4:31-33.

MOLES—Animal

Moles are cylindrical bodied creatures who spend their lives pushing through tunnels in the soft earth with their enlarged, long-clawed forepaws. Because they seldom come into sunlight, and to protect the delicate tissue, their tiny eyes are buried in their facial skin. They feed on insects and plow the meadows to help the grass grow.

Isaiah prophesied that the time would come when men would cast their idols to the moles, or bury them in the earth, while they fled to the caves for safety.

References: II Nephi 8:36-37; Isaiah 2:20-21.

MONEY

The monetary system devised by the Nephites differed from that used in Jerusalem before the Lehites left. Money was used for wages and purchase of grain. The lawyers of the Nephites were famous for seeking to accumulate money to gain prestige. Priestcraft, preaching for money, was started by Nehor. Though he was forced to repent and was executed, the practice continued among dissenting groups. On occasion, unjust judges, like Gadianton, decided cases on the basis of money paid for a decision. When confronted, they tried to buy a confession from Nephi, the high priest son of Helaman.

The Jaredites also had a monetary system and used their money in hopes of buying power.

Isaiah told men that they who work to build Zion for wealth shall perish. God has promised the righteous milk and honey, without money and without price. In the latter day, churches will offer membership for money.

References: II Nephi 11:99, 109; Alma 1:8-9, 28-30; 8:53-66; Helaman 3:2-4, 89-90; III Nephi 9:76; Mormon 4:41, 50; Ether 4:12-14.

Table of the Nephite Monetary System
SILVER COINS

Coin	Value	Value in Leah
1 Leah	Smallest Coin	1
1 Shiblum	2 Leah	2
1 Shiblon	2 Shiblum	4
1 Senum	2 Shiblon	8*
1 Amnor	2 Senum	16
1 Ezrom	2 Amnor	32
1 Onti	5 Senum	40

GOLD COINS

Coin	Value	Value in Leah
1 Senine	1 Senum	8*
1 Antion	3 Shiblon	12
1 Seon	2 Senine	16
1 Shum	2 Seon	32
1 Limnah	5 Senine	40

*equal to 1 measure of grain.

MORIANCUMER—Old World Land

When the Jaredites were told to leave Babel, they traveled under the direction of the Lord until they came to Moriancumer near the ocean. There they stopped for four years to rest. During that time, the brother of Jared forgot to call on the Lord. For this he was chastened and he repented. He was told to build eight barges like those he had built before to cross the seas, but these were to be made watertight like submarines. In these, they were to cross the ocean.

It was in Moriancumer that the brother of Jared encountered God face-to-face and was told everything related to this world. From this experience, the brother of Jared was told to write in a book what he had seen. He was to seal the book and bury it along with two stones that would be used later to interpret the record.

When everything was prepared, the Jaredites set out across the ocean to the New World.

References: Ether 1:36-93; 3:1-5.

MORIANTON—Dissenter (c. 72 B.C.)

The people of Morianton were Nephites. They fought with their neighbors, the people of Lehi, over the location of the border that separated the two lands. When the matter could not be settled peacefully, the people of Morianton declared war on Lehi.

The people of Lehi fled to Moroni. When Morianton, the leader of the people of Morianton, heard this, he gathered his people and headed north.

Moroni heard about this exodus from a maid-servant of Morianton who had been mistreated. Moroni sent an army to stop Morianton, lest he create dissension among the Nephites.

Teancum led the army that eventually stopped Morianton, and after slaying Morianton brought the people back to their own land and established peace between Morianton and Lehi.
References: Alma 22:26-39.

MORIANTON—King (Ether)

Morianton was a descendant of Riplakish. His forefathers after Riplakish had been driven out from among the Jaredites because of their wicked-ness. Morianton gathered an army of the outcasts and went to reestablish himself among the people. He succeeded so well that he was made king.

As king, Morianton was just, but he continued his wicked ways for himself. The Jaredites pros-pered under his reign. He lived a long life, then at his death turned the kingdom over to Kim, his son.
References: Ether 1:6; 4:52-57.

MORIANTON—Land

Morianton was a land between Lehi and the sea inhabited by the Nephites under their leader, Mori-anton. They disputed with the people of Lehi over the location of the border between the two lands. When the people of Lehi went to Moroni for protec-tion, Morianton took the people northward. Tean-cum was sent by Moroni to bring them back. In the process of turning the people back, Morianton was slain.

Later in 63 B.C., Morianton was captured by Amalickiah who was a dissenter leading the Lamanite army. The Lamanites used Morianton for a stronghold into which new forces and supplies were brought for distribution. It was not until 61 B.C. that the people were able to return to Morianton in peace.

References: Alma 22:26-39; 23:31-32; 25:61-62; 27:5-7; 29:47.

MORIANTUM—Land

The Nephites in Moriantum during the last war of the Nephites with the Lamanites had become more wicked than the cannibalistic Lamanites. They captured Lamanite women, raped them, tortured them to death, then devoured their bodies. Only a few short years earlier they had been a righteous people.

References: Moroni 9:10-12.

MORMON—Father of Mormon (c. A.D. 230)

Mormon, in the midst of very wicked times, reared a son so righteous that at the age of ten he was chosen to become a high priest and recorder for the Nephites.

References: Mormon 1:6.

MORMON—Recorder (c. A.D. 250)

Ammoron, when he was about to die, was told by the Holy Ghost to hide the records of the Nephites along with the precious relics and find Mormon, a lad of ten, to tell him where the plates were buried.

Mormon waited as he was instructed until he was

twenty-four, witnessing while he grew older the beginnings of the last great war between the Nephites and the Lamanites. At the proper time, he took the record from its hiding place and prepared an abridgment, then added his own record. The original plates he reburied where he found them.

Having been called a disciple of Christ, he was selected to be the military leader for the Nephite army. After many battles, he saw that the people refused to be humbled but rejoiced in the shedding of blood. He put down his weapons and refused to lead them further. Once more, when the people appeared to humble themselves, Mormon took up the sword, but put it away when he saw that their repentance was not genuine. He followed their struggles and mourned for their souls.

When the battles seemed most hopeless and he was losing his strength, Mormon committed the abridgment of the plates of Nephi, Zeniff, Ether, and others to his son, Moroni, to record the finish of the Nephite civilization.

References: Words of Mormon 1:1-13, 16-17; III Nephi 2:96-102; 12:5, 6; 13:37; IV Nephi 1:26; Mormon 1:1 - 3:33; 4:1, 17; Ether 6:83; Moroni 7:1-3; 8:1 - 9:28.

MORMON—Land

Mormon was a land not far from Nephi which contained a fountain of clear water. Alma went there when he fled from King Noah and his army. While there, Alma wrote the words of Abinadi, the prophet, and preached them to all Nephites who would listen. In the waters of Mormon he baptized those who would covenant with God and established a church there. When King Noah came upon them with an army to destroy them, Alma led his people out toward Zarahemla.

Mormon, the abridger of the records of the Nephites, was named after his father and that land.
References: Mosiah 9:32-72; Alma 3:3, 4; 13:1; III Nephi 2:96.

MORON—King (Ether)

Moron was the son of Ethem. He reigned in wickedness as had his father before him. The secret combinations he allowed to be built gained strength, battled with him, and took half the kingdom from his rule. Later Moron regained strength in his own army and recovered that part of the kingdom.

A mighty descendant of the brother of Jared arose who overthrew Moron and held him in captivity the rest of his life. Moron was the father of Coriantor, who also lived in captivity.
References: Ether 1:6; 4:105-110.

MORON—Land

The land of Moron of the Jaredites was near the land of Desolation of the Nephites. It was there King Kib lived. Corihor, his son, came with his army, overthrew his father, and held the people there in captivity. Shule, son of Kib, was taken into Moron to be held in captivity by Noah, the son of Corihor. Noah was slain there for trying to execute Shule and Shule was released and reestablished on his throne.

References: Ether 3:42, 43, 55-57.

MORONI—War Chief (c. 74 B.C.)

Moroni was appointed by Alma to be chief captain of the Nephite army when he was about twenty-five years old. He led the army against the Lamanite invasion into Jershon, repelled them, then, through instructions from Alma, surrounded and defeated the army at Manti.

Moroni, angered by the Amalickiahite dissenters' efforts to make Amalickiah king, tore his coat to make a flag. Using this flag, he gathered a loyal army and put down the dissension, although Amalickiah himself escaped.

Moroni taught the Nephites to fortify the land and cities. He had strong walls and structures built from which the citizens could fight to preserve their cities while being protected from the slings and arrows of their enemies. His forts were so impregnable that when Amalickiah, who had made himself a Lamanite king, sent his army against the Nephites, they returned without fighting for fear of their enemies.

In a border dispute between Lehi and Morianton, Moroni sent Teancum to bring the fleeing people of Morianton back.

When Amalickiah brought his Lamanite army against the Nephites, the king-men, friends of Amalickiah, refused to prepare to defend the country. Moroni obtained permission and put down that group while Amalickiah was taking possession of many of the Nephite cities. In a battle that lasted seven years, Moroni marched against the Lamanites in defense of the Nephites. He, with the help of Helaman, Lehi, Teancum, and Antipus, was able to establish peace again in the land. In the midst of the war, he had an insurrection against Pahoran, the chief judge, to put down.

After the long war, Moroni turned the armies over to the leadership of Moronihah, his son, and spent the remainder of his life in peace.

References: Alma 20:18-98; 21:40-72, 128-180; 22:1-15, 28-37; 23:17-27; 24:8-13, 21-62; 25:1-63; 26:4 - 29:53; 30:3.

MORONI—Last Prophet (c. A.D. 380)

Moroni was the son of Mormon, son of Mormon. Mormon gave his son the relics and the abridgment of the plates of the Nephites. He commanded him to keep a record of the end of the Nephites.

In the last war of the Nephites, Moroni led a band of ten thousand warriors against the Lamanites. When that battle was over, only twenty-four Nephites were known to remain alive and many of them were wounded.

The Lamanites pursued those twenty-four and the others who had escaped the battle. Moroni hid and continued his writing, although he was hunted continually. He had no opportunity to make more plates, so he filled the ones he had with the record of the end of the Nephite civilization and true doctrine.

He abridged the record of the Jaredites, warning Joseph Smith, Jr., not to touch the sealed portions of the records of the brother of Jared. He also refused to record the secret oaths used to organize the secret combinations.

Before burying the plates with the relics, Moroni wrote a note of farewell to his Lamanite brothers, looking forward to his rest in the paradise of God.

References: Words of Mormon 1:1-3; Mormon 3:8, 13-14; 4:1-17; Ether 1:1-5, 82-83; 2:1-5; 3:1, 94-102; 4:1; 5:6-10, 30, 39-40; 6:1; Moroni 1:1-4; 7:1; 8:1, 2; 10:1-31.

MORONI—City - Land

Moroni was a city built by the Nephites in about 72 B.C. It was on the east by the sea and south by the Lamanite border. To the west of it lay Nephihah and to the north was Zarahemla.

Just five years later, the Nephites were driven from Moroni by the Lamanites under the leadership of Amalickiah, the Nephite dissenter. The people fled to Nephihah.

Later the Lamanites fled from Moroni, who was recapturing Nephihah. All the Lamanites from the other Nephite cities fled to the land of Moroni also. It was in the land of Moroni that the war ended after Teancum slew Ammoron, the brother of Amalickiah who had taken over Lamanite leadership after Amalickiah was slain. Teancum was slain by the servants of Ammoron.

In the cataclysm that preceded the coming of Christ to the New World, the city of Moroni

was sunk and covered by the sea and the people were drowned because of their wickedness.
References: Alma 22:14, 15; 23:27-30; 27:5; 29:29, 36-47; III Nephi 4:8-9, 29.

MORONIHAH—War Chief (c. 60 B.C.)

Moronihah, the son of Moroni, took over his father's position as war chief when Moroni got too old. In 53 B.C., Moronihah led his first defense of a Lamanite army and was successful in quickly defeating the invading army.

In 51 B.C., Coriantumr boldly led his Lamanite army into the heart of the land before Moronihah had time to gather defenses. The troops he had stationed around the borders had let Coriantumr pass.

When Moronihah discovered the invasion, he sent for Lehi to head them off before they came to Bountiful. This allowed Moronihah to completely surround the Lamanite invaders and soundly defeat them. Coriantumr was slain.

Again in 42 B.C., the Lamanites invaded, this time with such strength that it took Moronihah eleven years to drive them out. The Nephites had become full of pride and wickedness. They refused to aid in the support of the poor. Because of this Moronihah spent much of his time preaching and prophesying to call the people to repentance. When at last the people did repent, Moronihah was successful in helping the Nephites drive out the Lamanite army from half of their land, but at this point they ceased their effort.

References: Alma 29:53; 30:18, 19; Helaman 1:27-37; 2:38-53.

MORONIHAH—Captain (c. A.D. 385)

Moronihah led his ten thousand soldiers against the Lamanites in the greatest battle of the last Nephite war. He and all his Nephite warriors were slain.

References: Mormon 3:15.

MORONIHAH—City

Moronihah was a city built by the Nephites in prosperous times. The people who dwelled there had become so wicked that during the great cataclysm which occurred before the appearance of Christ in the New World the city was covered with earth from a volcanic thrust in its center. The city, with all its inhabitants, was buried under a mountain.

References: III Nephi 4:8-9, 24-25, 30.

MOSES—Prophet (Old Testament)

Moses was a prophet to the children of Israel. He was responsible for these people as he led them out of Egypt, through the Red Sea, through the wilderness, and to the promised land of Canaan. Along the way, Moses was given a law to teach the people. Because he had not convinced the Israelites of their need to trust fully in God, even though they were given water from a rock, bread and meat from heaven, and healed from poisonous bites by looking at a serpent attached to the staff of Moses, the Israelites were not allowed to enter Canaan. Instead they were made to wander in the wilderness and to suffer affliction until a new generation arose who were obedient to the will of God. Moses, just before the Israelites were about to enter the promised land, was taken by God and seen no more. Alma, son of Alma, in telling this story to the Nephites, supposed that he was buried by God himself.

Moses testified of the coming of Christ to the world. Joseph, son of Jacob, testified of the coming of Joseph, son of Joseph, to be like Moses in leadership, responsibility, and need for a scribe and spokesman, among other likenesses.

When Christ made himself known to the multitude in the New World, he introduced himself as one prophesied of by Moses.

References: I Nephi 1:100, 159; 5:104-137; 6:3-5, 28-29 (Isaiah 48:21-22); 7:43-48; II Nephi 2:15-43; 11:37-39, 57; Mosiah 7:93-97, 106-107; 8:11; Alma 16:191-195, 205; 21:21-22; Helaman 3:44-49; III Nephi 7:5-9; 9:60-61, 98-99; 12:20.

MOSIAH—Father of Benjamin (c. 279 B.C.)

Mosiah was told by God to lead the people who would go out of Nephi in order to stay their destruction by the Lamanites. The Nephites wandered until they came to the land of Zarahemla inhabited by the Mulekites. The Mulekites had lost their original language and had to be taught by Mosiah and his followers so that they could communicate. The Nephites joined the

Mulekites and Mosiah was elected their king.

Mosiah interpreted the stone of the Jaredites that related the history of those who had come from Babel to the New World but had all been slain. When Mosiah died, the kingdom was turned over to his son, Benjamin.

References: Omni 1:19-40; Mosiah 1:73-75.

MOSIAH—Son of Benjamin (c. 154 B.C.)

Mosiah was taught by his father in the reformed Egyptian language to read and write. When the time came, King Benjamin, being very old, conferred the kingdom on Mosiah. He also was given charge of the religious relics of the Nephites and the plates upon which he was to continue the record of the Nephites.

Even though he was a king, Mosiah supported himself by farming. During his grandfather's reign, a colony had left Zarahemla under Zeniff's leadership to return to Nephi. During Mosiah's reign a group of sixteen men asked permission to go to Nephi to see what had become of this colony, since nothing had been heard from them since their departure.

Alma and his people who had fled out of Nephi from King Noah and his army were received by King Mosiah with great joy when they arrived in Zarahemla. Also, the Nephites, under the leadership of King Limhi from Nephi, were received as descendants of those who had left Zarahemla.

King Mosiah gathered the people of Zarahemla

244

and read to them the record of Zeniff. He then called on Alma to speak. When he had finished his report, he gave Alma charge of the church.

Alma brought to King Mosiah those who had dissented and refused to repent. Mosiah returned them to Alma and refused to judge them. When persecutions arose between the believers and the dissenters, Mosiah sent out a decree that no one was to be persecuted because of his faith or lack of it.

Later when his sons asked Mosiah's permission to go to preach to the Nephites, it was granted because God promised Mosiah that they would return unharmed. This came to pass. Using the Urim and Thummim, Mosiah then translated the records of the Jaredites brought to him by King Limhi.

When this work was done, King Mosiah asked the Nephites who they would have for their king. They asked for first one and then another of the sons of Mosiah, but they all refused, and Mosiah would not compel them. Instead, he persuaded the people to establish a system of judges. Alma was elected the first chief judge. Shortly thereafter King Mosiah died.

References: Mosiah 1:2-15, 22-28, 67-69; 4:3-11; 5:1-3; 9:170; 11:76-91, 97, 110, 114-119, 151-155; 12:1-26; 13:1-68; Alma 1:1-2, 19-21; 8:26-28, 48, 54-55; Helaman 2:54-57; III Nephi 1:43; Ether 1:95.

MOTH—Animal

The moth is an insect which develops in four

stages. The first stage is the egg which hatches into a worm-like second stage or grub. It is during the grub larva stage that the moth is most harmful. What the grub eats depends on the variety of moth. Some eat portions of crop plants; some devour cloth; some consume fruit. When the time is right the larva spins a cocoon in which it encases itself. A few varieties of cocoons can be spun into silk after the pupa or changing moth has been killed. The pupa changes into the adult moth and breaks free to fly about. It is during this stage that the moth mates to produce more eggs to start the cycle again.

The enemies of Christ and Isaiah are compared to old garments eaten by moths and rendered useless. Christ tells the Nephites to attend to their stewardsip responsibilities rather than accumulation of wealth that moths can damage beyond usefulness. Treasures given to God never are destroyed.

Later Christ mourns for the fourth generation from those to whom he speaks, because they seek the accumulation of wealth and lose everything.

References: II Nephi 5:66 (Isaiah 50:6), 84 (Isaiah 51:8); III Nephi 5:110-112; 13:9.

MULEK—Son of Zedekiah (c. 588 B.C.)

All the sons of Zedekiah, the last king of Judah, were slain before the eyes of their father except Mulek. He had escaped one year earlier with a group of Jews who were led to the New World and preserved by God in the north part of the land.

References: Omni 1:26; Helaman 2:129; 3:56-57; Ezekiel 17:22, 23; II Kings 25:7.

MULEK—City

Mulek was located in the land southward and just east of the wilderness occupied by the Lamanites. It was near Gid and the sea.

Amalickiah came with his Lamanite troops to invade the Nephites in about 67 B.C. Among the cities taken was Mulek. When Amalickiah was slain, the Lamanites retreated to Mulek and used that city as the center of their activities. Ammoron, the brother of Amalickiah, took charge of the Lamanite army.

Teancum, who had slain Amalickiah, was sent to recapture the city of Mulek. This was done by leading the Lamanites out with a small decoy force and heading them into an ambush with Lehi in front and Moroni, who went into Mulek while the troops were gone and recaptured it, behind.

Later Nephi and Lehi, sons of Helaman, came there to preach and reestablish the faith in the church.

References: Alma 23:31-32; 24:2, 18-59; Helaman 2:77-78.

MULEK—Land

In about 29 B.C., there was peace in the land, so much so that the borders between the Lamanites and the Nephites were erased. For a while they called the land northward

Mulek because it was first inhabited by the
Mulekites who had come with Mulek, the son
of Zedekiah, from Jerusalem.
References: Helaman 2:129.

MULEKITES—Descendants

Mulekites are the descendants of the followers
of Mulek who left Jerusalem just one year
before the rest of the sons of Zedekiah were
slain and the city was overthrown. They traveled
to the New World and were preserved by God
in the north part of the land. Many years
later they were discovered by the Nephites who
had left Jerusalem about ten years before Mulek.
The Nephites had established a colony in the
New World but were driven northward under
the leadership of Mosiah by their Lamanite
brethren. They encountered the Mulekites in
Zarahemla.

Mulek took no records with him, and so the
people forgot the Jewish traditions and lost the
Jewish language. After they were taught by the
Nephites to understand the reformed Egyptian
they had adopted, the Mulekites mingled with
the Nephites and were no more a separate people.

When the Jaredites annihilated themselves
through a prolonged civil war, the last survivor
of the war, Coriantumr, stumbled into the
Mulekite territory and remained for a while,
telling the Mulekites of the demise of the
Jaredites. He prepared a stone containing this

record to give to the Mulekites before he died.
References: Omni 1:21-38.

MULOK—Mulekite (Unknown)

Mulok is indicated as the forefather of Zara-hemla, the leader of the Mulekites. Some authorities feel that Mulok is another spelling for Mulek, son of King Zedekiah of Judah.
References: Mosiah 11:77-79.

MULOKI—Son of Mosiah (c. 120 B.C.)

Muloki was a companion of Alma, son of Alma. Together with his brothers and Alma, they hindered the development of the church by flattering away the weaker members to idolatry. The people of the church, through prayer, stopped this activity by sending them angelic ministry. From the time of the angel's visit, Muloki and his companions sought to repair the damage they had done in the church and extended their ministry to the Lamanites. Many Lamanites were converted who never did fall away from righteousness.

When Mosiah grew old and asked the people who should be their next ruler, Muloki was among those chosen, but he declined. Instead he went with his brothers to the Lamanites.

Armed only with weapons to obtain food and faith, diligence, knowledge of the Scriptures, fasting, and prayer, they went to preach. Because of the preparation of the sons of Mosiah, they received power and authority from God to teach for fourteen years without coming to harm, though imprisoned, starved, and left without water.

After the brothers separated in the land of the Lamanites, Muloki was found by Aaron preaching in Ani-anti. When the Lamanites there refused to listen, the evangelists went on to Middoni. There Aaron and Muloki were put in prison without food, clothes, or water, until Ammon and King Lamoni came to rescue them. After this Muloki fell into obscurity. He probably continued to work with Aaron until they returned safely to their father in Zarahemla.

References: Mosiah 11:159-176; 203-207; 13:3-6; Alma 12:1-28; 13:15-22.

MUSICAL INSTRUMENTS

The Jaredites had trumpets that they used to call their warriors to battle. All other references to musical instruments are in prophecy.

See the articles on *Harp, Pipe, Tabret, Trump,* and *Viol.*

N

NAHOM—*Old World Place*

Nahom was the farthest point south that the Lehites traveled before they turned eastward following the directions of the Liahona, or compass, instead of the Red Sea. There Ishmael died and was buried, causing much tribulation among the group because of the mourning and ranting of the children of Ishmael.

References: I Nephi 5:43-55.

NAPHTALI—*Old World Land*

Nephtali was the fifth son of Jacob, through Bilhah, handmaid to Rachel. His inheritance lay west of the Sea of Galilee and the upper Jordan.

Isaiah prophesied that the people of Naphtali would be cut off lightly. They were the first tribe west of the Jordan to be taken captive by the Assyrians. Later they would see a great light among them. The light was Christ who spent much of his time preaching there.

References: II Nephi 9:61-62; Isaiah 9:1-2.

NAZARETH—*Old World City*

Nazareth was an obscure and scorned village on the southern border of Zebulan. It lay around sixty miles north of Jerusalem and east of the south end of the Sea of Galilee. Just one mile south of the town was the junction of many important highways and trade routes.

It was there that Mary and Joseph took Jesus to live after their return from Egypt. It was just north of there that the first recorded miracle of Christ occurred. The preaching of Christ was rejected and he had to go elsewhere to do his ministry.

Nephi, son of Lehi, in a vision saw Nazareth and Mary, the mother of Christ. It was to that city that Gabriel went to tell Mary of the

son to come as she was about to marry Joseph.
References: I Nephi 3:53; Luke 1:31-32.

NEAS—Plant

Neas was a crop raised by the Nephites. They probably brought the seed with them from Jerusalem. There is no other record to tell us what the nature of the plant was.
References: Mosiah 6:12.

NEHOR—Dissenter (c. 91 B.C.)

Nehor taught that all men should be saved into heaven no matter what they did during their probation on earth. He contended so hotly with Gideon that he slew him. Because of this, Nehor was condemned by Alma, the chief judge, to die. Before he died, he was forced to declare that all he had taught was false.
References: Alma 1:3-23, 76; 4:8.

NEHORS—Dissenters

Nehors were the followers of Nehor. They believed that God didn't care what men did and that he would forgive them when they died. They preached for wealth and persecuted the poor.

Amlici was a follower of Nehor who sought to be king. He was slain by Alma. The people of Ammonihah were Nehors and those who would not repent when Alma, son of Alma, and Amulek, his second witness, ministered to them. They cast out Alma and Amulek and were later utterly destroyed by the Lamanites. The Amalekites and Amulonites were also Nehors.

252

They refused the word of Aaron, son of Mosiah, and were destroyed at the hands of the Nephites.
References: Alma 1:24-34, 53; 4:8; 10:58-61, 106; 11:14-19; 13:2-12; 14:56-58.

NEHOR—City - Land

Nehor was a city among the Jaredites in which Corihor kept his father, Kib, captive. Shule, brother of Corihor, fought Corihor in Nehor, released their father from prison, and reestablished him on his throne.

Nehor was not too far from the land called Desolation by the Nephites.

The land of Nehor surrounded and included the city of Nehor of the Jaredites.
References: Ether 3:41-46.

NEPHI—Son of Lehi (c. 600 B.C.)

Nephi was the fourth son of Lehi. Though his brothers constantly refused to believe their father, Nephi sought a witness of God and received it. Because of his faith, he was called to be ruler and teacher of the Lehites when his father died.

He had been taught by his father to read and write Egyptian and the scriptures of the Jews. In Egyptian he recorded the visions and prophecies of his father an abridgment from his father's records.

When his father was told to leave Jerusalem with his family, Nephi inquired of the Lord and was visited and convinced that the move was right. He then went to his brother Sam and told him of the visit. Sam believed him. Thus encouraged, he approached Laman and Lemuel with his message. Instead of believing him, his two oldest brothers reacted with jealousy and began from that time to rebel against their father and threaten Nephi, often with his life.

When the brothers were sent back to Jerusalem for the records of Laban, it was Nephi who was finally able to obtain them, but only by slaying Laban. Before they left, Nephi received his first beating at the hands of his brothers. The second time they returned to Jerusalem for the family of Ishmael, the trip was less eventful.

When Laman and Lemuel, with some of the children of Ishmael, desired to return to Jerusalem, Nephi gave them warning that if they did they would be destroyed. For his insolence, his brothers bound Nephi with cords and were about to leave him in the wilderness to be slain. With strength from the Lord, Nephi burst his bonds and stood free before his brothers. Again the brothers tried to bind him, but the family of Ishmael pleaded for Nephi, so they let him go.

When Lehi reported his vision of the tree of life, Nephi went to the Lord in prayer to receive understanding concerning it. He not only received the interpretation of Lehi's vision but also a vision of the history of the people of this continent to the end of the world.

Nephi took one of the daughters of Ishmael for a wife.

When in their journey, Nephi's bow broke,

his brothers were angry and began to whine so fervently for the lack of food that they made their father murmur also. Instead of joining the chorus, Nephi went out and made a bow of wood, then asked God for help to obtain food. He was blessed in this venture also. The Lehites were then able to return to their sanity and continue their journey.

When Ishmael died in the desert and was buried, Laman and Lemuel decided it was time to kill Lehi and Nephi and make good their return to Jerusalem. The Lord himself spoke to Laman and Lemuel to stop them in their desire.

When at the end of their travels by land, Nephi, in obedience to the commandments of God, began to prepare a ship for the ocean journey to the promised land, Laman and Lemuel began to call him a fool. Nephi rebuked them, comparing them to the unfaithful followers of Moses.

Laman and Lemuel made another attempt to slay him. Nephi called upon God to wither their hands if they touched him. The brothers shrank before him for many days. After time had passed, God told Nephi to break the spell by touching them but to shock them to their frames. When Nephi did as he was commanded, his brothers felt his power with such force that they fell down and began to worship him. Nephi rebuked them, reminding them that he was their younger brother. Only then would the work on the ship be done and preparations made to set sail.

Once aboard ship, Laman and Lemuel left off their work and worship to cavort about the deck and party as they had in Jerusalem. Nephi reprimanded them. For this, Laman and Lemuel again attacked Nephi, binding him so tightly that he could not move. Without Nephi at the helm, the compass ceased to work, Lehi and Sariah were sick to death, and storms came upon them to drive them back on their journey. Though Laman and Lemuel became frightened, they would not give in until it became obvious that if they did not loose Nephi they all would be drowned. After Nephi was loosed, the ship returned to course and they safely reached the New World.

Once they were settled, God commanded Nephi to begin a record of the Lehites upon plates of ore so that time could not destroy them and they could be kept for his posterity.

Nephi selected from the plates of brass those passages from Isaiah related to events of interest to the people of this land, recorded them on the plates of gold, and interpreted them in plain language. He also recorded the blessings given by Lehi to his children.

Again, after Lehi died, Laman and Lemuel set out to kill Nephi. This time Nephi was told to gather all who would follow him and flee to the wilderness. He took his family, Zoram, Sam, Jacob, Joseph, and their families and his younger sisters to a new area. They called this land Nephi and called themselves Nephites. There they began to dwell in righteousness according to the Law of Moses and to prosper.

Nephi kept with him the relics, including the sword of Laban, the Liahona, and the plates of brass, and continued his record on the plates of gold. He had a replica of Solomon's temple built there.

Nephi consecrated his younger brothers, Jacob and Joseph, to be priests and teachers with him.

Shortly after this God commanded Nephi to prepare other plates to contain the revelations and teachings. After many years of ruling his people Nephi turned the plates over to Jacob and commanded him to continue the record. He anointed a man to be their king whose name is not mentioned and then died. Being a descendant of Nephi added to the authority of the leaders of the Nephites who could claim it.

References: I Nephi 1-7; II Nephi 1-5; 8; 11 - 15; Jacob 1:1-18; 2:1, 69; 5:46; Mosiah 6:48-52; 9:2; 11:48-49; Alma 1:104, 112-116; 8:3; 21:119-120; 22:24; Helaman 3:5-8, 59; Mormon 1:6; 4:17.

NEPHI—Son of Helaman (c. 46 B.C.)

Nephi was the oldest son of Helaman, the chief judge of the Nephites and recorder of the records of Nephi. When his father died, Nephi took his place. He judged in righteousness. In spite of this, the people fell into pride, then open rebellion. Dissenters went to the Lamanites and brought their armies back against the Nephites so mercilessly that the Nephites were nearly driven from their land.

Nephi and his brother, Lehi, went to call the Nephites to repentance, for Nephi knew that God could not help them when they turned their back on him. The people repented but not fully enough to regain all their lands.

In 31 B.C., Nephi gave up his judgment seat to Cezoram and began to spend all his time bringing the people to repentance. He and Lehi preached with such power and authority among the Nephites that even the dissenters repented and returned to righteousness. When they preached to the Lamanites with such conviction, eight thousand were converted.

When they went to the Lamanites in Nephi, they were cast into prison without food. When the Lamanites came to execute them, they saw that Nephi and Lehi were surrounded by a protective ring of fire they dared not penetrate. The Lord himself called three times out of the darkness that overshadowed the Lamanites for them to repent. Their eyes were opened after a period of time and they saw that Nephi and Lehi conversed with angels.

When the Lamanites began to call to the voice that cried repentance to them, the darkness was lifted and they too were surrounded by a pillar of fire. As they continued to wonder, the Lord commended them for their faith and sent angels to minister to them. Those who were converted witnessed to others until the larger part of the Lamanites were converted and the boundaries between them and the Nephites were erased. Their righteousness began to develop so that they became greater than the Nephites in obedience and faith. Nephi and the converted Lamanites went into the north country to preach to the Lehites there.

When Nephi returned to the Nephites he saw that they had fallen into wickedness, developing secret combinations and committing great wickedness. Nephi went to pray on a tower in his garden about the wickedness of the people. He was seen there by a few who gathered others until there was a crowd watching and waiting. Nephi arose from his prayer, convicted them of their sins, and called them to repent. A contention arose in which the most wicked judges called the people to slay Nephi, but they were put down by those who believed Nephi. Nephi continued even more fervently to call them to repent.

As a witness of their wickedness, Nephi told them of a murder that was taking place at the judgment seat. The judges agreed that if what Nephi said was true concerning the murder, they would believe. They sent messengers who saw exactly what Nephi had predicted. The messengers fell in astonishment. The true murderers cried out that the messengers had committed the act and seized them and threw them into prison.

When the mourning for the judge had passed,

the Nephites asked what had become of the messengers. The judges called the messengers from prison to ask them what had happened. When they heard that Nephi had told them of the murder, they seized Nephi as an accomplice. Nephi told them who the real murderer was and what would happen when they went to arrest him.

Instead of being converted by this prophetic testimony the people debated the issue, became divided, and ceased to listen to Nephi, turning their backs to walk away. A dejected Nephi, as he returned home, heard the voice of the Lord praise him for his diligence, then give him a key to seal heaven and earth.

Thus encouraged, Nephi turned and went back to the wayward multitude to preach repentance and prophesy of their fate if they refused to repent. He was put in prison for his efforts but was conveyed away out of their grasp to return to his preaching.

Using the key he had been given by God, Nephi sent famine among the Nephites in hopes that they would repent. The famine continued for three years. When they had repented somewhat, Nephi called to the Lord to end the famine. In nine years, the Nephites returned to their fullness of wickedness.

The Lamanite, Samuel, was sent to prophesy among the Nephites concerning the signs to begin in just five years, of the coming of Christ. Those who believed Samuel went to Nephi for baptism. Those who did not drove Samuel from their midst.

Nephi gave his son, Nephi, charge of the relics and plates and departed, never to be seen again. Some think that he was one of the wise men who went to Bethlehem to see the Christ child.

References: Words of Mormon 1:5; Helaman 2:19, 33-124; 3:1-132; 4:4-29; 5:110-114; III Nephi 1:2-3, 46; 2:93-94.

NEPHI—Son of Nephi (c. A.D. 1)

When he departed, Nephi, son of Helaman, left the plates of the record of the Lehites and the relics in the charge of his son, Nephi. At that time the Nephites were divided between those who believed that the signs of Christ would soon appear, as prophesied by Samuel the Lamanite, and those who did not believe. Those who did not believe established a dead-line for the appearance of the signs. If the signs did not appear by the deadline, they intended to slay all who believed Samuel.

On the eve of the deadline, Nephi bowed down to the earth and wept for the misery of the Nephites who believed. He opened his whole heart to God all day long. In the evening God came to him and told him that on the next day he would come among men, subject to the flesh, to be called Christ, to minister to the inhabitants of Israel, to be resurrected to bring all men to him through atonement. And so it was. Nephi rejoiced. Those who fought against the believers fell as if dead because they knew judgment would soon come upon them.

Nephi baptized all who would repent, and peace was established for four years. Then the more stubborn Nephites returned to their wicked ways and the Gadiantons again flourished through secret combinations. By the thirteenth year after the sign of the birth of Christ, war came among them again.

From that time the Nephites changed like the tides, from wickedness to righteousness to wickedness again. Nephi had been strengthened by visits from angels, the voice of the Lord, and being eyewitness to the ministry of Christ. He went about calling all the men in the land to repent. He performed miracles in the name of Jesus, yet he was hated out of jealousy.

Then the cataclysm spoken of by Samuel as the sign of the crucifixion of Christ occurred in the thirty-fourth year after the sign of Christ's birth. Through all the upheaval Nephi remained steadfast, awaiting the appearance of Christ, his Lord.

When Christ appeared, Nephi moved with the multitude of the remnant left of all the people, for most had perished in earthquake, fire, avalanche, volcano, and flood. Christ called to him by name. Nephi was given authority to baptize in such a manner that all knew of his authority. Eleven others were called also and ordained to be disciples, or special witnesses, of Christ. Hungrily, Nephi listened at his Master's feet, consuming all that Christ had to offer him of the new testimony of the gospel and fullness of the law.

When Jesus ascended after that first visit, Nephi and the rest of the twelve began to teach the multitude, each with one portion of the crowd. Nephi led the multitude to baptism in obedience to the instructions, first himself, then the twelve, then his portion of the remnant. After all were baptized, the endowment of the Holy Ghost was received. Jesus came again among them and Nephi eagerly listened.

Jesus called for the records Nephi kept. He was displeased that the prophecy of Samuel concerning the appearance of the dead saints at the time of the crucifixion had been left out along with the fulfillment of that prophecy. Nephi corrected that error.

Nephi continued to work miracles in the name of Jesus after Jesus returned to heaven. Before Nephi died, he gave the record of the Nephites to his son, Amos, to keep.

References: III Nephi 1:2-46; 3:56-69; 5:17-21, 44; 9:4-16; 10:34-41; IV Nephi 1:6-7, 21-22.

NEPHI—City - Land

The first city-land established by the Nephites when they separated themselves from the Lamanites was called Nephi. There Nephi, son of Lehi, built his replica of Solomon's temple. There the Nephites thrived for about four hundred years.

The contentions between the Lamanites and the Nephites continued until the Nephites were forced to abandon Nephi and move to the wilderness where they found Zarahemla of the Mulekites and lived there.

King Benjamin fought in defense of Zarahemla and drove out the Lamanites who had moved into Nephi and had come to Zarahemla to do battle.

In 130 B.C., Zeniff took a group from Zarahemla back to Nephi to see what had become of it and reinhabit it if possible. The first expedition ended in bloodshed among the expeditioners. The second expedition was more successful.

Zeniff kept a record of the Nephites who had returned to Nephi, their prosperity under the false peace afforded them by the devious Lamanite king, and their subsequent wars to maintain their peace.

After Zeniff, Noah took over the city-land. Under his wicked and burdensome reign, the buildings were garnished with precious metals and fine carvings in wood. He exacted taxes to pay for these ornaments, his upkeep, and to support his gentlemen and ladies at court.

Abinadi came to prophesy against them and was executed. Alma, who was a priest of Noah, believed Abinadi and was forced to flee with the more righteous inhabitants to Zarahemla.

In righteous indignation, Gideon arose to slay Noah, but was stopped when Noah sounded the alarm for another Lamanite invasion. In the confusion, Noah and his priests and nobles fled. His son, Limhi, took over the abandoned throne and surrendered to the king of the Lamanites, agreeing to pay tribute to maintain peace.

The nobles of King Noah's court saw their leader encouraging them to abandon their families. They rose up and burned him and returned to Nephi. The priests of Noah abandoned their families. They stole daughters of the Lamanites for new wives and hid behind their skirts to save their own necks from the swords of the infuriated Lamanites. Then they joined the Lamanites to torment both the Nephites who remained in the land of Nephi and those who had fled.

Ammon led a group of men from Zarahemla to find the inhabitants of Nephi and share the news between the two cities of Nephites. He found King Limhi in a state of bitter confusion. Limhi had fought the Lamanites to attempt to throw off the burden of taxes but had failed. He had resigned himself to living humbly but could not conquer his desire to escape.

With the help of Gideon and Ammon, Limhi and his people did escape and returned to Zarahemla with the plates of Ether found in an earlier expedition sent out to find Zarahemla. The abandoned city was once more filled with Lamanites.

Later Aaron, son of Mosiah, asked permission of his father to go to Nephi to preach to the Lamanites there; he also received the Lord's promise of protection. He went to Nephi from Middoni, offering himself as a servant to the king, father of King Lamoni. He converted the father of Lamoni, and with his protection and the help of his brothers, Aaron converted all the civilized Lamanites.

The converts joined to become the Anti-Nephi-Lehies, who never did fall away from righteousness. When the less civilized Lamanites were roused by Nephite dissenters to destroy the converts, Ammon moved them to Jershon near Zarahemla, a land given them by the Nephites for an inheritance and maintained as a protectorate.

Other Nephites dissented and moved to Nephi to stir the Lamanites to invade Zarahemla from time to time.

Nephi and Lehi, sons of Helaman, went to Nephi about 30 B.C. to convert the Lamanites there. They were so successful that the Lamanites became more righteous than the Nephites. Those Lamanites sent converts to Zarahemla to preach to the Nephites.

References: II Nephi 4:12, 21-26; Omni 1:2-22, 48-52; Words of Mormon 1:19-22; Mosiah 5 - 10; 11:39-42; 12:1-13; 13:5-6; Alma 1:79-81; 12:8-13, 77-78, 181; 13:30 - 14:77; 15:1-14; 21:78, 101-113; 22:8, 11-12; 25:6-8; Helaman 2:44-46, 82-117.

NEPHIHAH—Chief Judge (c. 83 B.C.)

Nephihah, a wise elder in the church, was selected by Alma to succeed him as chief judge so that Alma could go reunite the church. His appointment was sustained by an election. For fifteen years Nephihah judged the people in righteousness before God.

Alma had asked him to take over the record keeping on the plates but he refused.

When Nephihah died, his son Pahoran was elected to fill the judgment seat in his stead.

References: Alma 2:22-28; 6:10-15; 22:40-43.

NEPHIHAH—City - Land

Nephihah was built by the Nephites about 72 B.C. between Moroni and Aaron and south of Lehi. When the Lamanites, under Amalickiah's leadership, invaded about 67 B.C., the Nephites from Moroni and Lehi fled to Nephihah to join for a collective defense.

Instead of trying to attack Nephihah, Amalickiah surrounded the city with soldiers and laid seige by cutting off outside supplies. Thus the Lamanites gained possession of all the surrounding cities but not Nephihah.

It wasn't until 62 B.C. that the Lamanites actually gained the courage to attack Nephihah. By this time, Amalickiah had been slain and Ammoron, his brother, was their leader. They had been forced out of some Zarahemla territory by Moroni and Helaman, so the Lamanite army that laid seige to Nephihah was now more numerous. Moroni had supposed that Nephi-hah's defense had been sent more forces by others, so he did not reinforce Nephihah himself. Thus Nephihah was lost to the Lamanites.

A year later, after Moroni had settled internal affairs for Pahoran, whose life was in jeopardy from men who sought to be kings of the Nephites, he took his army to develop strategy to retake Nephihah.

Moroni came by night to spy out the city to see how it could be taken. Seeing all the Lamanite soldiers asleep, he took his men over the wall by ladders so that in the morning there was an army of Nephites within the city. They drove the Lamanites out and followed after them, slaying many and capturing the rest. Thus Nephihah was wrested from the hands of the Lamanites.

References: Alma 22:15; 23:30-32; 26:28; 27:4-11; 29:16, 20-34.

NEPHITES—Descendants

When he wrote in the record of the Lehites, Jacob, son of Lehi, divided the descendants of Lehi into two great clans, the Lamanites and the Nephites. Because Nephi had to flee from his brothers with all who would join him, the division had been physical as well.

The Nephite clan included the tribes of Jacob, Joseph, Nephi, and Zoram. Those of Sam had joined with Nephi's descendants and were not a separate tribe.

Pride set in among the Nephites beginning with their second king. From that time, the Nephites fluctuated between pride and righteousness throughout their history. A period of righteousness brought prosperity. Prosperity led to pride, pride led to dissension, dissension led to desertion, desertion led to war, war led to grief, grief led to repentance, repentance led to righteousness, and righteousness led to prosperity; thus the cycle began again. The time required to pass through a cycle depended on the leadership at the time.

In periods of prosperity, great building, machinery development, and weapon improvement occurred. The Nephites were fine craftsmen, farmers, and husbandmen over their cattle. When repentant, they received great prophecies, visions, and endowments of portions of God's power.

They were almost always one step ahead of the Lamanites in armory development. Because they retained a written record, they retained a common language and remained relatively civilized. They maintained a democratic form of government, electing either a king or judge to rule them.

Toward the time when Christ was about to come to them, they began to foster secret combinations to such an extent as to become barbaric. From time to time they threw off these combinations but never completely.

Priestcraft, working for the church for personal pride and profit, was another sin that would make an entry from time to time in periods of pride, to be squashed in periods of repentance.

Eventually, near the time of the coming of Christ, the Lamanites became more righteous and steadfast than the Nephites and sent prophets like Samuel to preach repentance and warn of an impending fall.

After a cataclysm at the death of Christ, only a more righteous remnant of the Lamanites and Nephites survived. Christ came to the remnant and established his church in such righteousness that it lasted for two hundred years before pride began the cycle to their complete destruction. After that, all the preaching of their prophets together led only to brief periods of partial repentance.

By A.D. 250 the Gadianton secret society of robbers was rebuilt. By A.D. 322 war began with the Lamanites, dissenters who marked themselves as the Lamanites of old. In a single battle in A.D. 385 all but twenty-four Nephite soldiers were wiped out. The record of the Nephites ends about 421 A.D. with Moroni, alone of the Nephites, who is fleeing for his life.

References: II Nephi 12:68-72; Jacob 1:13-15; Jarom 1:15-16; Enos 1:41; Alma 1:102-109; 12:22-30; Helaman 5:1; III Nephi 1:18-53; IV Nephi; Moroni.

NEUM—Prophet (Old Testament)

Neum prophesied to the Jews of the coming of the Messiah and that the Jews would rise

up and crucify him. Since he prophesied against the Jews, making them appear to commit a horrible sin against the very one who was sent to save them, his writings were lost. They must have been kept by Laban, however, and included in the plates of brass because Nephi, son of Lehi, refers to this prophecy.
References: I Nephi 5:241.

NIMRAH—Son of Akish (Ether)

Akish, in jealousy, shut his own son in prison and had him starved to death. Nimrah, another son of Akish, in anger against his bloodthirsty father, fled the kingdom and joined his enemy, Omer, the rightful king of the Jaredites who had been displaced by Akish for Jared's sake.
References: Ether 4:8-10.

NIMROD—Son of Cohor (Ether)

Under Shule, the kingdom of the Jaredites was divided, with Cohor taking half. Cohor fought Shule for the rest of the kingdom but was slain. When Nimrod, his son, came to Cohor's throne, he reunited the Jaredites under Shule. Because of this righteous act, Nimrod was allowed freedom in the land and was favored by Shule.
References: Ether 3:58-61.

NIMROD—Old World Valley

Nimrod was a descendant of Ham, son of Cush. He was a great hunter and founder of Nineveh and Calah in Assyria. His valley was probably just west of Nineveh and north of Babylon.

When the Jaredites left the tower of Babel, they were instructed to travel into the valley northward. They obeyed these instructions, taking with them their domestic animals, including fish and bees, and seeds for crops of all kinds. It was there that the Lord and the brother of Jared conversed while the Lord hid himself in a cloud.

From the valley of Nimrod, the Jaredites were led into a wilderness not yet explored by man, toward their destination in the New World.

References: Ether 1:17-26.

NOAH—Ark Builder (Old Testament)

Noah spent 120 years prophesying to the people as he prepared the ark with the help of his three sons. The people laughed him to scorn but too late discovered that the prophecies were correct. After the flood in which all but eight people perished, God promised that no other such flood would come. This promise was first given to Noah's great-grandfather Enoch.

The covenant God made with Enoch (that the flood which encompassed the earth would not be repeated) was recorded on the plates of brass and repeated to the Lehites by Alma and Christ.

References: Alma 8:31-32; Ether 3:8-9; III Nephi 10:17; Genesis 7:56-58; 8; 9.

NOAH—*King of Nephi (c. 178 B.C.)*

Noah succeeded his righteous father, Zeniff, to the throne of Nephi. Unlike his father, Noah demanded the financial support of his subjects by taxation of 20 percent of their substance. He required the building of ornate structures, including a palace and temple.

He set aside all the righteous priests ordained by his father, and gathered a new order who were willing to preach as Noah desired while they lived in the lap of luxury at the expense of the people. They condemned those whom Noah did not like and turned their backs on Noah's wickedness.

Noah gathered to his palace, also at public expense, a gaggle of wives and concubines to keep him entertained. He set about having a vineyard planted and a winery installed. When the crop was harvested and fermented, he and his court became jolly drunks.

The Lamanites began to pester the king by raiding his flocks. Noah sent guards but they were slain by the Lamanites. Noah sent his army which was successful in driving out the Lamanites, so Noah began to boast in his own strength. As Noah boasted, he began to delight in demonstrating his brutality even upon his own citizenry.

Abinadi rose up and began to prophesy against Noah and his lackeys. He began to call the people to repent, calling out the sins of Noah and his underlings. Noah, when he heard of it, was enraged. He called upon the people to refuse to listen to Abinadi's harangue and to capture him. Abinadi fled.

Two years later Abinadi returned in disguise and began again to preach repentance among the people. When he laid before them the ugliness and ultimate consequence of their sins, they were angry and captured him.

Abinadi was at last brought before the king in bonds. In presenting Abinadi to King Noah, the people demonstrated their blindness of mind by upholding Noah's wickedness. Noah had Abinadi cast into prison to await his judgment.

After Noah consulted with his court priests, a trial was held. When Abinadi continued to convict his judges, he was condemned to death, though Noah feared him. As Abinadi died he prophesied that Noah would die as he had, by burning at the stake.

No sooner had Noah rid himself of Abinadi when Alma, one of his priests, began to cause trouble. Alma believed the words of Abinadi and began to continue to call the people to repentance. Noah had him driven from the land.

Alma fled and took with him all who would join him in repentance. The kingdom that remained to Noah became divided. The citizens who opposed the king were led by Gideon who set out to kill King Noah. Just as Gideon was about to slay Noah, the king saw an invasion of the Lamanites coming and sounded the alarm.

Noah commanded the men to flee the city and leave their wives and children to contend with the Lamanites. Noah himself led the retreat. The priests of Noah ran at his heels, followed by many of the men. The rest refused to leave and submitted themselves to bondage to the Lamanites.

Those who fled with Noah soon decided it was time to see what had become of their families. Noah commanded them not to return. They turned on Noah and killed him as he had executed Abinadi, by burning at the stake.

Noah became the prime example of the consequences of unrighteous kings.

References: Mosiah 7:1 - 9:96; 11:9-10; 13:23; Alma 3:5.

NOAH—Son of Corihor (Ether)

Corihor inherited half the kingdom of the Jaredites but returned it to Shule, the rightful king of the Jaredites. Corihor's son, Noah, was angry when he discovered this. With the help of his brother, Cohor, he convinced many to join him to fight Shule. He succeeded in capturing Shule and taking him to Moron, intending to execute him. Before Noah could accomplish this goal, he was slain by the sons of Shule. The half-kingdom of Noah was taken over by his son, Cohor.

References: Ether 3:50-58.

NOAH—City - Land

Noah was a city surrounded by a land possessed by the Nephites. It was near Ammonihah. When the Lamanites in 81 B.C. destroyed Ammonihah, they continued their battle into Noah, slaying some and capturing many. Alma sent Zoram to recover the captives from Noah. Zoram found them abandoned by the Lamanites not far from Manti and safely returned them to their own land.

When the Lamanites returned ten years later to fight again in Noah, they were disappointed to find Noah fortified and under the command of Lehi. Nevertheless they attacked.

Because of the fortifications built by Moroni, the city was safe to the Nephites. When the Lamanites saw that they could neither go over nor tunnel under the wall, and that all their chief captains were slain, they fled into the wilderness.

References: Alma 11:3-13; 21:162-180.

NOB—Old World City

Nob was located between Anathoth and Jerusalem. Isaiah prophesied that the Assyrian would remain at Nob one day on the way to conquer Jerusalem. Nob was reinhabited when the Jews returned from exile.

References: II Nephi 9:113; Isaiah 10:32; Nehemiah 11:32.

O

OAKS—Plants

Oaks are trees of a very sturdy nature. The wood is hard and polishable. Furniture as well as tools can be produced from it. Wood from oaks was made into oars and idols by the Hebrews.

Isaiah used the oaks of Bashan to represent the elders of the tribe of Manasseh. He told the elders that they would be judged and then taken captive and scattered. Later Isaiah compared Jerusalem in the days of the scattering of the Jews to an oak that has shed its leaves but the life remains in it to create anew.

References: II Nephi 8:29 (Isaiah 2:13); 9:13 (Isaiah 6:13).

OLIVE—Plant

The olive is a tree which produced shade, wood, food, and oil for the Hebrews. It has been used since the time of Noah as a symbol of peace. Since the tame olive can grow to twenty feet in height, it is often the only tree visible for any great distance and acts as a landmark for centuries. If chopped down trees spring up from its large side roots.

The tame olive was maintained by removing branches from a sturdy wild olive tree and replacing them by grafting in tame olive branches.

Both Nephi and Jacob, sons of Lehi, quote from the allegory of Zenos concerning the olive tree grafting. In this parable the olive tree is used to represent Israel and its branches and tribes of Israel. According to Zenos, the good branches, or the faithful Israelites, would be grafted into widely scattered wild olive trees and wild olive branches, or gentiles, grafted in to maintain God's work in the desolate olive tree trunks. Later the process would be reversed when the tame branches are to be returned to the tame tree, or to become re-acquainted with the truth of God.

References: I Nephi 3:16-19; 4:8, 14-29; II Nephi 2:6-9; Jacob 3:30-153; 4:2-7.

OLIVER COWDERY—Scribe (c. A.D. 1830)

Though Oliver Cowdery is not mentioned by name, he is described by Nephi as the spokesman for Joseph Smith, Jr., as Aaron spoke for Moses. Oliver wrote as Joseph translated the plates of the abridgment of Mormon, the record of the Lehites. Oliver was the second priest, second elder, and the second in command. He served as one of the three witnesses and one of the founding members of the church of the Restoration.

Later Oliver left the church, but he never denied what he had witnessed.

References: II Nephi 2:36-38; Church History, Volumes 1 and 2.

OGATH—Place

During the last war of the Jaredites, Shiz was beaten in a battle with Coriantumr. Shiz's soldiers fled to Ogath and pitched their tents. Ogath lay south of the waters of Ripliancum.

References: Ether 6:80-82.

OMER—King of Jaredites (Ether)

Omer was the son of Shule. He reigned

righteously until his son Jared rebelled against him and carried him into captivity. After many years the other sons of Omer warred with Jared and returned the kingdom to their father.

Jared sent Akish to kill his father, Omer, and return the kingdom to Jared. Omer was warned of God in a dream of this plot and fled to the hill of Shim, then on to Ablom. Later the son of Akish, Nimrah, joined Omer after Akish had slain Jared and his own son and taken over the kingdom.

There followed a war among the sons and followers of Akish so that those who remained joined Omer. Omer was restored to the throne.

In his old age, Omer sired Emer who reigned after his death.

References: Ether 1:6; 3:67-83; 4.

OMNER—Son of Mosiah (c. 120 B.C.)

Omner and his brothers were leaders of a group of dissenters who tried to destroy the church of Christ Alma was trying to build. They were stopped in their endeavor when Alma, son of Alma, their companion, was visited by an angel. Alma fell into a trance-like state and had to be carried back to his father. Through prayers of the faithful, Alma regained his spirit and testified of the visions of eternal torment awaiting him if he did not repent. This witness converted Omner and his brothers so that from that time their lives were spent in repairing the damage they had done to the church, then going further, with the blessing of their father, to convert their Lamanite enemies.

When King Mosiah, Omner's father, became old, he asked the people to elect a new king. When Omner was elected, he refused because of the greater task at hand.

Omner had the protection of the king of the Lamanites to continue his ministry among the Lamanites until all who would were converted. These converts never did fall away but became righteous.

After their mission, the brothers rejoiced together, then met Alma who took them to his own house in Zarahemla to refresh themselves and relax.

After a time Alma ordained Omner a seventy and sent him among the Zoramites to try to convert them. That venture was less successful.
References: Mosiah 11:159-176; 203-206; 12:1-14; 13:1-6; Alma 13;82; 14:1-13, 78; 15:19; 16:83, 112-123.

OMNER—City

Omner was a city among the Nephites built on the seashore along the east border of Zarahemla. It sat among the cities of Mulek, Gid, Morianton, and Lehi. Omner was captured by Amalickiah in his invasion at the head of the Lamanites about 67 B.C., though it had been fortified by Moroni.
Reference: Alma 23:31-32.

OMNI—Recorder (c. 362 B.C.)

Omni was the son of Jarom. He had been

prepared by his father in reading and writing reformed Egyptian so that when the time came he could take over recording the history of the Nephites on the plates of Nephi. He was also to be a leader of the Nephites.

Omni calls himself a wicked man, not having kept the commandments of the Lord. During his life he was called upon often to lead the Nephites in defense against the invasions of the Lamanites.

When he was too old to continue, Omni gave the plates to his son, Amaron, to keep.

References: Jarom 1:32; Omni 1:1-5.

ONIDAH—Hill

Onidah was a hill, located in Antionum, first possessed by the Zoramites then the Lamanites. It was near the mountain Antipas.

Alma went to that hill to address the Zoramites. Only the poor would listen and not all of them were converted.

The Lamanites stored their weapons of war at Onidah. It was there that the unsuccessful Lamanite army fled from the more loyal Lamanites who were sent to destroy them. From there they fled to Antipas to fight their brothers rather than to be sent again to war with the Nephites.

References: Alma 16:124; 21:84.

ONIHAH—City

Onihah and its inhabitants were drowned as it sank and was covered by water in the cataclysm that changed the face of the land at the time of the crucifixion of Christ in Jerusalem. Christ told the remnant from the catastrophe that this was done to hide their wickedness.

References: III Nephi 4:32-33.

ORES—See Metals

OREB—Old World Place

Oreb was the name of a large block of rock on the west of the Jordan River. Isaiah prophesied that the Assyrians would be defeated just as the Midians were defeated on the Rock of Oreb.

Oreb, prince of the Midians, had been slain by Gideon on the rock that later bore his name. This event followed the defeat of the Midians by Gideon who had awakened the stuporous troops at midnight with trumpets, pitchers, and lamplights. In their confusion the Midian soldiers slew one another. The few who escaped were routed by Gideon's small band of Israelites.

References: II Nephi 9:107; Isaiah 10:26; Judges 7:25.

ORIHAH—Son of Jared (Ether)

Orihah was the only son of Jared who would agree to lead the Jaredites after his father. Many were elected before him but refused the responsibility. When he was elected almost as a last resort, he accepted. He was anointed to be their king.

Orihah was a humble man, sustaining himself and his family by farming. He remained righteous throughout his long life. He had twenty-

three sons and eight daughters. His youngest
son, Kib, reigned in his stead when Orihah died.
References: Ether 1:6; 3:16-38.

OWLS—Animals

Owls are birds of prey. They are often found
to live in abandoned barns and houses, living
on the rats and mice that come for the scraps
of feed.

Isaiah prophesied that Babylon would be left
to the owls and other doleful creatures, because
men would not stay there after it fell.

Babylon now stands in ruin, inhabited as Isaiah
predicted. The Arabian guides who go there
with tourists refuse to stay when the shadows
grow long as the sun sets.
References: II Nephi 10:21; Isaiah 13:21.

OXEN—Animals

Oxen are very muscular bovines or cows
trained to pull. They were brought to the New
World by the Jaredites from the tower of Babel.
When the Jaredites were scattered and later
destroyed themselves by civil war, their oxen
roamed free. Oxen were later found in the
wilderness by the Nephites and domesticated.

In Isaiah's prophecy concerning the reign of
Christ the carnivorous lion is to learn to eat
straw like an ox.
References: I Nephi 5:216; II Nephi 9:120-124; 12:91-95;
Isaiah 11:5-9; Ether 4:21.

P

PAANCHI—Son of Pahoran (c. 52 B.C.)

When Pahoran died three of his sons, including Paanchi, contended for the judgment seat that was left unfilled. When his brother, Pahoran, won the election, Paanchi could not accept the defeat. Instead he rebelled, drawing his followers with him. Before his rebellion led to war, Paanchi was arrested and tried for conspiracy and condemned to death. When his followers learned of his condemnation, they sent for Kishkumen who murdered Pahoran by secret combinations.

References: Helaman 1:1-10.

PACHUS—Dissenter (c. 62 B.C.)

While Pahoran sat on the judgment seat Moroni was busy with a long war with the Lamanites. While the battle continued, a group of men seeking honor and prestige set about to remove Pahoran from his office and establish a king. They succeeded in chasing Pahoran from Zarahemla to Gideon. Once in Gideon, Pahoran gathered those opposed to the king-men around him, but the king-men held Zarahemla and established Pachus as their king. Pachus in turn sent a message of allegiance to the Lamanites, hoping that once the Nephites were conquered he would be made king over all the land.

Moroni, receiving a letter from Pahoran concerning this turn of events, took a small army and came toward Gideon, gathering the civilians opposed to Pachus as he came. By the time he united his forces with Pahoran in Gideon, his army was larger and more powerful than the forces of Pachus.

The united armies of Moroni and Pahoran went to Zarahemla and fought Pachus. Pachus was slain, his army captured, and the judgment seat restored to Pahoran. The men of Pachus were forced to join the army of Moroni or suffer execution so that peace in Zarahemla was once more established.

References: Alma 28:3-10; 29:3-11.

PACUMENI—Chief Judge (c. 52 B.C.)

When Pahoran died, he left the judgment seat vacant. Three of his sons sought this position and Pahoran was elected. Pacumeni relinquished his claim and united with his people. Out of jealousy, his brother Paanchi had Pahoran slain by Kishkumen. After the deed was done, Kishkumen fled, so Pacumeni was elected to fill the judgment seat.

In the next year, Coriantumr led a swift army of Lamanites into Zarahemla before the alarm could be sounded and a defense established. Once inside the city Coriantumr slew all who opposed him. Pacumeni tried to flee but was slain.

References: Helaman 1:1-23.

PAGAG—Son of the Brother of Jared (Ether)

When Jared and his brother became too old to rule the Jaredites, they gathered the people together to decide who would follow them. Pagag, oldest son of the brother of Jared, was the first elected to be the Jaredite king but he refused, and his father would not compel him to be king.

References: Ether 3:29-31.

PAHORAN—Chief Judge (c. 68 B.C.)

When Nephihah died his son, Pahoran, was elected to be chief judge and governor over the Nephites. His duty was to judge all major matters, keep the peace, and maintain freedom, particularly freedom of religion.

As he sat in office, some people came to Pahoran asking him to change the law so that a king could be established, but he refused. The Nephites divided over this issue into the freemen and the king-men. When Pahoran called for a vote to settle the matter, the freemen won. The freemen forced the king-men to be silent.

When the king-men heard that the Lamanites under Amalickiah were coming to invade Zarahemla, they refused to join in defense of the country. Moroni, in anger at this rebellion, asked Pahoran's permission to compel the king-men to arms. With the majority of the Nephites behind him, Pahoran granted Moroni's request.

As the war against the Lamanites progressed, Moroni wrote a letter to Pahoran asking for more men and supplies for Helaman so that he could maintain the land already recaptured. When he received no supplies and no reply, Moroni again wrote a letter to Pahoran condemning him for his refusal.

Soon after Moroni sent his second letter, he received a letter from Pahoran explaining that he couldn't send troops because of a civil strife going on in Zarahemla that was getting out of control. Again those who considered themselves nobility sought to overthrow Pahoran and establish a king. Pahoran fled to Gideon with those who refused a king and began preparations to attack the king-men. He begged Moroni to come help him put down this civil strife.

Moroni, upon learning that Pahoran was not the traitor, left the army in the charge of Lehi and Teancum, took a small force, and went to the aid of Pahoran. He picked up volunteers along the way so that by the time he reached Zarahemla he was able to overthrow the king and slay or capture all the king-men. Pahoran was established again as governor and Moroni returned to war with the Lamanites, taking Pahoran with him.

When the war ended with victory and freedom for the Nephites, Pahoran returned to his judgment seat.

Pahoran had many sons but died without recommending any of them to follow him as governor.

References: Alma 22:42-44; 23:2-9, 15-20; 27:3, 13-15; 28:1-27; 29:1-12, 16-30, 54; Helaman 1:1-4.

PAHORAN—Son of Pahoran (c. 52 B.C.)

Pahoran died leaving the governorship without naming someone to follow him. Three of his sons vied for this post and Pahoran was elected by the people. Pacumeni, his brother, surrendered claim to that position but Paanchi would not. Paanchi rose up in rebellion and began to divide the Nephites. He was arrested and executed for conspiracy to overthrow the government. His followers did not give up but sent for Kishkumen who slew Pahoran.

References: Helaman 1:1-13, 39.

PALESTINA—Old World Land

Palestina or Palestine refers to the whole of the promised land of Abraham, including the coastal plains as well as the mountainous regions.

Isaiah warned the people that Palestine in its entirety would be destroyed by an army from the north.

Palestine was conquered several times from the north. The conquerers included Assyria, Babylonia, and Rome.

References: II Nephi 10:51-53; Isaiah 14:20-32.

PATHROS—Old World Land

Pathros is the area of upper or southern Egypt. Isaiah prophesied that in the latter days the Lord would recover a remnant of the Israelites from Pathros.

References: II Nephi 9:216; Isaiah 11:11.

PEKAH—Son of Remaliah (Old Testament)

Pekah served as army commander under Pekahiah. With the help of a company of Gileadites, he slew the king of Israel and reigned in his stead. As king, he contacted his friend, Rezin, king of Aram-Damascus, and established an alliance to go against Judah with the intent of putting one of their friends on that throne. When that was accomplished, they planned to go to war against Assyria.

They went so far as to surround Jerusalem and lay seige to it when Tiglath-pileser III brought his Assyrian armies against the Phoenecians and, having been bribed by Ahaz, turned against Israel. At the same time, the Assyrians attacked Damascus. Pekah was slain by Hoshen, son of Elath.

Isaiah told Ahaz of the coming conspiracy of Pekah against him and warned Ahaz to remain neutral because God would remove the threat through Assyria.

References: II Nephi 9:14-22; Isaiah 1-9.

PIPE—Musical Instrument

A pipe is a short tube with no fluting at the end. The player attaches reeds to one end and blows through the reeds to produce music.

The pipe produced a plaintive melody and was used in ceremonies where a sad or mystical mood was desired, such as at a funeral.

A warning is given by Isaiah to those who are winebibbers indulging in wine all day. He saw them in dens or small rooms in groups playing instruments to provide a solemn atmosphere, but no worship of God was there.
References: II Nephi 8:81-82; Isaiah 5:11-12.

PLANTS

Many plants are mentioned specifically in the record of the Nephites. Among the crops planted by the Nephites for food are corn, barley, wheat, neas, sheum, and grapes.

Trees, mentioned mostly in prophecies, include the oak, cedar, sycamore, teil, and olive.

For more information see each plant listed separately—those already mentioned and briers, grass, reeds, and thorns.

PLATES OF BRASS

The plates of brass were kept by a designated priest or elder of the family. It was his responsibility to keep the genealogy records up to date. He also recorded all the prophecies for easy reference.

Laban was responsible for the records of the tribe of Joseph. He was very proud of his position. He kept the records up to date even of prophets with whom he disagreed or who had been stoned for supposed blasphemy. He refused to give, trade, or sell the records, guarding them with his life, even when commanded to relinquish them.

Because of this, when Nephi obtained the records for the Lehites by slaying Laban, he had at his fingertips prophecies which are no longer available to men.

Lehi lists the records as the five books of Moses—Genesis, Exodus, Leviticus, Numbers, Deuteronomy—through Jeremiah. Also included were the prophecies of Zenos, Zenock, and Neum. These records were omitted from the old records by many of the family record keepers because they prophesied that the Jews would crucify their Messiah. Malachi was not included but was later named by Christ when he appeared to the Lehites and taught them.

The records were handed down from generation to generation along with the plates of Nephi.

When the Jews returned to Jerusalem from their Babylonian captivity the records of the priests were missing, because they were in the New World.

References: I Nephi 1:17, 61-170; 3:163; 5:239-244, 264; 6:2; 7:1, 66-67; II Nephi 3:1-5, 28-29; 4:17; Omni 1:25; Mosiah 1:4-6, 23-24; 6:52; 12:15-17; 13:1-2; Alma 17:31-33; III Nephi 1:2-3; 4:71-73; Ezra 2:59-63.

PLATES OF GOLD

The plates of gold were the records prepared by the Jaredites and hidden up by Ether. They were found by a party of explorers sent out by Limhi to find Zarahemla. They were corroborated by a stone kept by the Mulekites in Zarahemla, prepared by Coriantumr, the last Jaredite.

Mosiah was called upon to translate the records found by Limhi and the Mulekites using the Urim and Thummim to aid the work. The translation is the book of Ether.

References: Omni 1:35-39; Mosiah 5:60-64; 12:16-26; Ether.

PLATES OF JACOB

The plates of Jacob were an addition to the record of Nephi of the days of Jacob, brother of Nephi and son of Lehi.

References: Jacob 2:69.

PLATES, LARGER

The larger plates were prepared voluntarily by Nephi, son of Lehi. On these plates he wrote a detailed record of their genealogy and an abridgment of his father's record. He recorded the history of the Lehites including their wars and contentions. These were handed down with the rest of the records, usually from father to son, throughout the generations to Mormon.

References: I Nephi 5:218-225; II Nephi 4:45-50; Jacob 2:68; 5:42-44; Jarom 1:31-32.

PLATES OF NEPHI

By the command of God, Nephi, son of Lehi, prepared plates of ore, probably gold, on which he recorded things pleasing to God. These records were handed down from generation to generation with the command to add to the records new prophecies or fulfillment of prophecies, laws, and judgments.

Mormon abridged the records so that they were more compact. The original records he buried. The abridgment he gave to Moroni to complete.

Before Moroni died, all the other Nephites were slain by the Lamanites. He completed as much of the records as he could, then buried the records to preserve them from destruction by the Lamanites.

Centuries later the records of Moroni, the abridgment, were given to Joseph Smith, Jr., to translate. The original records have not yet been uncovered.

References: I Nephi 1:17; 2:92-95; 5:218-225; II Nephi 4:46-49; Jacob 5:42-48; Jarom 1:31-32; Words of Mormon 1:4-13; Mosiah 1:10, 23-24; 12:14-17; 13:1-2; Alma 17:31-34, 38-49; 20:100; III Nephi 2:92-101; 12:1-5; IV Nephi 1:22-24; Mormon 1:5, 44, 45; 3:6-8; Moroni 10.

TABLE OF THE RECORDERS ON THE PLATES OF NEPHI

Nephi—Son of Lehi
Jacob—Brother of Nephi
Enos—Son of Jacob
Jarom—Son of Enos
Omni—Son of Jarom
Amaron—Son of Omni
Chemish—Brother of Amaron
Abinadom—Son of Chemish
Amaleki—Son of Abinadom
Benjamin—Righteous King
Mosiah—Son of Benjamin
Alma—High Priest

Alma—Son of Alma
Helaman—Son of Alma
Shiblon—Brother of Helaman
Helaman—Son of Helaman
Nephi—Son of Helaman
Nephi—Son of Nephi
Amos—Son of Nephi
Amos—Son of Amos
Ammoron—Brother of Amos
Mormon—Upright Boy
Moroni—Son of Mormon

PLATES—Twenty-Four

Twenty-four bound plates were given to Helaman by Alma, his father, that contained the secrets of the oaths and combinations of Satan for doing evil. They had been written by the Jaredites for instruction of Shule's band. That book also contained a record of the abominations committed by the wicked followers of the secret orders.

Helaman was forbidden to reveal its contents to the Nephites or Lamanites lest they destroy themselves as did the Jaredites. Though Helaman did as he was commanded Satan taught again those oaths to Kishkumen and Gadianton and they were available to the weak men who desired to do evil.

References: II Nephi 7:22; Alma 17:52-70; Helaman 1:11, 12; 2:140-160; IV Nephi 1:49-50; Ether 3:89-102; 4:30; 6:16.

PLOWSHARES—Tools

Plowshares are metal plates fastened to a plow to speed up cutting through the soil to make furrows for planting or cultivation of crops.

In times of war, much metal was needed to make swords. In the last days a promise is given that peace will be so complete and lasting that the swords will be beaten into plowshares, for there will be no more war.

References: II Nephi 8:20; Isaiah 2:4.

PRISONS—Buildings

Prisons are buildings constructed to keep the people who have been condemned by the judges confined for trial, punishment, or execution.

In trying to describe the depths to which the Jews had fallen in sin, Nephi, son of Lehi, tells his brothers that even the prophet Jeremiah had been cast into prison.

In the New World a prison was built in Nephi, the first large city built by the Nephites. Ammon and three of his brethren were kept there until they could be questioned by King Limhi. Abinadi had been cast into that same prison earlier by Limhi's father, King Noah. He was kept there until his execution.

Alma and Amulek were cast into prison in Ammonihah, a city of Nephite dissenters. They were released from this prison by the power of God. The prison tumbled upon their jailers and tormentors but Alma and Amulek left unharmed.

Lamoni had a prison built in Ishmael among the Lamanites. Ammah, Aaron, and Muloki, sons of Mosiah, were kept in prison in Middoni, nearby. They were released by the intercession of King Lamoni, a Lamanite, and Ammon, their brother.

The king-men were cast into prison in Zarahemla by Moroni, the chief of the Nephite army, because of the dissension they caused during a time of war. They were later tried and executed.

Coriantumr, leader of the Lamanites, invaded Zarahemla and cast into prison the Nephites who had not been slain or had not escaped. They were released when Coriantumr was defeated.

Nephi and Lehi were cast into prison in Ishmael where Ammon had been kept by King Limhi. Their release by the ministrations of angels resulted in the conversion of their captors.

Nephi later came prophesying in Zarahemla concerning the murder of the chief judge of the Nephites. The five witnesses sent to ascertain the truth were cast into prison as accused murderers. They were released when the truth was known.

Gidgiddoni, chief of the Nephites, had the Gadianton robbers put into prison. There they received ministry and teaching until they were converted.

After the coming of Christ to the New World, his twelve disciples were cast into prison as they continued their witnessing to the inhabitants of the land. The prisons could not hold them until all the survivors were converted.

In Moron among the Jaredites, Noah put his grandfather in prison in order to obtain the kingdom. Noah would have slain Shule had not his uncle slain Noah.

Akish put his own son in prison and starved him to death. This led to the eventual death of Akish.

Shez had prisons built to hold those who could not or would not pay the heavy taxes he laid on his Jaredite subjects.

Through all this history, God displayed his power and mercy for his saints imprisoned after they demonstrated their faith.

References: I Nephi 2:22; Mosiah 5:7-11; 7:69-70; 8:23; 9:8, 164; Alma 6:38-40; 7:47-49; 8:19-20; 10:60-85; 12:30-32, 182-221; 13:18-32; 14:2, 114; 17:25; 21:54-56; 23:23-24; 29:9-10, 59, 60; Helaman 1:24; 2:83-110; 3:76-129; III Nephi 2:86-88; 5:73-75; 13:29-31; IV Nephi 1:31-33; Mormon 4:30-31; Ether 3:56-57; 4:8, 49-50; 5:14-18.

PRUNING HOOK—Tool

A pruning hook is a curved metal blade attached to a long pole. To prune a tree, the orchard keeper catches the curve of the hook over an old limb and by pulling sharply down, the branch is lopped off.

Through Isaiah we are told that in the last days of peace, the spears no longer needed for war will be reshaped into pruning hooks.

References: II Nephi 8:20; Isaiah 2:4.

Q

QUIVER—Weapon

A quiver is a long leather pouch in which arrows were kept at hand by an archer. For convenience on the field of battle, the quiver was worn either over one shoulder and across the back or hung from the loincloth belt.

Isaiah compares himself to an arrow kept ready in a quiver by the Lord to do battle against evil.

In the time of Jarom, the Nephites made quivers and filled them with arrows in preparation for their defense against the constantly invading armies of Lamanites.

References: I Nephi 6:32-33; Isaiah 49:2-3; Jarom 1:19-21.

R

RABBANAH—Title

Rabbanah is a title of respect given by the Lamanites to the great persons who came to their courts. Often such persons were feared to be the Great Spirit come to visit them in the flesh.

The term probably comes from the Hebrew title *Rabboni*, a heightened form of Rabbi which means teacher. It thus means a great teacher or great master.

Ammon, after demonstrating prowess among the enemies of Lamoni and great faithfulness in obedience to the king's orders, was called Rabbanah when asked to remain in the king's presence while King Lamoni, king of the Lamanites, decided how he should inquire of Ammon who he was.

References: Alma 12:82-85.

RAHAB—Old World Land

Rahab was the symbolic name for Egypt and the Dragon was the master of Rahab or the pharaoh. When Isaiah asks, "Art thou not it that hath cut Rahab, and wounded the dragon?" he is reminding Israel of their exodus from Egypt and the death of the son of Pharaoh which wounded the dragon sufficiently to make him let the Israelites go.

References: II Nephi 5:87-89; Isaiah 51:9-10.

RAMAH—Hill

In the last struggles of the Jaredites, Coriantumr, the king, settled his army near Ramah. This hill is noted to be the same as Cumorah, the hill in which the Lehite records were hidden by Mormon, the Nephite, before he died.

References: Ether 6:83; Mormon 3:7-8.

RAMATH—Old World City

Ramath or Ramath-Gilead is a city which lies considerably east of Jordan. Isaiah in describing the march of the Assyrians lists Ramath as a city conquered by them.

It was a city of refuge selected out of the inheritance of Gad.

References: II Nephi 9:110; Isaiah 10:29; Deuteronomy 4:43.

RAMEUMPTOM—Building

Rameumptoms were towers built in the center of Zoramite synagogues on which prayers were offered. The Zoramites gathered at their synagogues once a week wearing their finest apparel. If not dressed richly enough, even members of the church were forbidden to enter.

Each Zoramite would climb, one at a time, to the top of this holy stand, raise his hands to heaven, and put God in his place as a nice spirit by their one prayer of pride repeated word for word by each member of the church every week.

After this period of prayer the Zoramites returned home to forget the ordeal until the next week.

Alma on seeing this was sickened by their perverse worship of their self-created God. He tried, but was unable to convince them of their need to repent.

References: Alma 16:89-90.

RAZOR—Tool

The Egyptian cleaning process involved the shaving of the whole body with a razor. To the Israelites the head was shaved in mourning but otherwise the beard was considered sacred, not to be shaved even at the corners. The Levites alone were called upon to shave all their flesh in purification rites preparatory to ordination.

Thus when the Lord is prophesied to shave with a hired razor the whole body, the people are to be purified in preparation for a revolution.

References: II Nephi 9:33; Isaiah 7:20; Genesis 41:14; Leviticus 19:27; 21:5; Numbers 8:6-16; Ezekiel 5:1.

RED SEA—Old World Sea

The Red Sea divides Egypt and northeastern Africa from Arabia. It is a long narrow body of water extending 1,200 miles in a southeastern direction between the Mediterranean Sea and the Indian Ocean. It played an important role in nearly every phase of the history of Israel and still does.

When Lehi was commanded to take his family out of Jerusalem, he headed for the Red Sea borders. He camped there with his family, sending his sons back to Jerusalem for the records of Laban and again for the family of Ishmael, who had wives for his sons. Then they folded their tents, turned their backs on Jerusalem, and followed the fertile areas of the Red Sea borders southeasterly for many days.

Along the way, the sons of Lehi fought for their right to return to their luxurious past in Jerusalem and were prodded on by Lehi, Nephi, angels, and God himself. Nephi broke his steel hunting bow and made another of wood. Lehi was given the Liahona, a compass or director for their path. Ishmael died and was buried. The sons of Lehi were married. Children were born.

From somewhere along the southern region of the Red Sea, the family turned eastward away from the Red Sea, never to see it again.

Four times the story of Moses concerning his parting of the Red Sea for the preserving of the children of Israel is recounted to remind the Lehites of the goodness of God.

Isaiah speaks of the life of Christ and his influence which extended to the Red Sea, which as a babe Christ crossed twice, upon entering and leaving Egypt.

References: I Nephi 1:29-36, 100; 5:18, 107-109; II Nephi 9:61 (Isaiah 9:1); Mosiah 5:28-29; Alma 17:25-28; Helaman 3:44.

REED—Plant

The reed is a common grass-like plant growing in marshes. Its tough stalk was used for arrows, roofing, weaving mats and partitions, scales, flutes, and pens. When the reed withers it turns dry and brittle.

When the brothers threatened Nephi, son of Lehi, beyond his ability to endure, he called upon the power of God to wither his brothers as a dried reed if they dared touch him. This stopped their molesting so that the ship could be built that was to carry the Lehites from the Old World to the New.

References: I Nephi 5:155.

REMALIAH—Father of Pekah (Old Testament)

Remaliah or Remaljah has not been mentioned as having any claim to the throne of Israel. Through ambition, his son, Pekah, took the kingdom and usurped his power as king until he was slain.

References: II Nephi 9:14-22 (Isaiah 7:1-9), 43-46 (Isaiah 8:5-8).

REZIN—King of Aram-Damascus (c. 732 B.C.)

Rezin or Rasjan was the last king of Aram-Damascus. He allied with Pekah, king of Israel, against Judah, beginning under Jotham and continuing under Ahaz, in an attempt to depose Ahaz and install one of their own men. They laid seige against Jerusalem but could not overthrow it.

While they were busy at war with Judah, Tiglath-pileser III brought the Assyrian troops against the Phoenicians and then began to whittle away Israel's territory because of a bribe from Ahaz. When Damascus was captured by Assyria, Rezin was killed.

This whole plot had been revealed to Isaiah who was told to warn Ahaz to refuse to ally with Rezin and Pekah.

References: II Nephi 9:14-22, 43-46, 71-72; Isaiah 7:1-9; 8:5-8; 9:11-12.

RIPLAH—Hill

Riplah was located near the river Sidon on the north bank.

Lamanites were attempting to invade the land of the Nephites. Moroni as captain of the Nephites had met the invasion head on with such a show of force that the Lamanites fled without a fight. Before they could recoup their forces and return, Moroni set up his forces to trap them at their point of return near Manti. A portion of the army under Lehi's command were concealed on the south of the hill Riplah. Moroni's strategy to surround the Lamanite army succeeded perfectly. References: Alma 20:35-38.

RIPLAKISH—Son of Shez (Ether)

Riplakish followed his father, Shez, to the throne of the Jaredites. He was not obedient to the commandments. He took many wives and concubines and supported himself and his nobles by taxing the populace. He spent his revenue on building huge, ornate structures including an elaborate throne.

Even if his subjects were unable to pay their taxes, Riplakish had prisons built to hold them and those who on principle refused to pay. His prisoners worked or were slain. The imprisoned artisans prepared gold ornaments for his pleasure.

After forty-two years of suffering under Riplakish's cruel fist, the citizens rose up in rebellion, slew him, and drove his descendants into exile. It was many years before Morianton, descendant of Riplakish, could reestablish the Jaredites' kingdom. References: Ether 1:6; 4:47-53.

RIPLIANCUM—Lake

In the last war of the Jaredites, Coriantumr fled before Shiz until he came to a large lake called Ripliancum. It was south of Shurr and Comnor and north of Ogath where Cumorah is located.

There the two armies came together. The tide turned in favor of Coriantumr though Coriantumr was wounded and had to be carried from the battlefield. Shiz fled to Ogath before the army of Coriantumr.

References: Ether 6:79-82.

ROADS—See Highways

ROBE

Robes were garments made to cover the body. They were pictured in carvings to be loose fitting, belted, and reaching to below the knees or just above the feet.

The angel that visited Nephi, son of Lehi, wore a white robe, as did Christ, in both visions and in the flesh. Nephi hoped that his reward would include a white robe signifying his cleanliness from sin.

References: I Nephi 2:44; 3:238-239; II Nephi 3:56; 6:34-35; III Nephi 5:9-10.

ROE—Animal

A roe or roebuck is also known as a gazelle. This is an antelope, a sleek, graceful, delicate, horned animal. When it flees from its enemies on the wide-open plains where it roams, it runs at great speeds, leaping high and changing directions frequently to avoid being caught. The roe does not claim a certain territory as do some other animals.

Isaiah compares humanity to a chased roe in the days of the judgment of God—a people fleeing swiftly from their enemies, but without a place to go.

References: II Nephi 10:14; Isaiah 13:14.

ROOT MEDICINE

Helaman recorded a time of peace during his dispensation when many people died only of disease or old age. This was in sharp contrast to the many years in which wars with the Lamanites took the greater toll.

Helaman mentions here the use of plants and roots to cure the sick. In modern times many are returning to natural remedies for illnesses as the Indians reveal the sources for their root medicines. These remedies have been successfully used for thousands of years and knowledge of them has been passed on from generation to generation through the tribal medicine man who specialized in this knowledge for the tribe.

Usually prayer sessions accompany the administration of the root medicine in the form of teas and poultices. This practice stems from the laying on of hands for the healing of the sick performed from ancient times by the elders under God's commission.

References: Alma 21:75-76.

S

SALEM—Old World Land

Salem was the land surrounding and including

the city Salem. It was ruled by the righteous King Melchisedec who established the church there. He convinced the citizens of the city that they should repent and establish peace. Abraham went to Melchisedec at Salem to pay his tithes.

Later Salem became Jerusalem, the capital of Israel and Judah.

References: Alma 10:8-14.

SAM—Son of Lehi (c. 600 B.C.)

Sam was a rather quiet, unassuming lad. He seemed to follow whoever was leading at the time. He was the first to believe Nephi concerning his vision. Only once did he stand up for Nephi, his younger brother. That was at Jerusalem when the sons of Lehi were sent back to acquire the plates of Laban. For his attempt to make a stand, he with Nephi was beaten by his envious brothers, Laman and Lemuel. After that he seemed to back away from decisions, though Alma calls him a just and holy man.

When the sons of Lehi divided, Sam and his family joined Nephi but were never a separate tribe as the Josephites were. Lehi told Sam in his patriarchal blessing that his seed or children would join with Nephi and be numbered with the Nephites.

References; I Nephi 1:32, 49-52, 131-133; 2:12, 42, 55-58; II Nephi 1:52-54; 3:18-21; 4:8; Alma 1:104.

SAMARIA—Old World City

When the ten northern tribes broke away

307

from Benjamin and Judah, Omri built Samaria about 880 B.C., on a hill belonging to Shemer, to be the northern capital. It became the center of idol worship as well as the location of the palace for the center of government. The tribe of Ephraim took leadership over the ten tribes and through them the line of kings was established. When Pekah, son of Remaliah, came to the throne, the end of the Samarian government was near. Because of his alliance with Syria against Judah and Assyria, Samaria was overthrown and the ten tribes scattered by Sargon II in about 122 B.C.

Isaiah was sent to Ahaz, because of the Israelites' idolatry, to tell them of these woes to come to Samaria as an example of what would happen to Jerusalem if there was no repentance.

References: II Nephi 9:21-95; Isaiah 7:8-10:14; I Kings 16:24; II Kings 18:9-37; 19:9-37.

SAMUEL—Prophet (c. 6 B.C.)

Samuel was a Lamanite. By 6 B.C. the Lamanites had become more righteous than the white Nephites. Samuel was sent by God to declare repentance and to prophesy of the signs of the coming of Christ to Jerusalem and of his death.

After Samuel preached among the Nephites for a while in the land of Zarahemla, he was cast out. He was told by God to return to the city of Zarahemla and to say what came to his mind. He was not allowed to enter by the gate, so he climbed up on the wall of the city and shouted his message to the citizenry below.

This time Samuel included in his message the destruction of the Nephites in four hundred years. He told them of the destruction of Zarahemla by fire, which occurred at the time of the crucifixion of Christ in Jerusalem. He explained the curse that would make their weapons seem to disappear, not to be found, calling them and their treasures "slippery."

The Nephites who heard this dire message sought to slay Samuel by casting stones and shooting arrows at him. None were able to hit him as he continued his message, shielded by the Holy Spirit.

Many believed him and repented, calling upon Nephi, son of Helaman, to baptize them. But most did not believe him and tried to drown out his message with shouting. The citizens of Zarahemla sent for the army to bind him, but Samuel jumped off the wall and sped away.

Samuel never returned to the Nephites, but took his message to the Lamanites.

References: Helaman 5:2-120; III Nephi 1:5-6, 9, 16-24; IV Nephi 3:25; 9:62; 10:35-41; Mormon 1:20, 34.

SAMUEL—Prophet (Old Testament)

Samuel was the son of Eldaha and Hannah. He was dedicated by Hannah before his conception to service in the temple. When he was about three, he was brought to the temple to serve the high priest, Eli. While still quite young, probably about eight, he was commissioned by the Lord to judge his people and to be the first of a long series of prophets to Israel.

Christ proclaimed Samuel as the first prophet to testify of his life in a long period of prophecy during which all prophets proclaimed his coming.

References: III Nephi 9:62; I Samuel 1-3.

SANCTUARY—Building

The sanctuary originally was a most holy room of the temple into which the high priest entered annually for a special sacrifice for the sins of the Israelites.

Later sanctuaries were built as places of high worship. They often contained an altar for a center of worship but not for blood sacrifice.

Sanctuaries were common among both the Lamanites and the Nephites as centers for worship. Preaching and prayer services were conducted there. As the evangelists went from the Nephites to the Lamanites, sanctuaries were built and used to call the Lamanites from their corrupted practices to purer repentance.

Sanctuary building was extended to the land northward as new colonies reached out for more territory.

Nephi, son of Lehi, prophesied that in the

latter days churches would be built of finery and sanctuaries adorned for the pride of the members by robbing the poor and needy and denying them access because of their lack of fine apparel.

References: II Nephi 12:15; Alma 10:109-110; 11:22; 13:9, 39; 14:1-6; Helaman 2:9, 12-14; Ether 6:2-3.

SARAH — Wife of Abraham (Old Testament)

Sarah was the first wife of Abraham. She was a half-sister to Abraham, having the same father, Terah. When Abraham feared the reaction of a strange people as he wandered, he called Sarah his sister rather than his wife, often creating more problems than he solved.

Sarah was barren until she was ninety. She was then given Isaac, through Abraham, as her only child, as foretold in prophecy which she would not believe until it was fulfilled.

Sarah was always faithful and obedient to Abraham, though not always to God. She tried to remove her reproach for her barrenness by giving her handmaid, Hagar, to Abraham for a wife. Though Ishmael, the son born of this union, was denied the rights of firstborn because he was born out of wedlock, he was the firstborn of Abraham. Upon Sarah's insistence, Ishmael and Hagar were sent away when Isaac was weaned.

Nephi repeated Isaiah's plea that the descendants of Israel look to Sarah as their ancestor and remember the covenants with God and remain a faithful people.

References: II Nephi 5:71 (Isaiah 51:2); Genesis 12-17; 20-23.

SARIAH—Wife of Lehi (c. 600 B.C.)

Sariah was the faithful wife of Lehi. She clung loyally to her husband whenever she was instructed to pack and move. She did not complain when Lehi told her to leave her life of ease in Jerusalem and head for the wilderness. Only once did she murmur against her husband.

When Lehi sent his sons back to Jerusalem to obtain the records of Laban, their return was long delayed. Sariah greatly feared that her sons were slain in the wilderness and she was to be left, childless, to perish in the wilderness. She voiced the same complaint against Lehi as Laman, her son—that Lehi was a visionary man.

Gently Lehi admitted that she was right. But the vision she feared would be to her and her family a great blessing. He assured her that her sons were under the protection of God and that even the cruel and powerful Laban was no match for the power of God.

Silently Sariah stood by her tent mourning and watching for the appearance of her sons as the weary days passed. When at last they did return, her joy was full. She was completely convinced of the truth of the mission of her husband. Never again did she question his leadership.

Stalwartly she continued to move or stay as her husband directed, bearing Lehi two more sons and possibly more daughters on the journey to the promised New World.

On the boat, as it crossed the wide ocean, Sariah was almost brought to her death by the vicious quarreling of her sons. In grief she was so weakened that she could not rise from her bed. She lay in deep depression beside her husband until a severe storm on the seas drove the ship backward tossing them almost to the depths of the sea. Only then would her older sons release her younger son, Nephi, so that the journey could be finished.

She recovered, but not all of her strength returned. There is no mention of her death or whether she reached the promised land.

References: I Nephi 1:31-32, 146-156; 5:200-213.

SATAN—Father of Lies

Satan contended with God for his throne. He sought to take on the glory of God by taking away the agency of man. For this sin, he and his cohorts were cast out of heaven from the face of God into eternal misery.

When he fell to earth, Satan was allowed to tempt man, to sift the righteous who would resist him from the evil who would submit themselves to him. He went to Eve and with lies enticed her to disobedience; she in turn enticed Adam to join her in sin. Contrary to Satan's lie, Adam and Eve were cast out of the presence of God and eventually had to suffer death.

Satan used anger and jealousy to entice Cain to murder, and to accept secret oaths and secret combinations. Those ordinances were used over and over again whenever pride weakened the resistance of men.

Satan used the appearance of luxury to instill pride, and pride to wedge away the righteous to covetousness. Covetousness led to stealing and all manner of iniquity.

Satan uses subtle lies to lull others away from worship and prayer on a regular basis, to bind the eyes from study. He founded the great and abominable church for those who refuse to study but attend for the praise of men.

Satan uses gossip to instill contention to separate the weak from worship with the stalwart. Satan whispers to the miracle workers to accept monetary reward and leads them to priest-craft and a loss of their gift and their soul. Satan can appear as an angel bringing new revelations that are very near the truth but are salted with a little lie to turn away the hearts of men.

Once a soul is captured first with flaxen threads, then with chains, Satan laughs and brings that soul to his domain in hell. At resurrection all men will receive the knowledge of all good and all evil and will have perfect remembrance of their deeds in their time of probation. Those who have followed the path of Satan will come to a state of eternal torment and misery because of that knowledge and guilt. Yet Satan would tell men that there is no hell and he is not.

Christ has power over Satan. He can remove devils from the hearts of men and cleanse the soul for renewal of life. The wisdom of God is greater than the cunning of the devil. When men resist evil, Satan can have no power over them. When all men come to a state of resisting evil, Satan will be bound for a long time.

References: I Nephi 3:83-85, 124-127, 141, 175, 201-209, 235-237; 4:50-63; 7:32-35, 60-62; II Nephi 1:31-32, 101-104; 6:20-40, 89-93; 7:41-42; 10:34-39; 11:74-76, 93-94; 12:22-33, 99; Jacob 2:64-65; 5:23-24; Omni 1:45; Mosiah 1:98-104; 2:26; 8:70-89; 11:133-135; Alma 3:38, 65-70; 6:10; 7:41-44; 8:25-28, 36-37, 41, 68; 9:2-9, 15-32; 10:43, 104-110; 11:32; 15:12; 16:51-77, 218-219, 233-238; 17:46-48, 65-67; 19:16, 45-46, 77-107; 21:140; 25:24; Helaman 2:25, 26, 74-75, 145-162; 3:16-17; 4:53-55; 5:35-36, 117-118, 136-138; III Nephi 1:25-26, 38-42; 3:17-18, 59-61; 4:26-27; 5:29-31, 115; 6:34; 8:47-51; 9:97; 12:21-24; 13:9, 52-53, 59-60; IV Nephi 1:30; Mormon 2:47; 4:87-88; Ether 3:100-102; 6:92; Moroni 7:8-16; 9:3.

SCALPING

In about 74 B.C., in a war with the Lamanites, Moroni had his Nephite army surround the army of Zerahemnah, the Lamanite chief. Moroni asked Zerahemnah to agree to lay down his weapons and vow never to come to war with the Nephites again. Even though he knew by so doing his men would surely die, Zerahemnah raised his sword to slay Moroni. Moroni's guard raised his sword in defense, hacking the blade from Zerahemnah's upraised sword; when the blade flew off, it severed the scalp from the head of Zerahemnah. The scalp lay at Zerahemnah's feet. When he saw it, he backed away.

The soldier whose weapon had caused the scalp to be cut off, picked up the scalp and, placing it on the tip of his sword, raised it high so that all the Lamanites could see it. He cried out to the Lamanites that in the same manner the scalp had fallen from their chief, so should they fall to the earth. With this warning, the greater part of the Lamanite army surrendered.

The remainder were again stirred to battle by Zerahemnah. After another brief but bloody battle, Zerahemnah committed his army to the treaty proposed by Moroni.

References: Alma 20:81-86.

SEANTUM—Murderer (c. 23 B.C.)

Seantum was a member of the secret society of robbers founded by Gadianton. He crept up to the judgment seat and murdered his own brother, Seezoram, in order to obtain the judgment seat for himself. Afterward, he fled to his own house.

Nephi, son of Helaman, saw this act in a vision and proclaimed it to the crowds as proof of his authority. Instead of acknowledging Nephi, the Nephites accused him of conspiracy in the affair. The five witnesses sent to the scene fainted there and were imprisoned as the murderers.

When Nephi sent the judges to Seantum with an exact description of his reaction to their questions, the five were released and Seantum was taken.

Instead of the people being astonished to repentance by this event, they divided in contention as to whether Nephi was a prophet of God and left Nephi standing alone in the street.

Reference: Helaman 3:63-112.

SEBUS—*Water Source*

The Sebus provided water for the Lamanite shepherds in Ishmael to water their sheep. As a matter almost of tradition, the other shepherds came to drive away and scatter the flocks of the king. When Ammon, the Nephite, came among the shepherds as a voluntary servant of King Lamoni, he defended the right of the king's shepherds to water their sheep. Some of the other shepherds were slain, others had their arms hacked off, others fled.

This defensive action brought such fear to the king's shepherds that they brought the arms of the mutilated shepherds to the king as evidence.

Later one of the shepherds, who was present at the water of Sebus and whose brother had been slain by Ammon, tried to slay Ammon while he lay in prayer. This man was struck dead by God.

References: Alma 12:38-160.

SECRET COMBINATIONS—*See Plates—Twenty-four, Satan, Gadianton, Akish.*

SEEZORAM—Chief Judge (c. 20 B.C.)

Seezoram was slain by his own brother, Seantum, as he sat on the judgment seat. Seantum committed the murder in a cloak of secrecy because he was jealous of his brother's position, then fled.

Nephi, son of Helaman, saw this action in a vision and reported it to the Nephites as a testimony of his divine authority. Instead of impressing the people, the incident was a center of contention which divided the Nephites still further.

References: Helaman 3:63-112.

SERAPHIM—Angels

Seraphim are mentioned only once in biblical literature. They appear in Isaiah's vision of the Lord on his throne. They stand above the temple awaiting the command of God, appearing as men having six wings; two cover the face, two cover the feet, and with two they fly.

One of the seraphim performed the ritual of cleansing on Isaiah by placing a coal from the altar on Isaiah's mouth. When this was done, Isaiah felt sufficiently healed to volunteer as messenger to Israel until its destruction and scattering.

References: II Nephi 9:1-8; Isaiah 6:1-8.

SERPENTS—Animals

Serpents referred to snakes or lizards. The Lehites were reminded by Moses of the poisonous serpents sent to the Israelites because of their iniquity. To heal the people, Moses raised a serpent before them. Those who looked at the serpent were healed of their bites.

An endowment of power was given to the twelve disciples, chosen as leaders by Christ at his appearance in the New World, to protect them from the bite of poisonous serpents.

In the land of the Jaredites, King Heth ordered the slaying of the prophets sent to call them to repentance. Because of this and other iniquities, a great drought was sent upon the land. The drought brought the poisonous serpents out of hiding and the people and their herds fled from the serpents. Many were bitten and killed. Others died of starvation as they fled southward toward the land where the Lehites would soon come.

After the Jaredites moved far enough southward, the serpents ceased to pursue them but acted as a barrier preventing their return to their previous homeland.

After two righteous kings, the Jaredites were sufficiently humbled that the barrier of serpents was removed. Since the people had by that time reestablished themselves, they did not return to the land northward but continued to look to the land southward for their sustenance.

References: II Nephi 11:38; Numbers 21:5-9; Mormon 4:30-31; Ether 4:35-38, 66.

SETH—Son of Shiblon (Ether)

Seth was the son of a king, slain for his

unrighteousness. He was held in captivity all his life. His son, Ahah, regained the kingdom.
References: Ether 1:6; 4:99.

SHARED—*Rebel (Ether)*

Shared gathered an army and led it against Coriantumr, an unrighteous king of the Jaredites. He fought Coriantumr for three years before he was able to wrest the kingdom from Coriantumr.

Shared reigned only one year before Coriantumr was able to gather an army to depose him. By this time, the whole nation was in upheaval. Every leader in the land fought with his neighbor and their friends for possessions.

Coriantumr again fought Shared and was able to slay him after days of battle where victory switched sides with every skirmish. Before Shared died, he wounded Coriantumr so deeply that he was unable to go to war again for two years.
References: Ether 6:25-34, 37, 42.

SHAZER—*Old World Place*

As the Lehites traveled out of Jerusalem along the border of the Red Sea, they came to a wilderness where they set up their tents to rest. This was four days' travel south-southeast of the river they had named Laman.

While the family rested, the sons of Lehi went into the forest and obtained meat using their bows and arrows. After a rest they con-

tinued on their way, traveling in the same south-southeast direction.
Reference: I Nephi 5:16, 17.

SHEAR-JASHUB—Son of Isaiah (Old Testament)

Shear-jashub accompanied his father, Isaiah the prophet, when Isaiah was sent to meet Ahaz to warn him of the conspiracy of Ephraim that was rising against him.
References: II Nephi 9:16-17; Isaiah 7:3-4.

SHEEP—Animals

Sheep are gentle four-legged domesticated animals. They produce milk, wool, meat, and leather. They have been domesticated since the beginning of man.

Jaredites brought sheep with them to the New World from the tower of Babel. Many of these animals were left free to roam after the Jaredites were destroyed in their last civil war. Some of these developed into wild strains. Others were captured and domesticated by the Lehites who came to inherit the land.

Sheep are herded in flocks by their shepherd. At night the shepherd gathers them together into a pen or fold. In Israel there is no gate to the pen, only an opening for the sheep to enter. The shepherd counts the sheep as they enter through the opening which is wide enough for only one sheep to enter at a time. If any of his sheep are missing, he must leave his flock and search the area, calling for the missing animal until either the live animal or the carcass is found. When all have entered, the shepherd sits or lies down across the entrance, preventing the sheep from leaving or predators from entering. Thus the shepherd uses his own body as the door to the fold.

During the day, the shepherd leads his sheep to pasture and water. He uses his crook to pull sheep back when they stray too far. He often has a flute to soothe the sheep and keep them from stampeding. If he should shout too harshly at his flock, they would scatter, each sheep taking off in a different direction. Then he would have to spend all day rounding them up again.

Sometimes goats are mixed in with the sheep to help in herding. Goats will go voluntarily where sheep have to be pushed or pulled. The goats are used to lead the sheep over difficult terrain. When the sheep are brought in to be sheared, the goats are used to lead them to the gates where they are taken one at a time to be shaved or sheared to obtain the wool for cloth. If goats are used, the sheep are quiet as they come. Some of the sheep may be slaughtered for meat at this time, with goats used to lead them to the butcher.

Christ used these facts about sheep to explain his love for his people. He offered himself as their protector and their judge. Like a sheep, if man wanders too far from the path of righteousness, he is subject to the enemy who would take him. Man is told to listen for his shepherd's voice.

Christ declared that there are other followers of the Good Shepherd whose history is not yet revealed when he told the Nephites that he had other sheep not of their pasture.

Christ quietly offered himself as the lamb for the slaughter or the sacrifice. He was led quietly by his goat-like enemies, not uttering complaint and thus being the Lamb of God.

References: I Nephi 7:56-59; II Nephi 9:34-35 (Isaiah 7:21-22), 120-124 (Isaiah 11:5-6); 10:14 (Isaiah 13:14); 12:91-95 (Isaiah 11:5-9); Mosiah 8:21-22, 33-34; 11:127-128; Alma 3:61-64, 103-106; 14:71-72; Helaman 5:102-104; III Nephi 6:27; 7:16-28; 8:63; 9:51-52, 98-99.

SHEM—Army Leader (c. A.D. 385)

Shem led his battalion of ten thousand Nephite soldiers into battle against the Lamanites in the last war of the Nephites. He and all his warriors were slain.

Reference: Mormon 3:15.

SHEM—Land

Shem was a land north of Jashon. Nephites fled there in the early part of the last war of the Nephites. They were closely pursued by Lamanite enemies.

Nephites, led by Mormon, stopped in the city of Shem long enough to fortify the city and rest for two years before they were again attacked by Lamanites.

Mormon called upon them to stand firm

and fight. The Nephites stood and fought so valiantly that they eventually drove away the Lamanites.

The Nephites, three years later, signed a truce with the Lamanites so that they retained the land northward. The remainder of the land was given to the Lamanites. This provided the Nephites ten years of uncertain peace, time spent in preparation of weapons. Mormon moved his people out of the land Desolation for further protection after calling for repentance and finding the people even more hardened in heart.
Reference: Mormon 1:48-69.

SHEMLON—Land

Shemlon was a land of the Lamanites located south of and not far from the land of Nephi. After Zeniff and his followers reinhabited the land of Nephi, Zeniff sent spies to Shemlon to watch for war preparations so that the Nephites would be forewarned.

When Noah took over leadership of the Nephites in the land of Nephi, he had a tower built so that he could look over to Shemlon and watch for war build-up among the Lamanites. The last act of Noah as king was to cry out from this tower a warning of a Lamanite invasion. Noah had fled there from the wrath of Gideon who was about to slay him because of his unrighteousness.

In Shemlon, daughters of the Lamanites gathered in a meadow to dance. The escaped priests of Noah captured them there and took them for wives.

Later Ammon was instrumental in converting the people of Shemlon to belief in God.

References: Mosiah 6:36-39; 7:16-19; 9:78-80, 108-112; Alma 14:13-14.

SHEMNON—Disciple (c. A.D. 34)

Shemnon was one of the twelve chosen by Christ to be a leader of the people who survived the cataclysm at the time of the crucifixion of Christ in Jerusalem.

Shemnon helped a portion of the multitude gathered for teaching to pray. When the people were prepared, Shemnon was baptized by Nephi then helped to baptize the rest. Shemnon was ordained by Christ and endowed with the gifts of the Spirit and protection of the Holy Ghost from harm.

For the rest of the story, see *Disciples*.

References: III Nephi 9:4-15.

SHEREM—Apostate (c. 500 B.C.)

Sherem was a wicked man who had been deceived by Satan into believing that there was no Christ. He went among the Nephites flattering them so that they might believe him. Sherem sought out Jacob, the younger brother of Nephi, and tried to convert him to this belief.

Jacob had a testimony, from angel ministry and from Christ himself, of the truth so that he would not be shaken. Sherem asked Jacob for a sign of the power of the Holy Ghost. The sign Jacob gave Sherem was so overpowering that he fell into a coma and had to be nourished many days. During this time, he was allowed to see the awfulness of his sins.

When he awoke he called the people together to publicly confess his sin and convince his followers of the trap into which they were falling. After his confession, he died. His followers repented.

Reference: Jacob 5:1-38.

SHERRIZAH—City

Sherrizah was one of the last strongholds of the Nephites before their annihilation. In the city was a high tower in which many took refuge.

The Lamanites attacked and overthrew the Nephites, taking the people from the tower captive. They slew the men and fed their bodies to the women and children, providing them little water to wash down the flesh. The Lamanites took the food from the land and left the Nephites behind to wander and starve.

The Nephites at that time were even more sadistic than the Lamanites.

References: Moroni 9:8-16.

SHEUM—Plant

The exact nature of sheum is not explained; it is merely listed among the crops raised by the Nephites.

References: Mosiah 6:12.

SHEZ—Descendant of Heth (Ether)

In the time of the vindictive Jaredite King Heth, the prophets were slain because they revealed too much truth. To stop this wickedness, a drought came upon the land. All of the household of Heth moved southward and perished in famine except Shez. It became his responsibility to gather and rebuild the nation.

Shez remembered the goodness of God and gathered his citizens together in righteousness. They had long years of relative peace and prosperity even though there were robbers in the land. His first son, Shez, was slain for his riches by robbers.

A younger son, Riplakish, took over the kingdom when Shez died.

References: Ether 1:6; 4:43-47.

SHEZ—Son of Shez (Ether)

Shez was a proud and vain man. He rebelled against his righteous father and would have created a civil war to dethrone the king had not he been stopped. Before Shez could gather enough of an army, robbers saw the riches he possessed and flaunted openly. The robbers attacked, stripped away his wealth, and left him to die. Thus peace was maintained for many more years.

References: Ether 4:45.

SHIBLOM—Son of Com (Ether)

Shiblom reigned over the Jaredites after his

father. Almost immediately his brother divided the kingdom and started a civil war.

During Shiblom's life, his brother ruled his portion of the kingdom and ordered all the prophets of doom slain. The prophets warned them of the terrible destruction that would come among them if they refused to repent. Because of their secret society for civil uprising, the Jaredites refused to listen. Famine followed pestilence which followed destruction until a great many people perished. The Jaredites began to repent and call upon God for their salvation instead of their demonic leaders.

Shiblom was slain; Seth, son of Shiblom, was brought into captivity and Ahah succeeded to the throne.

References: Ether 4:92-99.

SHIBLOM—Captain (c. A.D. 385)

Shiblom commanded a battalion of ten thousand men in the last war of the Nephites. In a single bloody battle, he and all his men were slain.

References: Mormon 3:15.

SHIBLON—Brother of Shiblom (Ether)

Shiblon, son of Com, rebelled against his brother who had succeeded his father to the throne of the Jaredites. He gathered his friends about him and fought Shiblom in a great civil war.

Shiblon overcame Shiblom and ordered that

the prophets of the day, who testified of impending doom, be slain. The civil war continued, building on secret combinations for murder and plunder. Soon famine and pestilence were added to this wanton destruction until the prophecies of the martyred prophets came to pass.

At last the people saw that they must repent or die. Shiblom and Shiblon were slain. Seth, son of Shiblon, was brought into captivity and Ahah, son of Seth, was crowned king of the Jaredites. The people repented and destruction began to abate.

References: Ether 1:6; 4:93-99.

SHIBLON—Son of Alma (c. 74 B.C.)

Shiblon was taken by his father to preach among the Zoramite dissenters in hope of turning them away from their apostasy. Though he was bound and stoned by the Zoramites, he patiently waited for the power of God to deliver him.

His father, in giving Shiblon his patriarchal blessing, described Shiblon as strong, steady, faithful, patient, and diligent.

When he returned from an unsuccessful mission among the Zoramites, Shiblon continued to preach among the Nephites, showing by example the benefits of obedience to the commandments of God. When his brother, Helaman, grew too old to keep them, Shiblon was given charge of the plates of Nephi and the treasures of the church. He recorded the colonizing efforts of the Nephites in prosperity as they reached northward into the land and westward across the sea in expanding their territory.

Before he died, Shiblon passed the plates and treasure to Helaman's son, Helaman.

References: Alma 16:84; 18; 21:185-186; 30.

SHIELDS—Arms

Shields were plates fashioned of brass or leather to be held in one arm while the soldier wielded his sword or javelin in the other.

The Nephites, under Moroni's instruction, made shields before the Lamanites did. The Lamanites declared that these shields, not the power of God, served as their protection and were severely punished for this attitude.

Later the Lamanites prepared shields of leather for themselves.

Gidgiddoni, war chief in A.D. 17, armed the Nephites with shields against the Gadianton robbers and successfully defended the Nephites while driving off the robbers.

The Jaredites armed themselves with shields when they entered their last war that led to their annihilation. Limhi's men, sent to find Zarahemla from Nephi, discovered the field of battle. The shields of copper and brass that littered the field were still perfectly sound centuries later.

Reference: Mosiah 5:65; Alma 20:21, 24, 77; 21:42, 154-155; Helaman 1:15; III Nephi 2:38; Ether 6:87, 96.

SHILOAH—Waters

The waters of the springs of Gihon in the king's garden in Jerusalem were called Shiloah or Shiloam.

While he ministered to the Jews in Palestine, Christ sent a man blind from birth to Shiloah to wash off the clay he had used to cover the blind man's eyes. When the man did as Christ bade him, he gained his vision.

Those who refuse the waters of Shiloah remain blind to the truth of God.

References: II Nephi 9:43-46; Isaiah 8:5-8; Nehemiah 3:15; John 9:1-7.

SHILOM—Land

Shilom was a land of the Lamanites north of the land of Nephi. When Zeniff and his Nephite followers left Zarahemla they went to Nephi and treatied with the Lamanites to live in the land. The Lamanites gave them Shilom as part of their land to settle. Lamanites surrounded the Nephite settlement, keeping watch as they prospered.

After years of watching, the Lamanites began to raid the Nephites. King Noah, the Nephite ruler of Nephi, had a tower built to overlook the land so that he could be warned in cases of Lamanite invasions.

When King Limhi, son of Noah, decided to leave the land because of the harshness of the treatment accorded the Nephites and the tribute required by their captors, Gideon led the Nephites around Shilom toward Zarahemla.

When the Lamanites reinhabited the land of Shilom, Amulon, a devious priest of Noah, was established as teacher of the people there.

Later Ammon and his brothers came to the land and converted the Lamanites to a belief in God.

References: Mosiah 5:6-9, 23-24; 6:9-11, 17, 37-38; 7:16-19; 10:11-14; 11:44-47; Alma 14:13-14.

SHIM—Hill

Shim was located in the land of Antum. There Ammoron hid the record and treasures of the Nephites until Mormon, then ten years old, was old enough to care for them. Later Mormon came to the hill and uncovered the records and relics as he had been commanded.

Omer, king of the Jaredites, had passed by there many centuries before in his flight from Akish.

References: Mormon 1:2-4; 2:25; Ether 4:3-4.

SHIMNILON—City

Lamanites who inhabited the city of Shimnilon were converted by the preaching of Ammon and his brothers to faith in God.

Reference: Alma 14:13.

SHINAR—Old World Land

Shinar is thought to mean the land surrounding the city of Babylon. On the plain of Shinar the tower of Babel was built.

Isaiah prophesied that the Lord would gather

a remnant of Jews from Shinar in the last days.
References: II Nephi 9:126; Isaiah 11:11.

SHIPS—Boats

In about 588 B.C., Nephi was instructed to build a ship to carry the Lehites across the ocean to the New World. The exact nature of the ship is not known, though it was described as unlike common ships of that day and made tight so that it would not sink. It had a tiller and rudder of sorts and could be steered. It was large enough to carry about forty people and their seeds and provisions across a stormy ocean.

From Isaiah, Nephi, son of Lehi, quotes the prophecy that the Lord will bring destruction upon the ships of Tarshish. These ships carried wealthy cargoes of ore or metal to and from smelters located along the ancient Spanish and Portuguese coasts.

In about 57 B.C., Hagoth, a Nephite, built a large ship to launch from Bountiful to carry colonists to the land northward.
References: I Nephi 5:68-96, 156-213; II Nephi 8:29-32; Isaiah 2:13-16; Alma 30:6-15; Helaman 2:12-14.

SHIZ—Traitor (Ether)

When Lib died at the hand of Coriantumr, king of the Jaredites, Shiz, brother of Lib, took up the fight. Shiz took over leadership of Lib's Jaredite forces, pursuing Coriantumr, destroying cities, and slaying citizens as he went. So awful was the carnage that the people divided themselves between the army of Shiz and the army of Coriantumr.

Death came to multitudes. Bodies piled high on the land were left to rot or to be carrion for vultures.

After years of destruction Coriantumr wrote a letter to Shiz surrendering on condition that his life be spared. Shiz replied that he would accept the surrender only if Coriantumr would come to be executed. Coriantumr was angered by this demand. The war resumed.

Carnage continued until only Shiz and Coriantumr remained of all the warring Jaredites, with Ether the lone witness. Shiz fainted. Coriantumr rested on his sword and then, before Shiz came to his senses, used his sword to hack off the head of Shiz. Thus were the Jaredites annihilated.

References: Ether 6:51-105.

SHULE—Jaredite King (Ether)

Shule, son of Kib, was born in captivity under the rule of his older brother, Corihor. When he grew to be a strong, intelligent young man, he was angry with his brother for holding their father in captivity.

Shule set about preparing swords for his followers. When ready, he led his army against his brother and restored the kingdom to his father. In turn, Kib returned the kingdom to his son Shule when he was too old to rule.

Shule reigned in righteousness and prosperity. When his brother, Corihor, repented of his envy, Shule forgave him and gave him a position of power in the kingdom.

Later Noah, son of Corihor, rebelled against Shule. He battled Shule for the kingdom, taking half, then later the remainder, and placing Shule in captivity in Moron. Before Noah could execute Shule, Shule's sons killed Noah and rescued their father. For a while Shule and the son of Noah reigned jointly, Cohor having half the kingdom and Shule the remainder.

Cohor gathered his people to unite the kingdom under his own rule, but was slain. Nimrod, son of Cohor, turned the half-kingdom back to Shule. The kingdom was united at last. Nimrod was rewarded with freedom in the land.

When prophets came among the people to prophesy of the curse that would come if they did not repent, the Jaredites began to persecute them. Shule administered justice so that the prophets could work unhindered.

After Shule became too old to reign, he turned the kingdom over to his son Omer.

References: Ether 1:6; 3:44-67.

SHURR—Valley

Shurr was a valley in the land of Jaredites, located near the hill Comnor.

Coriantumr pitched the tents of his army there when he went to war with Shiz, the rebel. Three times battles raged before Coriantumr

was so deeply wounded and so many soldiers from both armies slain that the war was temporarily halted.
References: Ether 6:65-71.

SIDOM—Land

Sidom lay near Ammonihah and Zarahemla. It was inhabited by dissenters from the Nephites.

After Alma and Amulek were released from prison in Ammonihah, they went to Sidom. There these Nephite preachers found the exiles from Ammonihah, including Zeezrom, the lawyer. Alma healed Zeezrom of illness due to guilt. Zeezrom was baptized and the church established among the inhabitants.

Sanctuaries were built in Sidom for the worship of God before the altar.
References: Alma 10:86-110.

SIDON—River

The river Sidon flowed swiftly by the land of Zarahemla as its east border then out to sea. Dissenters often crossed to the east of Sidon to establish apostate colonies and gather Lamanites to battle the Nephites.

The river carried away the bodies of Lamanites who died aiding the Amalekites.

Sidon was also a site of baptisms of converts.

Gideon was built on the east of the Sidon from Zarahemla. Melek lay west of Sidon near Zarahemla. Sidon separated the Lamanite wilderness from Manti, a Nephite land. The hill

Riplah was not far from the Sidon on the east.

Near Riplah and Manti, Moroni, with the help of Lehi, surrounded Lamanite forces led by Zoramite dissenters. The Zoramites were soundly defeated and peace established temporarily among the Nephites. Again the dead from this battle were cast into the rushing waters of the Sidon.

Later, Moroni built fortifications along the Sidon to further protect the Nephites from Lamanite invasions. The city of Nephihah was built at the head of river Sidon.

The last war of the Nephites that led to their ultimate annihilation began beside the Sidon.

References: Alma 1:70-71, 84-86, 91-101; 2:4-5; 4:7-8; 6:4-5; 11:8-12; 13:68-69; 20:25-59, 97; 21:168; 22:11-12; 26:28; Mormon 1:10.

SILK—Cloth

Silk is produced by larvae, a worm-like stage, of some moths as they construct cocoons preparatory to the pupa sleeping stage. Cocoons are boiled to kill the pupae, then carefully unwound. The long thin strands are twisted together to form fine strong threads. When the threads are woven together, a light, filmy cloth is produced.

Both Lehites and Jaredites were able to produce fine silk. When the peoples prospered enough to produce silk, they made fine garments. Those who could afford these precious things often suffered from pride which led to wickedness then failure in progress until repentance removed pride.

In his vision of the great and abominable church, Nephi, son of Lehi, saw much silk. It was interpreted to be the desires of the great and abominable church, a sign by which it would be known.

References: I Nephi 3:142-144; Alma 1:43-44; 2:8-21; Ether 4:18-19, 73.

SILVER—Metal

Silver, an element, does not combine easily with oxygen. It tarnishes, turning black when in contact with sulfur, but it is easily cleaned. Silver presents a durable, shiny, metallic-white surface. It is easily shaped into ornaments and drawn into fine wires.

Silver was mined by Jaredites and Lehites for coins and ornaments. Accumulation of silver during periods of prosperity often caused the more affluent to persecute those less prosperous. Jealousy and strife led to wars until the people were brought to repentance by disaster that inevitably followed.

Lehi left his silver behind in Jerusalem. Loss of these riches caused eternal bitterness between the Lamanites and the Nephites. The silver was gathered and taken to Laban in an unsuccessful attempt to purchase the records of the Lehites.

In a vision of the great and abominable church, Nephi, son of Lehi, saw silver in abundance. The angel interpreted this to be the desire of the great and abominable church.

Isaiah predicted that the New World would have silver in abundance. In the latter days, he prophesied that men would bury their idols of silver and try to hide from calamity in caves. He also prophesied that the Medes would be chosen to overthrow Babylon because they did not seek to accumulate silver.

King Benjamin reminded his people that he had not taken wages of silver for his many years of service to the Nephites and so should they serve one another.

King Noah, apostate king of Nephites in Nephi, taxed the citizens in the land to adorn buildings he had built and to support his household of wives, concubines, priests, and their wives and concubines.

Amulek, second witness and friend of Alma, gave up all his precious things to serve the Lord and was greatly blessed because of it.

Jesus quotes Malachi in parable of the refiner of precious metals to remind them of his chastening the people in order to keep them in the path of righteousness. He prophesied that by the fourth generation the Nephites would again turn to silver for comfort and power. And so it was.

References: I Nephi 1:29, 38-41, 75-90; 3:142-144; 5:217; II Nephi 4:21; 8:23-24, 36-37 (Isaiah 2:7, 20-21); 10:17 (Isaiah 13:17); Jacob 1:15-17; 2:14; Jarom 1:19; Mosiah 1:43; 2:32; 7:6-12; 9:88-90; 10:15; Alma 1:43-44; 2:8-10; 8:52-70; 10:107; 12:22-25; 16:100; Helaman 2:128-130; 2:157-158; 3:22, 23; 4:48-55; 5:37-39; III Nephi 3:2-3; 11:6 (Malachi 3:3); 13:9; IV Nephi 1:55; Ether 4:18-19, 71.

SINAI—Old World Mountain

Sinai, Horeb, is a mountain in the Sinai peninsula. Scholars disagree concerning its location.

Much of Moses' religious life centered around Mount Sinai. It was there that he first met God after being attracted to the mountain by a burning bush. He was taught there concerning his responsibilities to the Israelite nation. Later he brought the Israelites there after securing their release from the clutches of Pharaoh of Egypt. God met him and gave him the ten commandments in a forty-day period of separation and communion.

References: Mosiah 7:93-95, 106; Exodus 3:12; 19:1 - Numbers 10:11.

SINIM—Old World Land

Some authorities agree that Sinim refers to China by its referral in early writings by the name Sinae or Tain, a dynasty of 255 B.C.

Isaiah prophesied that people from Sinim would join Israel in the latter days of the gathering of the Jews.

References: I Nephi 6:42; Isaiah 49:12.

SIRON—Land

Siron, a land of the Lamanites, bordered the land of the Zoramites. When Alma took his sons with him to preach to the apostate Zoramites, Corianton was beguiled by the harlot Isabel and followed her to Siron.

References: Alma 19:5.

SLAVES

In Jerusalem, slaves were people owned as chattel by masters. The masters had power of life and death over their slaves. They were traded and sold like oxen at the market—men for their strength, women for their beauty and skills.

Slaves were obtained by capture in battle, purchase at the market, birth from other slaves, restitution of stolen property from a thief who could not pay for goods he had been caught stealing, default on bad debts, self-sale to avoid poverty, and abduction. Only abduction, kidnapping, and sale into slavery by parents and kidnappers were considered criminal offenses.

Most forms of slavery were temporary, ending in the seventh year or the year of jubilee. At that time the slave was given the choice of freedom or permanent slavery.

Lehi took no slaves with him to the New World except Zoram, the servant of Laban. Even he was considered a free man. Only the Lamanites desired and kept slaves.

King Benjamin reminded the Nephites that they had not to that time (about 130 B.C.) taken slaves.

Later, King Limhi decided that he and his Nephite followers at Nephi would rather be slaves to their own brothers in Zarahemla than serve the Lamanites any longer. Plans were made for their escape which proved successful.

Ammon, son of Mosiah, gathered the Lamanites who were converted to righteousness out of the land of the father of Lamoni and took them to Zarahemla because they preferred being slaves to the Nephites rather than the Amalekite dissenters.

Neither of these groups were accepted as slaves by the Nephites but were given land and freedom as brothers.

As time passed, Moroni became a valiant war chief because of his love of freedom and abhorrence of slavery.

In about A.D. 16 Giddianhi, the chief of the band of robbers, in a letter to Lachoneus, offered to take the righteous Nephites in peace as brothers, not slaves. Lachoneus recognized this as a lie and refused.

References: Mosiah 1:44; 5:21-22; Alma 15:9, 10; 21:132; III Nephi 2:5-8.

SLING—*Weapon*

A sling consisted of a strap with a hollow, wider patch of leather in the center. A stone was held in the patch. The two ends of the strap were held in one hand, one end between the thumb and index finger, the other between the index and middle fingers. The sling was whirred rapidly above the head of the warrior. When the strap held by the thumb was released, the stone flew in a straight line toward the intended target. Extra stones were carried in a leather pouch on the belt of the marksman.

This weapon was used in ancient times primarily by shepherds to guard sheep. The Israelite army used slingsmen, mainly of the tribe of Benjamin, in their wars.

The men who returned with Zeniff to Nephi were armed with slings to stop the invasions of the Lamanites. They found the Lamanites likewise armed.

The sons of Mosiah took little with them when they went to convert the Lamanites except slings to obtain food.

Using his sling, Ammon, one of the sons of Mosiah, was able to drive off the enemies of the shepherds of King Lamoni; thus the way was opened for him to minister to the Lamanite king and to convert him to righteousness.

Slings were not mentioned as a weapon of the Jaredites.

References: I Nephi 5:19-20, 28; Mosiah 6:19, 37-38; Alma 1:64-67, 103; 12:10-13, 52-89; 20:23; 21:172.

SNARES

Small traps or snares were used to catch animals. They were made of leather, metal, or rope set with a trigger of some kind. Animals were drawn to the snare by some kind of tempting bait. The animal would overlook the camouflaged trap as it concentrated on the prize offered.

Jaredites used snares to catch birds to bring to the New World. These were probably the net type meant to capture but not kill the animal.

Christ offered miracles of healing and methods of obtaining peace to the multitudes in Jerusalem while he taught there. Isaiah saw this as a snare to the inhabitants of Jerusalem.

Nephi warned his people not to lay traps or snares of words for those who tried to convince them to repent.

In spite of this warning, Alma was caught by a snare laid by King Noah who baited the trap with easy living and promises of riches if Alma would preach what King Noah wanted to hear. It took Abinadi the prophet to remove the bands of the snare from Alma's heart.

Often the unrepentant would try to ask evangelists questions designed so that any answer could be twisted to be used against the minister. The Lord provided a vision of the snare laid and an exit so that the true men of faith were not ensnared.

References: II Nephi 9:52 (Isaiah 8:14); 11:157; Mosiah 11:9; Alma 8:26; 9:8; 25:59; 26:52; Helaman 2:26; Ether 1:23.

SODOM—Old World City

Sodom was one of five cities located on the southern tip of the Dead Sea. Lot, the nephew of Abraham, was attracted to this area by the abundance of water and luxurious pasture for his cattle. He was given this land for an everlasting inheritance.

Later the inhabitants of Sodom and Gomorrah in particular had reached such depths of sin because of pride that their sins became infamous. They sank to such measures as sexually attacking any traveler who dared enter their city. God overthrew this city and its sister cities with fire and brimstone (sulfur), after removing Lot and his daughters, and buried the inhabitants so that this form of perversion would be hid for a time from the curiosity of men.

Both Jerusalem and Babylon were described by Isaiah to be subject to the same sins as Sodom. God promised that as complete a devastation would come upon Babylon and Jerusalem would not escape.

References: II Nephi 8:46-47 (Isaiah 3:8, 9); 10:19.

SOLOMON—King of Israel (Old Testament)

Solomon was the third king of Israel, following David to the throne. Most of the inheritance of the tribes of Israel in Canaan was conquered under Saul and David. The task of establishing the kingdom in peace and building a temple to replace the worn tabernacle of Moses was left to Solomon. He received wisdom as a gift of the Spirit, which he used to establish the throne of David in the land. His fame for wisdom spread to the whole civilized world, even to the queen of Sheba (Ethiopia), who came to learn from him.

To gain Solomon's favor, many rulers sent him gifts, among them young maidens to serve as wives or concubines and to establish political ties with the Israelite kingdom. Solomon accepted all these gifts in his pride until he had brides by the hundreds. This brought foreign influence and paganism into the palace. Such a great household placed formidable financial burdens on the people for their support. Also, to keep the many wives from battling among themselves, special homes had to be built to keep them and their eunuch guards.

When the Lehites separated into the divisions of Lamanites and Nephites, Nephi, son of Lehi, had the Nephites build a replica of the temple of Solomon in the New World.

Jacob recorded that the Nephites in their prosperity began to take many wives and concubines, using Solomon's acts as an excuse. Jacob reminded the people that this was considered an abomination to the Lord and they must cease. They forgot that Solomon was driven to mental collapse by his many brides.

In repeating the Sermon on the Mount to the multitude in the New World, Christ compared the lilies of the field to the apparel of Solomon, giving preference to the lilies.

References: II Nephi 4:22-25; Jacob 1:15; 2:32-33; III Nephi 6:6-7; I Kings 2 - 11; Ecclesiastes.

SONS OF ALMA

Unlike Alma, the sons of Alma did not rebel. They accepted their missions to serve in the priesthood. Only Corianton fell from grace, and he repented. All three were renowned for their diligence to preach and minister to the people in righteousness and spent their lives in faithful service to God, not only in restoring the church to its strength but by reaching out to convert the Lamanites to righteousness. None sought to take over the kingdom after their father so a judgeship was established among the Nephites instead.

See also the articles on *Helaman*, *Shiblon*, and *Corianton*.

References: Mosiah 11:152-176; 203-207; 13:3-6; Alma 12:1-28; 13:1-82; 14:1-12, 78; 15:5-36; 16:83, 112; 17:5; 21:185.

SONS OF PAHORAN

When Pahoran, the chief judge of the Nephites, died, his sons all sought to follow him as judge. When the election was held among the Nephites, Pahoran was elected. Pacumeni withdrew his claim but Paanchi took his followers and began to revolt. Paanchi was captured and executed. Kiskumen, leader of the secret society, in anger slew Pahoran so that Pacumeni at last was made judge. He was able to retain control of the people for many years.

See also *Pahoran*, *Paanchi*, and *Pacumeni* for more details.

References: Helaman 1:2-13.

SPEARS—Weapons

Spears consisted of a shaft of wood which had a pointed blade attached to one end. The blade was made of stone or metal. Spears were used either by thrusting or throwing to obtain food or in defense.

Spears are mentioned as weapons taken to obtain food along the way by the sons of Mosiah as they went to convert the Lamanites.

Nephi quotes Isaiah's prophecy that after Christ comes to reign, spears will be reshaped into pruning hooks since they will no longer be needed for war.

References: II Nephi 8:20; Isaiah 2:4; Alma 12:10-13.

STAR

Five major classes of heavenly bodies are visible to the naked eye; planets, satellites, comets, stars, and nebulae. The sun is a star. The rest of the stars shine constantly but are hidden by day by the radiance of the sun. Light from a full moon obscures the light of the stars behind it but not the light of the sun. Most comets are visible only through telescopes but may have the brightness of the moon at times. Stars shine through the tail of most comets even when they are close to the earth. Nebulae are frail curtains of stardust.

When describing the glory of Christ upon his return, Nephi likened his brightness to the sun. The twelve apostles of Christ had brightness greater than stars.

In a description of the fall of Babylon and the great and abominable church, Isaiah speaks of a time when the light from the stars, moon, and sun will be blotted out by a darkness too thick to penetrate.

Lucifer was condemned because, through pride, he vowed to raise himself above the apostles or stars of God.

Five years before the birth of Christ, Samuel

the Lamanite prophet came to the Nephites to prophesy of Christ's coming. He spoke of a new star to arise to be the sign of Christ's birth. It was to have brightness equal to the sun for one night, then shrink in brightness. At the death of Christ, a darkness would arise to obscure the brightness of the sun, moon, and stars so that no light could shine for three days.

Nephi records that in accordance with Samuel's prophecy, a new star did appear on schedule. But skeptics debated the issue so that few were converted by it. Also according to the word of Samuel, the three days of thick darkness were caused by dust and ashes rising from the aftermath of a cataclysm of earthquake, storm, and volcano that changed the entire face of the land, burning, sinking, and burying a great many cities in the New World. The darkness was thick enough to be felt and not even a candle could be lit in it.

References: I Nephi 1:8-10; II Nephi 10:10, 35-36 (Isaiah 13:10; 14:13-14); Helaman 5:59, 75-76; III Nephi 1:24; 4:18-21.

STEEL—*Metal*

Steel is produced by mixing molten iron with other metals. When shined and tempered it becomes malleable and strong. It was prepared in Jerusalem for making armor. Nephi was familiar with its preparation and use. He recognized that the sword of Laban was made of fine steel and used it as a pattern for more swords for the defense of the Nephites. He also had a bow of fine flexible steel which broke on the journey out of Jerusalem.

Jarom, son of Lehi, used steel in the production of farm tools for the Nephites.

Jaredites used steel also. Shule, in rebellion against King Coriantumr, fashioned steel swords for his army. These steel blades were used for many wars.

References: I Nephi 1:109; 5:22; II Nephi 4:21; Jarom 1:19; Ether 3:46.

STONES OF THE BROTHER OF JARED

The Lord told the brother of Jared that the vessels he was building to carry the Jaredites across the ocean would have to be sealed to travel under water. Because of this there could be no windows nor fires for light. (Fires lit in a closed room produce poisonous carbon monoxide gas.) From this the brother of Jared knew that there would be no light for the long journey. He went to a high mountain and found minerals from which he prepared stones—round, smooth, colorless, and clear. He took these stones to God and asked God to touch them so that they might glow and provide light for the journey.

God did as the faithful brother of Jared requested. The stones were taken to the eight waiting vessels where two were placed in each boat, one on each end. They provided light for almost a year.

References: Ether 1:53-68; 3:1-3, 12, 13.

SUN

The sun is the star nearest the earth. It sheds its light so strongly that when one is in the light of it, all other light seems not to shine. The light of the moon and stars is hidden in its brightness. Only in the shadows of solid structures is the light dimmed, but even there the sun bends its rays and dances around to prevent total darkness. At night the whole earth stands between us and the sun, so the stars and moon shed their glories. Only then, when men hide behind solid walls, does darkness descend.

The rays of the sun give color to environment. At the end of a storm the sun penetrates to paint a rainbow to remind men of the love God has for them in his promise never to flood the earth again as in the days of Noah.

Plants take bits of sunlight and prepare fruit in its season. Their blossoms and leaves produce brilliant colors in variety to teach men beauty.

Nephi, son of Lehi, describes the luster of Christ as of the sun from whose rays none are completely hidden. Only by men's efforts can one be hidden from the light of the sun. So likewise can man through his own efforts hide himself from the Son. The heat and light from the sun will not harm the righteous; neither shall knowledge, or light, from the Son.

There will be a day, according to Isaiah,

when the light of the sun shall be darkened in Babylon and knowledge of the Son shall fail in the great and abominable church before it falls.

In describing the power of God, Mormon, the abridger of the records of Nephi, interjects a comment into the words of Helaman. Mormon tells that God has power to stop the spinning of the earth and turn it backward so that the sun appears to stand still. Thus the astronomical knowledge of the ancients is demonstrated as well as the power of God.

Samuel, the Lamanite prophet, told the Nephites that there would be a day and night and day as one day because a star equal in brightness to the sun would appear to signal the day of the birth of Christ. In just five years from the giving of that prophecy, such a star did appear, but its brightness did not outshine the rising of the sun so the Nephites in the New World did know of the coming of the second day.

Samuel predicted the sign of Christ's crucifixion to be three days of total darkness. Light from the sun was completely absorbed by a thick layer of ash and dust so that not even a candle could be lit for those three days following the three hours of destruction of the face of the New World by earthquake, wind, and fire.

Christ gives as the law of sunshine that the

sun must shed its light on the evil and the good.

In the last days of the Nephites, their destruction by the Lamanites is described as complete as the dew's evaporation by the sun.

References: I Nephi 1:8; 6:40 (Isaiah 49:10); II Nephi 10:10 (Isaiah 13:10); Alma 16:166; Helaman 4:62; 5:56-58, 75-78; III Nephi 1:16-23; 4:18-21; 5:90-91; Mormon 2:20; Ether 5:2-4.

SWINE—*Animals*

Swine or pigs are animals that have cloven hoofs but do not ruminate or chew cud. They eat both flesh and vegetables. Because of their habit of eating flesh even to cannibalism, eating of their own offspring, their bodies harbor many disease organisms that cannot be killed even by thorough cooking or curing. Because of this, the Jews were forbidden to eat swine. When they saw gentiles eat the flesh of swine, they loathed both the gentiles and their swine. The gentiles harbored swine because they reproduce rapidly and convert 80 percent of their food into meat.

Swine have very poor cooling systems. To keep from overheating, they like to cover themselves with mud and dust by wallowing in mire.

The Jaredites, who left the Old World before the law concerning meats was given, brought swine with them. When the Jaredites annihilated themselves in a civil war, the swine ran free. They were not gathered and domesticated by the Mulekites or Lehites because these people were Jews. The swine continued to live in the wild and are still hunted by southerners.

Christ, knowing the attitude the Jews exhibited toward swine, told the remnant who heard him in the New World not to cast their pearls before swine.

References: III Nephi 3:43; 6:18; Ether 4:20.

SWORD—Flaming

When Adam and Eve were evicted from the Garden of Eden for eating from the tree of knowledge, God placed cherubims and a flaming sword on the east of Eden to prevent their reentry. God knew that if they ate also of the tree of life they would have no chance to repent.

The exact nature of the flaming sword is not known but it was formidable enough an obstacle to perform its function.

References: Alma 9:35-46; 19:82-87; Genesis 3:31.

SWORD—Isaiah's Words

Isaiah referred to his mouth as a sharp sword. Through Isaiah's prophecies, many nations had a foreknowledge of their destruction, but they did not heed his warning.

References: I Nephi 6:31-33; Isaiah 49:1-3.

SWORD OF JUSTICE

The sword of justice, wrath, or vengeance was predicted to fall upon the heads of those peoples who sought to destroy the saints. In each case, such people were annihilated by an invading army, a civil uprising, or a natural calamity.

Isaiah foretells of civil conflicts that would lead to the annihilation of the great and abominable church.

Amulek called the citizens of Ammonihah to repent lest the sword of justice fall upon them. Since they refused to repent, the Lamanites at last did come and put the whole town to sword and destruction.

In his confession, Alma considered why the sword of justice did not fall upon him and his companions because of their acts to destroy the church headed by his father Alma.

In an epistle to Ammoron, leader of the invading Lamanite forces, Moroni, chief of the Nephite army, warned Ammoron of the sword of justice that was about to fall upon him if he did not repent. He refused and the Lamanites suffered terrible defeat.

Samuel, the Lamanite, prophesied to the Nephites that the sword of justice hung over them and would fall upon them in four hundred years after the coming of Christ to the New World. Just as Samuel predicted, the Nephites were eradicated by the Lamanites by that time because of the abominable conditions they had fallen to by pride.

Jesus himself told the Nephites of the sword of justice that would fall upon them in four hundred years. He also gave warning to the gentiles of later times that if they refuse to

355

repent, they will be destroyed.

Mormon reminded the people again of the sword of justice that was falling round them because of their secret combinations and abominations.

Moroni, the last prophet of the Nephites, reminded men again of the sword of justice set to fall upon those who join secret combinations to commit evil and those who allow such secret societies to exist.

References: I Nephi 7:26-27; Alma 8:32-34; 14:99; 25:6-8; Helaman 5:6-7; III Nephi 9:56; 13:57; Mormon 4:56; Ether 3:97.

SWORD OF LABAN

Nephi and his brothers were sent by their father, Lehi, to obtain the records of their tribe. After several unsuccessful attempts, Nephi went alone. He found Laban drunk upon the ground and was commanded by God to slay him to obtain the much needed records, since Laban refused to yield them up voluntarily. Nephi reluctantly took Laban's sword and cut off his head. The sword was of such fine workmanship that Nephi took it with him when he returned with the records to his father.

Nephi carried the sword to the New World. When his father died, Nephi was forced to separate himself and his family from his rebellious brothers. He used the sword of Laban as a model from which he prepared other swords for arming his followers for protection from his brothers. He wielded the sword of

Laban himself against the invading Lamanites who sought to destroy Nephi and his people.

King Benjamin obtained the sword of Laban along with the records and other treasures of the Nephites. He, too, fought off Lamanites with it in defense of the Nephites. When he became too old, he committed the care of the sword, records, and other treasures to Mosiah, his son.

The sword of Laban remained in the treasury handed down with the records from generation to generation until they were buried by Ammoron about A.D. 321. Mormon, the recorder, later dug them up as commanded by Ammoron. He later reburied them in the hill Cumorah, entrusting knowledge of the hiding place to his son Moroni.

Moroni took only Mormon's abridgment and the Urim and Thummim from Cumorah. Nevertheless, the sword has been seen by early witnesses to the record of the Lehites.

References: I Nephi 1:107-124; II Nephi 4:19; Jacob 1:10; Words of Mormon 1:20; Mosiah 1:23-24; Church History, Volume 1.

SWORDS TO PLOWSHARES

Isaiah recorded that in the last days when Christ reigns and peace is established firmly upon the earth, the swords, or weapons of war, shall be beaten or remolded into plowshares, or tools of agriculture and productivity.

References: II Nephi 8:20; Isaiah 2:4.

SWORD OF SCATTERING

Jews were warned that the sword of Babylon would come to scatter them from out of Jerusalem. And so it came upon Jerusalem shortly after Lehi took his family away. They were to continue to suffer for many generations because of their refusal to repent when Christ was sent to them.

Zion was scattered as was Jerusalem because of her pride. In 1838 Missourians drove out the Saints from the center place in Independence, Missouri. Again in 1846 they were driven and scattered from Nauvoo, Illinois. By this time polygamy had entered the congregations.

Babylon would have the same destruction fall suddenly upon it. The empire was overthrown by Persians by 275 B.C. The great and abominable church led by Satan is to undergo a similar fate.

References: I Nephi 1:12; II Nephi 5:104-105 (Isaiah 51:19); 8:63 (Isaiah 3:25); 10:15 (Isaiah 13:15), 41 (Isaiah 14:19).

SWORD—Weapon

The sword is the most frequently mentioned weapon in the record of the Jews and the record of the Lehites. It is a long thin piece of iron or steel which is sharpened to a cutting edge along one or both of its sides. It is usually drawn to a point and the other end fixed in a handle or hilt. In order to prevent accidents to the carrier, the blade or sharpened end is carried enclosed in a sheath. The hilt and sheath are decorated, often with gold and jewels, to show the owner's wealth.

Swords were made and used in war by the Nephites, Lamanites, Mulekites, Jaredites, and various other groups of dissenters. Only the Anti-Nephi-Lehies refused to use them, even in their own defense. The Nephites fashioned their swords after the model of the sword of Laban.

References: Omni 1:15, 29; Mosiah 6:19-21, 37; Alma 1:14, 18, 53, 65-67; 12:56-61, 160-163; 14:49-53; 15:32-34; 16:82; 20:20, 23, 78, 84-86, 91-92; 21:135-139; 22:23, 27; 23:23-24; 26:60-61, 86-90, 98, 165; 27:14-22, 28, 41, 47-50, 50, 56; 28:16; Helaman 1:15; 4:4-6, 17; III Nephi 1:57; 2:9-10; Mormon 3:16-17; Ether 3:46; 6:19, 38, 60, 72-73, 93-95, 101-104; Moroni 9:2.

SYCAMORES—Plants

The sycamore or sycamore-fig, is an evergreen tree bearing edible fruit. It grows to forty feet tall and its broad leaves provide shade as well as figs. Many prophets were known to sit under sycamores when prophesying in public. It bears wood similar to the cedars but is less durable and duller of finish. It was used as an imitation of cedar.

Isaiah in his prophecy says in replacing sycamore with cedar that a near imitation of true doctrine will be altered to the real doctrine of Christ when the time comes for Christ to reestablish his church on earth.

References: II Nephi 9:70; Isaiah 9:10.

SYNAGOGUES—Buildings

Synagogues were places of worship built by the Jews. The Nephites built them as a place for prayer, study, preaching, and giving of alms much like the gentile church buildings. Lamanites built them when the Nephites came to preach and teach among them.

Zoramites excluded the poor from their synagogues as unworthy because of their lack of fine clothes. They came only once a week to the high stand, or Rameumpton, built in the center. They thanked God for making them righteous. Their synagogues were not used for preaching or study.

The Amalekites used them for a center of debate. They apostasized their worship to omit revelation and looking forward to the coming of Christ.

Synagogues were built in every city by migrants to the land northward. Ruins, called kivas by those who lost knowledge of their proper usage as the centuries passed, of synagogues still stand.

Christ told the people that none were to be excluded from entering synagogues. The unrepentant should be gathered there and taught humility and truth until they were ready to rejoin the righteous.

In the last days of the Nephites, Mormon taught the people in their synagogues the true gospel, but still they refused to repent.

Today a synagogue is the center of Jewish life, having places for study, worship, debate, and general sharing. It is to be entered swiftly but left slowly as often as possible.

Synagogues were not known among the Jaredites because they were not Jews.

References: II Nephi 11:100; Alma 11:22; 13:5, 6, 21, 24; 14:2, 113; 16:88, 89, 121-135, 176; Helaman 2:9, 13; III Nephi 5:94, 97; 8:64; Moroni 7:1.

SYRIA—*Old World Land*

Syria was a short-lived empire from 312 to 128 B.C. The land lies south of Turkey and northeast of Lebanon.

Isaiah told Ahaz not to fear Rezin and his Syrian forces. They were defeated by Tiglath-pileser III about 732 B.C. Later Syria was to rise up and devour Israel. This occurred in 198 B.C. under Antiochus III.

References: II Nephi 9:14-21, 71-72; Isaiah 7:1-8; 9:12.

T

TABEAL—*Usurper (Old Testament)*

An alliance was formed by Syria, Ephraim, and Samaria against Israel under Ahaz. The intent was to overthrow Israel and place the son of Tabeal, or Tabeel, on the throne, who would be more willing to join the alliance.

Ahaz was forewarned of this move by Isaiah and told not to concern himself with the problem. God had plans to take care of the situation himself.

The exact identification of Tabeal or his son is unclear.

References: II Nephi 9:18-20; Isaiah 7:5-7.

TABERNACLE—*Building*

The first tabernacle was built according to

instructions given to Moses by God as the Israelites journeyed from Egypt to the promised land of Canaan. It consisted of a set of portable tents, each having a particular function. A portable fence was also constructed to set around it. There Moses met and talked with God as he came in a pillar of cloud or fire. In the tabernacle were kept the sacred laws and instruments to perform sacrifices. It was still used in David's time, until the temple of Solomon replaced it.

Mosiah, son of Benjamin, foretold the coming of God, referring to the flesh he would put on as a tabernacle of clay.

Alma referred to the flesh of God for his coming to earth as his mortal tabernacle.

Moroni tells us our bodies also are to be tabernacles.

References: II Nephi 8:70 (Isaiah 4:6); Mosiah 1:97-99; Alma 5:15; Moroni 9:6.

TABRET—Musical Instrument

The tabret or timbrel is similar to the tambourine. It is a flat, drumhead-like surface made to be held in one hand while it is struck in rhythm with the other. It was used to accompany singers and dancers in times of joy and gladness in triumphal pageants.

Isaiah warns men not to spend their days in frolic and gladness, forgetting to worship the Lord.

References: II Nephi 8:81-82; Isaiah 5:11-12.

TARSHISH—Old World City

Tarshish was a land rich in metals and ores. It was probably situated on Spain's western shore bordering the Mediterranean Sea. Phoenecians inhabited it and carried ore in ships, huge for that day, great distances for trade or sale. Tarshish ships were well known for swiftness and durability on long voyages.

Isaiah, in describing the catastrophe to come upon the proud and lofty, warns that even the rich merchants of the sea shall be brought low.

References: II Nephi 8:32; Isaiah 2:16.

TEANCUM—War Chief (c. 68 B.C.)

Teancum was second in command to Moroni and in equal command with Lehi. He led a battalion of Nephites. His first assignment was to head off the fleeing dissenters of Morianton. He was forced to slay Morianton in battle and to defeat the army to effect their surrender.

His next assignment was to aid in the defense of the Nephites against a Lamanite invasion led by Amalickiah, a dissenter who wanted to be king of the New World. To effect the demoralization of Amalickiah's troops, Teancum stole in to his tent and thrust a javelin into his heart, then crept back to his camp.

This strategy caused the Lamanites to give up their advance and begin a retreat. The brother of Amalickiah, Ammoron, took command of the Lamanites. He ordered the soldiers to defend what cities were already under Lamanite control.

Teancum received orders from Moroni to hold as many Lamanite prisoners as possible as ransom for a prisoner exchange. He was to prevent the Lamanites from further expansion of captured territory as well.

After holding his position successfully and strengthening it, Teancum received more troops and instructions to recapture Mulek. After several unsuccessful attempts, Teancum tried a decoy strategem which proved successful.

The prisoners taken in this battle were forced to rebuild and strengthen fortifications in the land Bountiful.

Teancum, tired after eight years of constant battle to drive out the stubborn Lamanites, decided that he would try to end the conflict by slaying Ammoron as he had Amalickiah. Though he was able to get to and slay Ammoron, he was not quick enough to prevent Ammoron from crying out. Ammoron's aroused guards chased Teancum and slew him.

Ammoron's slaying effected the routing of the Lamanites. The slaying of Teancum added to the fury of the Nephites. The Lamanites were driven from the land of the Nephites.

References: Alma 22:36-37; 23:35-44; 24:1-62; 28:20-26; 29:3, 14-15, 36-48.

TEANCUM—City

Teancum was a city built and inhabited by the Nephites. It was near the seashore and the land Desolation. The inhabitants of Desolation were driven from their homes by an invasion of Lamanites. The homeless Nephites went to Teancum to stay with their neighbors.

Together, citizens of Teancum and Desolation were able to repulse the first thrust of the Lamanites against Teancum. They boasted in their own strength and retook Desolation.

In the next sweep, the Lamanites, in a horrible battle, retook both Desolation and Teancum and sacrificed the survivors among the Nephites to their gods.

In revenge, the Nephites beat back the Lamanites in the last battle in which they would be successful. Afterward, the Nephites suffered continual defeat.

References: Mormon 2:3-20.

TEIL-TREE—Plant

The teil-tree is a linden tree. It is a tall deciduous shade tree bearing fragrant blossoms that attract bees. The bark is gray or brown, smooth on small trunks and deeply rutted on thicker ones. The inner bark is tough and stringy and used in making cords, mats, baskets, and even paper.

Isaiah compared the inhabitants of Jerusalem to the leaves of the teil-tree. The leaves are shed but the tree retains its life. So Jerusalem would shed its inhabitants but a tenth would maintain the lifeblood and holy seed in the city.

References: II Nephi 9:13; Isaiah 6:13.

TEMPLE—Building

The temple was the center of high worship. There the law of sacrifices was kept. There the high priesthood met with God for instruction, revelation, and prophecy. The first temple was built by Solomon according to plans given for the tabernacle of Moses by command of God.

Solomon's temple consisted of a porch where the people could come, a holy place where the priesthood could come, and a holy of holies in which the ark and eternal flame rested where only the prophets and seers could come to speak with God. Between the holy of holies and holy place was a curtain from the high ceiling to the floor. Around three sides of the temple were storage chambers for the various instruments of sacrifice.

Among the first buildings constructed by the Nephites was a replica of Solomon's temple. Not having all the materials available to them, they made substitutions for some of the materials used in its construction. The floor plan was the same as that used in Solomon's temple.

Isaiah recorded his vision of the Lord coming to his temple. It was there that Isaiah was called to be a prophet.

Jacob, brother of Nephi, claimed to have been ordained in the temple built under the direction of Nephi. Later, upon instructions from God, Jacob went up to the temple to call the Nephites to repentance.

When Mosiah, father of Benjamin, led the

people out of Nephi to Zarahemla, another temple was built there. Mosiah's grandson, Mosiah, gathered the Nephites to this temple to hear his father Benjamin's last message to the people and to be made king of the Nephites.

When Zeniff took a colony back to Nephi to reinhabit that land, he was succeeded by Noah, his son, who had the first temple refurbished with ornaments of wood, copper, and brass.

Later Limhi, son of Noah, gathered the Nephites in the land of Nephi to that first temple to hear Ammon tell them of their brethren in Zarahemla.

Alma, son of Alma, declared to the citizens in Gideon that God would not dwell in unholy temples. Amulek, Alma's companion, repeated this message later to the Zoramites. When Alma and Amulek went to preach, they taught in many temples. From this it is understood that temples had been constructed in the major cities in the land.

It was said that Aminadi, at one time, interpreted writing on the wall of the temple written by the finger of God. It is assumed that this event took place in the New World, but no more circumstances are known.

The Lamanites also built temples where the sons of Mosiah went to teach.

When the Lehites moved to the land northward to colonize it, they also built temples in every major city.

When the Nephites had dwindled into an

ungodly society, God gave Nephi, son of Helaman, power to destroy their temples.

The remnant who survived the cataclysm at the time of the crucifixion of Christ gathered around the temple in the land Bountiful to mourn for their lost kin.

Christ quoted Malachi in reporting that in the last day he would come suddenly to a temple built to receive him.

The Jaredites, not being Jews, did not construct temples in their lands.

References: II Nephi 4:22-25; 9:1 (Isaiah 6:1); Jacob 1:15-17; 2:2-3, 13; Mosiah 1:27-35, 80-82; 5:25; 7:13-16; 9:78; Alma 5:36-37; 8:1-2; 11:22; 14:1-6, 113; 16:235-236; Helaman 2:9, 13, 59-60; 3:121; III Nephi 5:1-3; 11:4; Malachi 3:1.

TENTS

When Lehi left Jerusalem, he left his house with all its conveniences behind and took only provisions and tents with him into the wilderness. For the next eight years he and his family would live in tents as they traveled across the world to their promised land.

The tent, made of cloth or skins, could be collapsed and rolled into a bundle along with its ropes and stakes. Poles were obtained wherever the traveler stopped.

When Nephi and his brothers were sent back to Jerusalem for the plates of Laban, they took their tents with them.

Once in the New World, after Lehi died and Laman and his followers caused such conflict as to threaten the life of Nephi and his followers, Nephi took his group into the wilderness with their tents.

Thirty-one years after leaving Jerusalem, in 569 B.C., the Nephites moved out of their tents into permanent structures. The Lamanites continued to live in tents.

The Nephites kept their tents for use in travel and for special occasions as seen by their gathering to hear King Benjamin.

Zeniff led a colony out of Zarahemla to Nephi to repossess it. Those pilgrims took their tents for the sojourn. When Ammon went in search of his brethren who had returned to Nephi, the search party traveled with tents. When Alma and his converts fled from Nephi because of the army of King Noah sent to slay them, they lived in tents until they returned to Zarahemla. When Ammon and Gideon led the remainder of the inhabitants from Nephi back to Zarahemla, they had tents.

When any army went to war, the soldiers used tents for their shelter in the fields.

The people who went to the land northward to colonize it dwelt in tents until their houses could be built.

The Lamanites continued to live in tents until about 400 B.C. Some never lived in houses but remained nomadic.

In the areas where trees were hard to find, the Lamanites took their poles with them. They continually refined their tents until they had sturdy structures able to withstand the more severe weather of northern latitudes.

Jaredites also lived in tents as they journeyed out of Babel to the New World. Whenever they traveled, they took their tents along for shelter.

When Babylon was destroyed, Isaiah prophesied that even the Arabians would refuse to pitch their tents there.

In preparation for the last days, men are called upon to enlarge their tents, lengthen their ropes, and strengthen their stakes. By so doing they will draw more men under the shelter of the church.

References: I Nephi 1:29, 33, 46, 59, 67, 145, 153-155; 2:11, 36-39, 92; 3:22; 4:1; 5:6, 11, 15-21, 39, 65-67, 213; II Nephi 4:10, 11; 10:20-21 (Isaiah 13:20-21); Enos 1:31-32; Mosiah 1:33-35; 5:6; 6:7; 9:72; 10:3-4; 11:5, 69-70; Alma 1:76, 83; 13:70-71; 15:27; 21:88; 23:39; Alma 23:41; 24:1; 26:139, 150; 29:21; Helaman 2:9; III Nephi 10:10-11; Mormon 3:5; Ether 1:37; 4:4; 6:64, 65, 80, 83.

TEOMNER—War Captain (c. 63 B.C.)

In a battle during the war against the invading Lamanites led by Ammoron, Moroni, chief of the Nephites, stationed the troops of Teomner in hiding outside Manti. Moroni drew the army of the Lamanites out of the city by retreating with a small force. Teomner waited in hiding until the Lamanites had passed in hot pursuit of the fleeing army of Moroni, then sent his men against the small guard left to protect the city. In that way, Moroni was able to recover Manti for a possession for the Nephites.

References: Alma 26:138-147.

THISTLE—*Plant*

A thistle is a short, spiny plant with thorny leaves. The pastel, many-petaled flowers look like round, thick brushes. When the seeds are set, each has a downy parasol. The wind catches the seeds and scatters them before it. When the stem is broken, the wound oozes white, milky, sticky sap.

Abinadi, in prophesying the fate of Noah and his hated priests, said that the priests would be driven as the seed of a thistle on the wind. The Lamanites as well as the Nephites chased and hunted the malicious priests till all were slain. Noah was driven, then executed by some of his own followers.

In describing a false prophet, Christ compares their fruit to the figs gathered of thistles. There is no known food value or fruit around a thistle seed.

References: Mosiah 7:63; III Nephi 6:28.

THORNS—*Plants*

Thorns are spiny projections on a variety of plants. Most are useless weed plants or vines that grow in neglected gardens or orchards. They were used in Jerusalem and Palestine around vineyards and pastures for the fencing of cattle and protection from wild beasts.

Isaiah prophesied that Jerusalem would be

overgrown with thorns after its destruction. He also prophesied that in the last days armies would come from Egypt and Assyria as flies upon the thorns. His other uses of thorn are yet unclear but they probably represent the enemies of Israel in the last days.

Christ, in describing the fruit of the false prophets, compares it to grapes born of thorns of which there are none.

References: II Nephi 8:76; 9:32-38 (Isaiah 7:19-25), 78 (Isaiah 9:17), 98 (Isaiah 10:17); III Nephi 6:28.

THRONE OF GOD

All the righteous who have seen the vision of the throne of God describe God as sitting on a throne high in the heavens. His train, or servants, fill the temple and concourses of angels surround the throne in an attitude of singing and praising God. The earth acts as the footstool of God. All men will be called at judgment to stand before God and be given full knowledge of good, and the evil which they have done in comparison.

Men are warned not to swear by heaven because it is the throne of God, nor the earth which is his footstool.

References: I Nephi 1:7, 13; 5:130; II Nephi 9:1; 12:29; Jacob 2:59; Alma 17:19-20; III Nephi 5:82-83; Mormon 1:75; Moroni 9:28.

THRONE OF MEN

The throne of David represented the authority to rule Israel. It was handed down from generation to generation. The incumbent selected the next of his kin to reign at his death unless he was slain by some foe. Christ was a direct descendant of David and received his authority to rule Israel from him. Since he did not remain dead, but lives still, he has not relinquished that authority.

Satan was condemned for trying to raise his throne, or seat of authority, above the apostles, or stars, of God.

Noah, king of the Nephite colony at Nephi, in his pride had a chair built and adorned to help him proclaim his proud authority over his fellow citizens.

Moroni, war chief of the Nephites, accused Pahoran, chief judge, of sitting pompously on his Nephite throne instead of helping with his authority to support the war against the Lamanites. Pahoran replied that he was not sitting idly by but was about to be evicted by a group of rebellious men who coveted his position.

Shule, the Jaredite, had a throne in Moron. He lost it to his nephew, Noah, but regained it in a quick rescue by his sons.

Akish took the throne of the Jaredite by slaying Jared, his father-in-law.

Riplakish was reported to have had built for himself an exceedingly beautiful throne at the expense of the Jaredites. Because of his arrogance, he and his descendants were driven from the land.

Shared, by contention and battle, placed himself

on the throne of the still living Coriantumr. He was slain as he sat at court by a more ambitious foe.

References: II Nephi 9:67; 10:31, 35-36; Mosiah 7:11-12; Alma 27:20, 27, 40; Ether 3:56-57; 4:6-7, 49-50; 6:39-40, 42-43.

TIMOTHY—Disciple (c. A.D. 34)

Timothy was a brother of Nephi, son of Nephi. Because of his righteousness, the jealous Nephites stoned him to death. In the name of Jesus, Nephi raised his brother from the dead.

Later when Christ came to the remnant who survived the calamities following the time of his crucifixion in Jerusalem, Christ called twelve to be disciples, special witnesses with authority to establish his church. Timothy was selected to be one of these witnesses.

As such, Timothy taught a portion of the repentant and expectant multitude to pray. He helped in the administration of communion and their baptism.

For further information read the article, *Disciples.*

References: III Nephi 3:60; 9:4-15.

TITLE OF LIBERTY—See Flag

TOOLS

In moving the Lehites from Jerusalem to the New World, Nephi, son of Lehi, made tools from molten ore for shipbuilding. He made bellows from the skins of animals to blow the fire to sufficient heat to work steel.

Later machinery and tools were made by the Nephites for building, agriculture, and war.

Samuel, the Lamanite, prophesied in 6 B.C. that the day would come when the Nephite tools would become slippery. That is, the Nephites would lay aside a tool and later be unable to find it. In A.D. 322 this slipperiness came to the tools, weapons, and treasures of the Nephites.

The Jaredites also had tools. They listed the plow, sower, reaper, hoe, and thrasher, in addition to tools for building and war. The Jaredites also were cursed with slipperiness of tools and treasures. They became afraid to let go of their weapons for defense of their families.

See also *Ax, Bellows, Ladders, Liahona, Plowshares, Pruning Hooks,* and *Yoke.*

References: I Nephi 5:71-74, 84; Jarom 1:19-21; Helaman 5:44-46; Ether 4:74-75; 6:35.

TOWERS—*Buildings*

In Jerusalem towers were built in the vineyards to facilitate watch over the fields. The watchmen would call out if enemies approached or if beasts broke through to ravage the vines. Isaiah foretold that the day would come when these towers and watchmen would prove useless.

King Benjamin of the Nephites had a tower built near the temple so that he could speak and be heard by the gathered multitude.

King Noah, a Nephite of the city Nephi, had a tower built near the temple so that he could overlook the valley below to be forewarned of Lamanite invasions. Another was built for the same purpose in Shilom. Because of his evil ways, Gideon chased Noah up to his tower near the temple. Before Gideon could slay him, Noah cried out that a Lamanite invasion was on the way. He called the men to flee and leave their families behind to plead for mercy of the Lamanites. Later, from the same tower, Limhi, successor to Noah, saw and gave warning of another invasion.

Towers were built by Moroni in the land of Zarahemla as part of their defense. Moroni had his flag, the title of liberty, raised at every tower to encourage freedom and peace. Later towers were built in every defensed city to look over the picket fences. Dissenters were made to hoist the flag on their towers or be executed, when they surrendered after the civil war of the king-men.

Nephi, son of Helaman, got upon the tower in his garden in the city of Zarahemla to pray for his people. The citizens of the city found him there and gathered in wonder. In the last war between the Lamanites and the Nephites, the Nephites sought refuge in the tower of Sherrizah. The Lamanites overcame their defense and took them prisoners.

References: II Nephi 8:31, 71-72; Mosiah 1:35-37; 7:16-19; 9:78, 79; Alma 21:71, 123; 22:3-4; 23:23-24; Helaman 3:10-12, 15; Moroni 9:8.

TOWER OF BABEL—Old World Building

The tower of Babel, or Great Tower, was built

by the people who were descendants of Noah. They remained in one location moving down to the plains after the flood. Satan enticed them to build a tower as a means of reaching into heaven to see God.

Rather than allow the people to continue forever on this useless endeavor, God dispersed the people by confounding or changing their pure language to a variety of less pure languages.

At this tower were Jared, his brother, and their families. In fear of separation, Jared asked his brother to cry unto the Lord to keep his family and friends together. The brother of Jared prayed to God, and his desires were granted.

Then, upon the request of Jared, his brother asked God where their families were to go at the time of the dispersal. They were guided to gather the most useful animals, including fish and birds, and crop seeds to take to a new land which had been preserved for a dwelling for the righteous. If they remained faithful, they could stay, if not, they would be swept off and a new civilization sent to inherit the land.

References: Omni 1:39-40; Mosiah 12:22-23; Helaman 2:153-155; Ether 1:1-5, 7.

TRAPS

Traps were set to capture animals, alive or dead. They were baited with food to entice the animal to overcome its instinctive fear and enter an unnatural enclosure.

Amulek accused the people of Ammonihah of laying word traps to catch the messengers of God and bring them to their death. In so doing, they brought the wrath of God upon themselves.

Reference: Alma 8:26.

TRIBES

A tribe is a group of people sharing the same ancestry or belief. The twelve tribes of Israel were all the descendants from each of the twelve sons of Israel.

The tribes of the people preceding the coming of Christ to the New World included those who shared common belief and government. They were joined by kinship or friendship and bonded to common protection. Their chiefs, or rulers, were at first elected, not for their holiness, but for their prowess.

In the year A.D. 231, a division among the people came again. They were divided by belief into tribes. The tribes took one of the first family of Lehi to be their patriarch and he of greatest prowess to be their ruler. The fathers taught their children their beliefs to maintain the tribal existence through generations.

References: I Nephi 3:115; 6:36 (Isaiah 49:6); 7:7-10; II Nephi 12:68-72; III Nephi 3:37-55; 7:15-28; 8:4; 10:5; 13:41; IV Nephi 1:39-43; Mormon 1:82-83.

TRUMP—Instrument

The trump or trumpet was a long horn

made of brass or ivory with a cupped mouthpiece. It was sounded to call people together. Certain tunes called people to assemble for worship, others for instruction, others for battle.

Alma compares spokesmen of God with trumps. These spokesmen are called to gather the repentant. A second trump will gather those who refuse the spokesmen.

Christ reminded men not to sound a trumpet or call attention to their good works for the praise of men.

Mormon, the recorder, warned men that all will be called from their places after their first death by a trump for judgment.

Coriantumr, the war chief, sounded a trumpet to call his Jaredite troops to battle.

References: Mosiah 11:133-134; Alma 15:52-53; III Nephi 5:94; Mormon 4:72-74; Ether 6:66.

TUBALOTH—King (c. 51 B.C.)

Tubaloth, king of the Lamanites, sent Coriantumr at the head of his army to conquer the hated Nephites. This venture ended by a fruitless surrender of the Lamanites and a hasty retreat.

References: Helaman 1:16-18.

U

URIAH—Priest (Old Testament)

Uriah was a high priest, chosen for his faithfulness by Isaiah to act as a witness to the prophecies concerning Maher-shalal-hash-baz, who would herald the destruction of Damascus, Samaria, by Sennecherib, king of Assyria.

Later Uriah abetted in the altering of religious practices initiated by Ahaz. This may have caused his silencing before the list of priests in Chronicles was made.

References: II Nephi 9:40 (Isaiah 8:2); II Kings 16:10-16; I Chronicles 6:4-15.

URIM AND THUMMIM — Seer Stones

Urim and Thummim, or interpreters, were transparent stones set in a bow. They had the power to give a righteous prophet, who possessed them, the gift of interpretation of unknown languages, revelation, prophecy, and manifestation of secrets. If an unrighteous man, not commanded of God, should try to use the Urim and Thummim, they would be darkened at best or cause the user to die at worst. They were handed down from generation to generation. The person who possessed and properly used the Urim and Thummim was known as the seer.

Mosiah was a seer. He used the Urim and Thummim to translate the records of the Jaredites, both the stone of Coriantumr and the plates of Ether. He then passed them with the records to Alma, son of Alma.

The brother of Jared placed a set of Urim and Thummim in the box with the records given him by God, not to be opened until the hearts of men were prepared after the

coming of Christ. These records were read to the righteous generations following the coming of Christ in the New World, but were resealed when wickedness began to come among the people.
References: Mosiah 5:72-80; 12:18-21; 13:1-2; Ether 1:88-101.

UZZIAH—King of Judah (Old Testament)

Uzziah, or Azariah, followed his father, Amaziah, to the throne of Judah when he was sixteen years old. His prosperous reign lasted fifty-two years. In his last years he contracted leprosy when he took it upon himself to offer incense on the altar of God even though he was told that he had no priesthood authority to do so.

Isaiah timed one of his great prophecies in accordance with the time of the death of Uzziah. Another came later in the days of his grandson, Ahaz.
References: II Nephi 9:1 (Isaiah 6:1), 14 (Isaiah 7:1); II Chronicles 26.

V

VINEYARD

A vineyard was a plot of ground set aside for the growing of grapes. The area was fenced in with briars and thorn hedge or rock to keep out animals and intruders. The wine dressers, or workers, dug the soil and fertilized it to keep the vines growing. The vines were pruned, or branches were cut off, because the grapes grow only on new wood. As the years pass, the trunk, or main stem, of the vine grows thick like a tree.

In the middle of the vineyard, a tower was built so that the grapes could be watched after they set on and the workmen could be kept at their tasks to assure an abundant harvest. The guard also kept watch against intruders who might try to break through the fence to steal the grapes.

When the grapes turned sour or the trunks too weak to produce grapes, the vineyard was destroyed and a new one planted.

Vineyards also were places for growing olive trees or an orchard. Their keeping involved grafting of tame olive branches into the trunk of a wild olive tree. This is because the trunk of the tame olive does not have an extensive enough root system to supply nourishment to its branches for a good harvest. The olives of a wild branch are shriveled and large pitted in comparison to the tame olive. Interchanging the branches makes both trees produce better fruit.

Isaiah used the example of both grape and olive vineyards to explain what would happen to the house of Israel in its scattering and gathering. A similar parable was given by Zenos.

King Noah had a vineyard in the land of Nephi and because of it became a drunkard.

References: II Nephi 8:52 (Isaiah 3:14), 71-80 (Isaiah 5:1-10); Jacob 3:30-146; Alma 10:21-22; 15:51.

VIOL—*Instrument*

The viol was a six-stringed musical instrument having a large base. It was generally made of cypress wood and played with a bow similar to a violin.

Isaiah warned men not to begin early in the day to drink and revel, listening to the viol, rather than the word of the Lord.

References: II Nephi 8:82 (Isaiah 5:12); 10:33 (Isaiah 14:11).

VULTURE—*Animal*

A vulture is a bird which eats only animals that are long dead, or carrion. They do not kill their prey but eat leftovers of other animals' prey, or animals who have died of natural causes or accidents. Jews were forbidden to eat vultures except to prevent starvation.

Abinadi prophesied that the carcasses of the priests of Noah would be eaten by vultures. This end was recorded later by Alma, son of Alma.

References: Mosiah 7:49; Alma 1:97.

W

WEAPONS

Both the Jaredites and Lehites armed themselves with a variety of weapons. Only the Anti-Nephi-Lehies refused to arm themselves. When an army was about to be annihilated, the commander was given the choice of surrender by ordering his warriors to lay down their arms and vowing not to take them up again in their lifetime, or death. When a warrior wished to join the peace pact of the Anti-Nephi-Lehies, he buried his weapons of war and went to live among the peace loving tribe.

Men are called to take up weapons only at the command of God to preserve their liberty, religion, peace, and families.

For specific information concerning the nature of weapons see the articles for arrow, ax, bow, cimeter, club, dart, javelin, quiver, sling, spear, and sword.

References: Jarom 1:19-20; Mosiah 6:19-21, 27; Alma 1:64-69; 12:10-13; 20:20-23, 70-95; 21:154-155; 23:22; 24:33, 40-48, 68-75; 25:19, 42, 48-49; 26:5-7, 64; 27:15; 29:17-18; Helaman 2:115-116; III Nephi 2:38; 10:25; Mormon 3:11, 26; Ether 4:76; 6:87.

WHALE—Animal

Whales are huge mammals that live in the sea. Their long trimline bodies slip easily beneath the waves to feed and travel. They bob to the top long enough to blow water and air from their noses or blowholes on the top of their heads, suck in a huge breath, and flip beneath the surface. They sound, or dive, deep into the waters, remaining there for long periods of time. It is the whale's tail that provides propulsion and the flippers that direct turns.

The boats built by the Jaredites were made

to be submerged in the ocean like a whale, diving into the angry sea then rising to the surface for renewal of air. They were strong enough that collisions with the whale would not break them apart.

References: Ether 1:56; 3:12.

WHEAT—Plant

Wheat is a cereal grass crop raised for food for people. It was raised in the ancient world lands and brought over by both the Jaredites and Lehites.

At harvesttime the stalks of wheat holding ears of grain were gathered in bunches. Men and animals gathered at the threshing floor to walk on the stalks to loosen the grain. When this was done, forks lifted residue into the air. The winds carried away inedible stems and chaff leaving the clean wheat behind. This was the sifting or winnowing process.

Christ told his followers that Satan desired men to become as chaff that he could scatter by winds of temptation.

References: Mosiah 6:12; III Nephi 8:51.

WOLF—Animal

The wolf is a type of dog that runs wild in packs. Together wolves spread the flock killing sheep in great numbers but only taking one each for food off to their lair.

One of the wolf's favorite meals is lamb. It is the duty of the shepherd to drive the wolf away from the sheep, slaying it when possible.

The wolf is symbolically the sheep's enemy. If it cannot scatter the sheep and grab a lamb openly, it tries to grab a stray lamb stealthily. False prophets who are selfish and ambitious can appear to be like sheep but inwardly want to scatter and overcome rather than gather and lead.

In the last days, men are told that peace will extend so completely that sheep will allow their natural enemies, the wolves, to abide with them.

References: II Nephi 9:120-124; 12:91-95 (Isaiah 11:5-9); Alma 3:103-106; III Nephi 6:27.

WOOD

Trunks and branches of trees were used in construction of wooden shafts for arrows, bows, darts, and axes. Sawed wood was used in construction of buildings, both in structural timbers and ornamentation. Wood not useful in other ways was burned as fuel. Dyes and medicines were also obtained from boiling bark and roots.

References: I Nephi 5:28; II Nephi 4:21; 9:96; Jarom 1:19; Mosiah 7:11-13; Helaman 2:10; III Nephi 4:18-20.

WORM—Animal

Worms are soft bodied, boneless, legless, elongated creatures that live by eating debris. Caterpillars of a variety of insects are also called worms.

Isaiah told the righteous not to fear the revilers, who would eventually be left for worms to consume. He also condemned Babylon to be inhabited by worms.

Ether reported that the Jaredites slew one another so rapidly in their last civil war that there was no time to bury their dead. Their bodies were left to the worms.

References: II Nephi 5:82-85 (Isaiah 51:7-8); 10:33 (Isaiah 14:11); Ether 6:58.

Y

YOKE—Tool

A yoke is a wooden or metal collar generally worn by a work animal. Leather straps hung from it were attached to burdens or machines. This allowed the harnessed animal to push against the yoke with the shoulders so pulling the burden with the greatest effort with the least injury to the animal.

When other animals were lacking, or for punishment, the yoke was placed upon the necks of men.

Symbolically the yoke represented suppression or servitude. When this yoke was broken, servants were freed.

References: I Nephi 3:140; II Nephi 9:64 (Isaiah 9:4), 108 (Isaiah 10:27); 10:47 (Isaiah 14:25); Mosiah 9:153; Alma 16:14, 35; 20:64; 21:156, 182-183; 28:17.

Z

ZARAHEMLA—Mulekite Leader (c. 200 B.C.)

Zarahemla was the leader of the Mulekites at the time the Nephites were fleeing from the Lamanites in Nephi and searching for a new home. The Mulekites came from Jerusalem shortly after the Lehites but brought no records with them. Consequently they lost their language and religion and had to be taught to communicate with the Nephites.

When they were able to communicate, Zarahemla told Mosiah, leader of the displaced Nephites, as much of the Mulekite history as was remembered. Zarahemla welcomed Mosiah and the Nephites, and the two peoples united under Mosiah's leadership.

References: Omni 1:25-34; Mosiah 5:4, 17; Helaman 1:16.

ZARAHEMLA—City

Zarahemla became the second capital city of the Nephites. It was located along the west bank of the Sidon River.

Mosiah was the first king of the united kingdom. His grandson, Mosiah, was the last official king, though several dissenters and traitors set up temporary self-appointed kingships later. After the second King Mosiah, the nation was governed by a chief judge, the first being Alma, who also served as the head of the church.

At one time Zarahemla was captured in a raid by Lamanites under Coriantumr, but was shortly released by the Nephite army under Moronihah.

Nephi, son of Helaman, returned to the land and found his native city so filled with wickedness that he cried to the Lord concerning Zarahemla. His efforts proved useless against the confusion that existed.

Samuel, the Lamanite prophet, came to Zarahemla in 5 B.C., to warn the Nephites of their impending doom unless they repented. He told them that but for the few righteous men among them, God would instantly send fire upon them.

In the cataclysm at the time of the death of Christ, Zarahemla burned because by then the citizens were ripe in iniquity. After the coming of Christ, and in a period of rebuilding, Zarahemla was reestablished.

References: Alma 1:83; 3:2; 4:1-8; 26:28; 27:14; 28:9-10, 23; 29:52; Helaman 1:19-35; 3:10-11; 5:14-19; III Nephi 4:8, 23, 28; IV Nephi 1:9.

ZARAHEMLA—Land

Zarahemla was established by the Mulekites who came from Jerusalem shortly after the Lehites left. It was located along the west bank of the river Sidon. The Mulekites brought no records with them, consequently they lost their ability to read and write and their language changed.

When the Nephites came to Zarahemla, they joined with the Mulekites, teaching them the Nephite culture. Mosiah, leader of the Nephites, became their king.

Benjamin, their second king, had all the citizens

gathered from the land in an attempt to give them a last message and unite them spiritually as well as politically under the leadership of his son, Mosiah.

A group left Zarahemla to reinhabit Nephi, but returned after internal conflicts split and nearly destroyed the group. A second group successfully established a colony in Nephi but returned many years later after sixteen men were sent to inquire of their safety and found them in captivity.

Mosiah, son of Benjamin, when he gave up his kingship many years later, changed the form of government to democracy with a chief judge as ruler. Alma was first to be selected. He also established the church in the land and a long period of prosperity followed.

From time to time dissenters arose who tried to destroy the government. When the Nephites were righteous, they were strengthened in their defense. When wickedness prevailed, they were trodden down and suffered defeat until the righteous again outnumbered the wicked. Between wars were short periods of prosperity and peace during which times much building and cultural advancements were made.

Mosiah, in his attempt to safeguard the inhabitants, had a wall built on the borders of the land of Zarahemla. He had the cities in the land fortified against their enemies, also.

In the end, A.D. 328, the Nephites were

permanently driven from the land by the Lamanites.

References: Omni 1:19-34, 42, 50; Mosiah 1:1-35; 5:1-2, 12, 18, 53-61, 75; 6:1-5; 9:165-168; 10:14-16; 11:76-90, 97, 104, 204-206; 13:64-65; Alma 1:101, 121-125; 2:1-6; 3:1; 6:12; 10:110; 11:1; 12:1, 10-13; 13:68-77; 14:60, 79, 89, 105; 15:5-6, 14, 19-20, 36; 16:7-13, 36-37, 80, 256-257; 21:19-20, 68, 75-90, 105-112, 123-127; 26:105-114, 121-124, 148-149; 27:4, 49-50; 29:6-16; 30:5; Helaman 1:18-35; 2:3, 27, 38, 78, 81, 122-123; 3:1; 5:2; III Nephi 1:2-3, 46; Mormon 1:7, 10-24.

ZEBULUN—Old World Land

Zebulun was the inheritance in Israel of the tribe of Zebulun. It made up the southwestern quarter of what became Galilee.

In the land of Zebulun is the city of Nazareth where Jesus spent his early years. Few of the inhabitants in that region recognized the light Christ tried to bring to them. This fulfilled Isaiah's prophecy that a light would be brought to Zebulun to afflict them lightly.

References: II Nephi 9:61, 62; Isaiah 9:1, 2; Matthew 5:14-15.

ZECHARIAH—Witness (Old Testament)

Zechariah, son of Jeberechaia, was called by Isaiah to witness a prophecy concerning the destruction of Samaria and Assyria. This was about two centuries before Zechariah, the Old Testament prophet, worked.

References: II Nephi 9:40; Isaiah 8:2.

ZEDEKIAH—King of Judah (Old Testament)

Zedekiah or Mattaniah, son of Josiah, was the last king of Judah, before Christ. He had been placed on the throne by Nebuchadrezzar, king of Babylon, to serve over the rabble left by the first captivity of citizens of Jerusalem.

During the first year of his reign, Lehi took his family from Jerusalem by commandment to the New World. Later in his reign, Mulek, son of Zedekiah, took his friends to the New World under the same authority. These two Jewish groups later joined together.

Shortly after Mulek left, unknown to him, his brothers were executed by order of Nebuchadrezzar in front of their father, Zedekiah, because of his treasonous acts in allying against Babylon with a coalition.

References: I Nephi 1:3, 161-162; Omni 1:26; Helaman 2:129; 3:56-57; II Kings 24:18-25; II Chronicles 34:10-21.

ZEDEKIAH—Disciple (c. A.D. 34)

Zedekiah was one of the twelve disciples selected by Christ to be leader and special witness of the gospel. As such, he taught a portion of the multitude as they awaited Christ's second appearance. He was baptized by Nephi and in turn baptized the repentant in his group.

For further information see the article, *Disciples.*

References: III Nephi 9:4-15.

ZEEZROM—Lawyer (c. 82 B.C.)

Zeezrom's goal in life was to accumulate wealth. To do so he caused trouble between people, then charged them a fee to settle the issue.

As was his habit, when Alma and Amulek came into his hometown, Ammonihah, to preach he went to argue hoping to get a case to settle. He asked questions trying to trap them in their words. Amulek, however, knew what Zeezrom was up to and openly confronted him. This caused Zeezrom to stand back and listen to what was being said. The truth began to play on his conscience and he began to tremble. Zeezrom's arguments changed to sincere inquiry. From sincere inquiry, he was led to guilt, as he realized the way he led his fellowmen into blindness. He then stood and tried to make the people heed the words of Alma and Amulek by his pleading. He was scoffed, spurned, spit upon, and exiled.

Zeezrom left the city in haste before a rock-throwing, maddened crowd. He arrived in Sidom so broken in spirit that he was taken to bed with a burning fever. When he heard that Alma and Amulek had arrived in Sidom, he called for them to administer to him. He was healed instantly and Alma baptized him.

With renewed vigor, Zeezrom went to pour his heart out to his fellowmen to convert them to righteousness.

Later Alma took Zeezrom to the citizens of Zoram to help call them to repentance. He was ordained by Alma for this mission and suffered much while there.

References: Alma 8:45-46, 64 - 9:14; 10:40-44, 89-102; 16:83, 112-123; Helaman 2:72, 107.

ZEEZROM—City

Zeezrom, a city established by the Nephites in the land of Manti, was captured by the Lamanites in the war of 66-60 B.C. It was probably released at the end of that long war.
References: Alma 26:15.

ZEMNARIHAH—Robber (c. A.D. 19)

Zemnarihah led his robber band to lay seige on Nephi hoping to capture and enslave the inhabitants. Gidgiddoni, leader of the Nephites, prepared for such an attack. The robbers were unable to find provisions to maintain their seige and suffered great losses as the Nephites marched out of the city upon them day and night. Consequently they were forced to retreat.

Gidgiddoni sent an army to meet the retreating robbers who were cut off and annihilated. Zemnarihah was hanged until dead.
References: III Nephi 2:63-76.

ZENEPHI—Army Leader (c. A.D. 400)

Zenephi led his portion of the Nephite army in pursuit of the Lamanites. After the Lamanites sacked the tower of Sherrizah, Zenephi heartlessly took all remaining provisions for his own impoverished forces leaving the few survivors at Sherrizah destitute.
References: Moroni 9:15.

ZENIFF—Colony Leader (c. 200 B.C.)

Zeniff was an educated young Nephite who returned to the land of Nephi to drive off the Lamanites from their first inheritance. This effort ended in a civil uprising in the Nephite ranks, when Zeniff tried to convert the war plans into a peaceful coexistence treaty. In the strife that broke out, the army was destroyed. The few survivors crept back to Zarahemla.

Zeniff was an ambitious young man who successfully led a second band of colonizers back to Nephi to reinhabit it. In his zeal to take possession of the city, he overlooked the obvious trap the king of the Lamanites, Laman, had laid for him and his followers. Laman intended to take the inhabitants of Nephi into bondage once they became prosperous.

Zeniff became king of Lehi-Nephi and nearby Shilom by a grant of peace from King Laman. The king allowed Zeniff and his followers to work in peace for twenty prosperous years, then he began to allow raiding parties to take what they could from the Nephite farmers. The raids led to battles, then to all-out war, as the Nephites struggled for freedom and the Lamanites for the wealth of the more industrious Nephites.

Zeniff, being old, conferred this troubled kingdom on Noah, one of his more ruthless sons, along with the careful records he had kept of the colony.

References: Mosiah 5:12, 17, 32-34, 53-54; 6:1-58; 7:1; 11:81.

ZENOCK—Prophet (Old Testament)

Zenock prophesied in Jerusalem of the life,

crucifixion, atonement, and redemption of Christ. He also spoke of the branch of Joseph broken off and carried across the sea.

Because of his zeal at a time when the Jews did not want to hear of their own wickedness to come, in slaying their own messiah, he was stoned to death.

Laban, in his eagerness to maintain a perfect record, kept the record of Zenock the prophet.

Perhaps because Zenock's message was a repetition of others, such as Isaiah, and contained nothing unique, or because what he said cut the pompous Jewish leaders to the quick, his message was not retained in the prophecies of the Old Testament.

References: I Nephi 5:240; Alma 16:188-189, 205; Helaman 3:54; III Nephi 4:70-71.

ZENOS—*Prophet (Old Testament)*

Zenos prophesied of the fate of a proud and pompous Israel, brought to destruction and captivity because of their refusal to heed their messiah. Instead, Zenos told them they would slay their own God. This was to bring about their scattering; but in time they would, through the gentiles they despised, be brought to a knowledge of what they had done, repent, and be gathered to become the great and perfect nation they were called to be. He incorporated his message in the parable of the tame olive tree.

The Jews took offense at being told of their condition of wickedness and slew Zenos. Most

Jews destroyed the record of prophecy. But Laban, in his zeal to maintain a perfect record, kept the prophecy. Thus when Nephi, son of Lehi, took the record prepared by Laban, the Lehites obtained the prophecy of Zenos. Jacob quoted it in the plates of Nephi with its interpretation for posterity.

References: I Nephi 5:242; Jacob 3:30-153; 4:2; Alma 16:177-188, 205; Helaman 3:53; 5:101; III Nephi 4:71.

ZERAHEMNAH—Leader (c. 74 B.C.)

Zerahemnah led a Lamanite army against the Nephites to try to force them into servitude. Knowing the cruel hatred the Amalekites and Zoramites, both Nephite dissenter factions, held for their brothers, he chose his captains from among them.

He led his forces toward Jershon, a land given to the Anti-Nephi-Lehies; repentant Lamanites who, because they had buried their weapons desiring only peace, were more hated than the Nephites. Because the Anti-Nephi-Lehies were known to rather die than fight, they were supposedly easy targets for the vengeful Lamanites. The Nephites, however, sent their own armies, fully armed, to protect the land of Jershon.

When Zerahemnah saw the preparations made by the Nephites to meet them, more armed than they, he ordered his men to stand off. He withdrew his troops into the cover of the wilderness and led them quickly around to Manti, hoping to catch the Nephites unaware.

Moroni, leader of the Nephites, forewarned by Alma the prophet, led his troops through the land to Manti and prepared to meet them. Moroni divided his warriors into three divisions and concealed them for a trap.

Zerahemnah boldly led his men into the valley of death prepared by Moroni. They were completely surrounded. When Zerahemnah saw this, he called his men to attack. Both armies fought valiantly, but the poorly armed Lamanites suffered destruction. The Lamanites refused to stand their ground in the slaughter and courageously tried to retreat and break through the wall of Nephites to the river Sidon to cross over to their own land. When they saw that was impossible, they tried to retreat farther into Manti. Zerahemnah and his Amalekite and Zoramite henchmen tried to spur the Lamanites on to victory, but there was to be no victory.

When Zerahemnah finally realized that his troops were surrounded, he was terrified. Moroni, seeing this, called a halt to the battle. He begged Zerahemnah to recognize that by the power of God, they were defeated and to vow that they would cease warring with the Nephites.

Zerahemnah stubbornly only credited the difference in armaments as the Nephites' power over them. Moroni refused to accept Zerahemnah's surrender and continued the battle. In his anxiety to be rid of his enemy, Zerahemnah rushed Moroni, but before his intent was accomplished, Moroni's guard lashed out at him with his sword and caught Zerahemnah's scalp. With his hair lying at his feet, Zerahemnah retreated within his own ranks. Many of the Lamanites became terrified at the sight of the scalp. The guard of Moroni raised the loathful thing on his sword to let them see it and waved it as a prophecy of their own fate if they continued to refuse surrender.

Seeing many of his army throw down their arms and retreat in shame, Zerahemnah commanded the army he had left to take up the attack with more fury. It was not until Zerahemnah saw that his great army was reduced to a frazzled few that he was willing to enter the treaty of peace demanded by Moroni. This time Moroni accepted his surrender, took his weapons, and allowed his shameful retreat.

References: Alma 20:5-8, 22-100.

ZERAM—Spy (c. 87 B.C.)

Zeram was sent out by Alma to keep watch over the camp of the Amlicites who were Nephite dissenters being pursued by the Nephite army. Together with Amnor, Manti, and Limher, Zeram crept toward Minon following the movements of the Amlicites. To their horror, the spies saw the Amlicites join an armed host of Lamanites heading toward Zarahemla, the land of the Nephites, to conquer it and put the inhabitants to bondage.

Quickly, they returned to camp, sought out Alma, and made their dreadful report. With this forewarning, the Nephites were able to stand prepared before the invasion and with the power of God maintained their liberty.
References: Alma 1:77-86.

ZERIN—Mountain

Zerin stood in the way of the brother of Jared. By the power of God, vested in him because of his great faith, the brother of Jared called for the mountain to remove and it was removed.

Whether this event took place in the old world or the new is not known.
References: Ether 5:30.

ZIFF—Metal

Ziff is included in the list of metals mined by the Nephites for the making of weapons and machinery. Its exact nature is not known.
Reference: Mosiah 7:6, 11.

ZORAM—Servant (c. 600 B.C.)

Zoram was an humble and much trusted servant of Laban. He had charge of Laban's treasury where records of the priests were kept. He stood ready at Laban's beck and call to admit him but no others to the sacred room. Zoram, as he had been taught, never looked in his master's eyes.

Nephi, son of Lehi, wearing the garments of

Laban whom he had just slain, approached the door. Zoram recognizing his master's robe and girdle, spoke to Nephi of the Jewish elders Laban had been visiting. Nephi, imitating the voice of Laban, asked Zoram to bring out the records of the priests. In unquestioning obedience to Laban, Zoram retrieved the record and followed Nephi, chattering all the while.

It was not until Zoram saw Nephi's brothers outside the city of Jerusalem hiding behind the wall, that he realized he had been deceived. They had come to Laban for the records and Zoram knew that Laban had stolen their treasure and sent his henchmen to slay them. Quickly he turned around to flee back to the safety of Laban's house, but the huge hand of Nephi halted his escape. Zoram struggled against Nephi but could not break his hold.

Zoram gave up the useless struggle and prepared to receive his blows. Instead Zoram heard the soft voice of Nephi promise him that he would be a free man, if he would but follow him. Zoram, knowing that his master was surely dead, and that he would be sold again into perhaps more awful circumstances, agreed.

Zoram, daily discovering that Nephi treated him only with kindness, began to trust him and serve him faithfully. He was given one of the daughters of Ishmael for a wife.

Before Lehi died, Zoram was blessed for his faithfulness to Nephi and told that his posterity

would be united with the posterity of Nephi.
References: I Nephi 1:123-145; 5:7; II Nephi 1:55-58; 4:8; Jacob 1:13; IV Nephi 1:40-41.

ZORAM—Chief Captain (c. 81 B.C.)

The Lamanites in their anger because of their indignation at not rousing the Anti-Nephi-Lehies to fight, came against Ammonihah, city of dissenters from the Nephites, and destroyed the city and its inhabitants. The Nephites mustered defense in time to prevent any further attack before the Lamanites penetrated into Zarahemla. The Lamanites took some captives of the citizens of Noah, a Nephite city, before they retreated.

Zoram was sent to look after the fate of the captives from Noah and see if anything could be done to free them. He went at once to Alma, the high priest, to find out through the spirit of prophecy where the Lamanites had gone.

Alma sent Zoram and his sons across the river Sidon toward Manti. Zoram found the nearly abandoned captives in the wilderness among the scattered Lamanites, took them without a struggle, and led them home.
References: Alma 11:5-12.

ZORAM—Apostate (c. 74 B.C.)

Zoram, in religious zeal, slew Korihor who had been reduced from proud liar to beggar. Alma, however, was not satisfied with the religion Zoram taught.

Zoram believed that there was no prophecy

or revelation, or Christ to come. Religion to him involved only one prayer on Sunday in the synagogue. All the rest of the time a man was free to do as he wished.

References: Alma 16:76-79.

ZORAMITES—*Apostates*

The followers of Zoram garbed themselves in their finest apparel one day a week to put in their appearance at the synagogues. One at a time, they mounted the Rameumpton, or Holy Stand, to shout to God their one prayer. They thanked God for making them righteous and saving them from foolish belief in a Christ to come. Having done their duty to God, they left, unaffected, to continue life as they pleased.

Those who were too poor to dress properly were despised and refused entry into the synagogue to worship.

Alma and his chosen companions came to retrieve Zoram and his followers from their apostasy, but they refused to repent. Instead the Zoramites cast out Alma and later joined the Lamanites.

The poor among the Zoramites listened to Alma and some repented because he taught them that they did not need an unholy temple in which to worship. The Zoramites counseled together after Alma left and cast out the repentant from among them, thus sealing their own doom.

These outcasts went to Jershon and were taken in by the Ammonites. Because of this, the Zoramites allied with the Lamanites against the Ammonites. The Ammonites retreated to Melek.

Together the Zoramites and Lamanites waged a fruitless war against the Nephites. It ended when nearly the entire combined army was annihilated by the Nephites.

Later Amalickiah used Zoramites for war chiefs because of their ruthlessness and their knowledge of Nephite defenses.

References: Alma 16:76 - 99, 241-256; 18:3, 15; 19:3, 17; 20:4-48; 21:126; 24:25, 41; III Nephi 1:35-37.

BIBLIOGRAPHY

Douglas, J. D., *The New Bible Dictionary*, William B. Eerdmans Publishing Co., Grand Rapids, Michigan, 1962.

Encyclopedia Judaica, Keter Publishing Company, Jerusalem, Israel, 1971.

Encyclopedia International, Grolier, Incorporated, New York, New York, 1969.

Hastings, James, *A Dictionary of the Bible*, Charles Scribner's Sons, Edinburgh, 1902.

The History of the Reorganized Church of Jesus Christ of Latter Day Saints, Volumes 1 and 2, 1805-1844, Herald House, Independence, Missouri, 1967.

New Catholic Encyclopedia, McGraw Hill Book Company, New York, New York, 1967.

Smith, Joseph, Jr., The Book of Mormon, Board of Publication of the Reorganized Church of Jesus Christ of Latter Day Saints, Independence, Missouri, 1953 (Authorized Edition).

Smith, Joseph, Jr., The Holy Scriptures, Inspired Version, Herald Publishing House, Independence, Missouri, 1974.

Starks, Arthur E., *A Concordance to the Book of Mormon*, Herald Publishing House, Independence, Missouri, 1950.

Wright, C. H., *Biblical Encyclopedia of the Holy Bible*, the Authorized King James Version, World Publishing Company, Cleveland, Ohio.